The Dragon
and the Eagle

The Dragor

THE PRESENCE OF CHINA I

A. Owen Aldridge

nd the Eagle

HE *AMERICAN ENLIGHTENMENT*

WAYNE STATE UNIVERSITY PRESS   DETROIT

Library of Congress Cataloging-in-Publication Data

Aldridge, Alfred Owen, 1915–
    The dragon and the eagle : the presence of China in the
American enlightenment / A. Owen Aldridge.
        p.   cm.
    Includes bibliographical references and index.
    ISBN 0-8143-2455-X (alk. paper)
    1. United States—Relations—China. 2. China—Relations—
United States. 3. United States—Intellectual life—18th century.
4. United States—Civilization—Chinese influences.   I. Title.
E183.8.C5A658   1993
303.48′273051—dc20   93-1060

DESIGNER

Mary Krzewinski

COVER ART

Portrait of Emperor Ch ' ien Lung, from <u>Memoires concernant L'Historie,</u>
<u>Les Siences, Les Arts . . .</u> (1776-1791). Reproduced with permission of
The Library Company of Philadelphia.

CONTENTS

PREFACE

Practically no previous scholarship has been devoted to intellectual relations between China and America during the period of the American Enlightenment. Critics and historians have assumed that the image of China did not penetrate North America until after inauguration of the trade between Canton and the East Coast shortly after the War for Independence came to an end. The paucity of scholarship on the period before this time has been noted by Stuart Creighton Miller in the introductory chapter of a book on nineteenth-century emigration from China to the United States. Finding no secondary studies in print, Miller made his own survey of eighteenth-century thought and came to the conclusion not only that American perception of China was "innocent and unstructured," which is true as far as the lack of method is concerned, but also that no strong interest was evinced concerning the Middle Kingdom, which is far from correct (1969: 13–15). Miller based his opinion on the presumed scarcity of books on China in colonial libraries, on the mistaken assumption that even Americans of "cosmopolitan tastes like Jefferson and Franklin . . . stumbled on the subject of China late in their careers," and on the completely erroneous affirmation that "the colonial press reflected the same lack of interest in China" as that allegedly revealed by the founding fathers. The following pages will show that, to the contrary, a lively curiosity about non-Western culture existed in America before the middle of the eighteenth century and that a good deal of accurate information about it was available during the American Revolution along with an almost equal amount of myth and legend.

My survey will cover the 120 years from the birth of Benjamin Franklin in 1706 to the death of Thomas Jefferson in 1826, essentially the period of the American Enlightenment. It could well be argued that the spread of ideas and concrete information concerning the Middle Kingdom represented in itself an important element of the intellectual ferment associated with the concept of Enlightenment both in America and Europe.

During colonial times, China existed in America as a mirage or a reflection of the attitudes and images of European writers, the majority of whom had never seen Asia themselves. After the War of Independence and the development of direct trade with China, many Americans walked on Chinese soil and many of them wrote about their experiences there. As a result a number of entire books about the Middle Kingdom were published in Philadelphia and elsewhere in the forty years between 1785 and 1825 together with a host of short pieces in newspapers and magazines. The evidence that I shall present indicates that by the end of the eighteenth century practically every idea or element of concrete information about China in print in London or in Paris had reappeared in some form or another in the United States. This is contrary to the received opinion and contrary also to my own view when I began my research.

At the end of the eighteenth century, China was the oldest empire on the face of the globe and the United States the youngest republic; China was conservative, traditional, and isolated; the United States, brash, energetic, and expanding. The history of their initial intercourse is, therefore, by no means a record of mutual understanding or cooperation, but in many ways a clash of contrasting cultures. Americans were curious and inquisitive about their counterparts in another hemisphere; the Chinese, indifferent and disdainful about theirs. The contact between America and China, like the earlier ones between Europe and the East, did not represent an intellectual mingling or exchange, but rather a one-way flow from East to West. The following pages will reveal some extraordinary instances of this relationship: Franklin at the age of thirty-two publishing in his Philadelphia newspaper an analysis of the thought of Confucius, Jefferson including a Chinese novel on a reading list of 200 books for his brother-in-law, Thomas Paine comparing Confucius and Christ as great moral teachers, Philip Freneau composing a poem hailing the first voyage of an American vessel to the Far East, a super-patriot writing another poem denouncing the British embassy of Lord Macartney to the Chinese emperor, the American Philosophical Society enquiring into the contents of a Chinese book unearthed in the midst of a camp of American Indians in Pennsylvania, and a shocked American sea captain viewing the corpses of Eurasian babies floating down the river in Canton.

The penetration of the image of one nation into the collective consciousness of another has much in common with the process by which a single writer from one part of the globe becomes known in another. The latter process is frequently described as "fortune" in such phrases as "the fortune of Dante in Victorian England." Fortune here signifies both influence and reception. In a broad sense, literary influence refers to any evidence that one author is known by any other author. Each appearance of the name *Confucius* in an American book or periodical could, therefore, be taken as an example of the influence of China. But in a narrow sense, influence exists only if the writer who uses the word *Confucius* incorporates in his text some evidence of his own thought processes or personality. In this light, influence is something which exists in the work of an author that would not have existed had he not read or known about the work of a preceding author.

I shall show that China exerted this special kind of influence upon several American authors, including Benjamin Franklin. The parallel notion of reception refers to the physical evidence that the work of an author from one cultural environment has entered a separate milieu, evidence comprising such criteria as editions, translations, and reviews. An author could, therefore, have a wide reception in a particular culture without influencing any writer within it. In recent years, the notion of reception has moved away from physical evidence such as the number of editions or reviews to embrace the individual reader and his or her response to a text. While I accept the basic notions of reception theory, I shall not be concerned in the following pages with reader psychology or epistemology, but with literary history. My purpose is not to speculate on the mental processes of American readers during the colonial and federal periods, but to describe the literary sources that were actually available to them. The latest trend in comparative literature, the method known as cross-culturism, comprises all the elements of what was known in the years when the discipline was dominated by French positivism as mirage study—that is, describing the notions reflected in one national milieu about the culture of a different one. The methodology of this book could be considered as either cross-culturism or mirage study.

Throughout, the reader will find various spellings of Chinese names, as these have multiple spellings in English.

ACKNOWLEDGMENTS

I have been indebted to many people during the years of the writing of this book and the even longer period of its gestation. My interest in East-West relations was awakened in 1971, when I was invited to present a paper at the First International Comparative Literature Conference in the Republic of China, and I have participated in each subsequent quadrennial congress, all of which have taken place at Tamkang University. In a plenary address at the fifth conference in 1987, I first broached the topic of early Chinese contacts with America. I am grateful to the administration of Tamkang University, particularly for the warm hospitality of Clement C. P. Chang, former president, and of Limin Chu, former vice president. In 1988, I used early drafts of some of my chapters as lectures at Korea University and at Seoul National University. My hosts at these institutions, where I served as Fulbright professor, Uchang Kim at the first, and Seongo-Kim at the second, graciously offered suggestions for improvement and expansion. Later in Taiwan, I received constant encouragement and advice from Heh-Hsiang Yuan of National Chung Ching University, Yiu-Nam Leung of National Tsing Hua University, and Kai Chong Cheung of Soochow University.

Among American institutions, I am chiefly indebted to the Library Company of Philadelphia, which awarded me a grant in 1989 to study the papers of Robert Waln, Jr. I am especially grateful for the personal attention accorded to me by John C. Van Horne, librarian, and James Green, curator. At the library of the American Philosophical Society, Roy Goodman, reference librarian, kindly drew my attention to various documents and supplied me with copies. I have received valuable bibliographical information and suggestions from Marcus A. McCorison, director and librarian of the American Antiquarian Society. Finally the Morgan Library of New York City provided me with a copy of a manuscript on Confucius by the botanist John Bartram.

I have also utilized the library resources of the following institutions: National Cheng Chi University (Taiwan), National Tsing Hua University (Taiwan), University of London, British Library, Pennsylvania State University, New York Public Library, and the University of Illinois.

An early version of parts of chapter 4 is included in the published proceedings of the Seventh Quadrennial Comparative Literature Conference held at Tamkang University, and chapters 3 and 10 have appeared in *Asian Culture Quarterly*. The Research Board of the University of Illinois provided funds for the illustrations.

The Pre-American Background

Ever since the Renaissance, people in Europe and America have shown a lively curiosity about China, considered in the eighteenth century as the richest and most populous nation in the world. This curiosity has thrived on China's isolation from the West for nearly all recorded history except for two or three brief periods in the nineteenth and twentieth centuries. The last fifty years have consequently seen the publication of many studies of the early links between China and the West. One of the most recent of these, *L'Europe chinoise*, in two volumes, 1988–1989, by the French comparatist Etiemble, brilliantly portrays the exploits of the earliest travelers to China, the proselytizing efforts of the Jesuits, the penetration of certain aspects of Chinese culture into European society, and the dissemination of European theories of the seventeenth and eighteenth centuries concerning Chinese racial origins, religion, and language. These two volumes reveal the process by which European Sinophilia of the seventeenth century gave way to Sinophobia toward the end of the eighteenth.

Broadly speaking, the same transformation took place in America in the shorter time span between 1725 and 1825. But the voices of disillusionment were, with two or three exceptions, limited to the few Americans at the turn of the eighteenth century who had actually visited China. Since the purpose of their travel was primarily mercantile, and only a handful of these traders had literary pretensions, their disparaging opinions were eventually rendered ineffectual by the burgeoning zeal of

Protestant missionary groups eager to grasp the opportunity of conquering fresh fields.

An American journalist in treating American attitudes toward China after World War II has ingeniously described the eighteenth century as the Age of Respect and the nineteenth as the Age of Contempt (Isaacs 1962:70–71). He bases his impression of modern American images of the Chinese upon a series of personal interviews. These images, clustered in paradoxical pairs, have strong resemblance to those reflected in printed texts of the Enlightenment: "The Chinese are seen as a superior people and an inferior people; devilishly exasperating heathens and wonderfully attractive humanists; wise sages and sadistic executioners; thrifty and honorable men and sly devious villains; comic opera soldiers and dangerous fighters" (Isaacs 1962:71).

A modern Chinese historian has suggested that Western attitudes toward the Middle Kingdom were on the whole favorable, however, during the eighteenth century because this was a period of "unprecedented peace and prosperity" and flourishing of the decorative arts, attributable in some measure to the Ch'ing dynasty and one of its most successful emperors, Ch'ien Lung, whose name was spelled in the eighteenth century K'ien Long (Hao 1980). Americans were certainly not aware of the internal politics of Chinese, but they had heard reports of the wisdom and benevolence of the ruling emperor.

In order to keep from duplicating previous scholarship, I shall confine my remarks on the European background to the major literary and intellectual texts before the eighteenth century. In treating subsequent sources I shall emphasize authors in English who have been previously neglected. I shall use as a focal point Samuel Miller's *A Brief Retrospect of the Eighteenth Century*, a comprehensive survey published in 1803 of the intellectual achievements of mankind during the previous hundred years. The author, a native of Delaware, was minister of the Wall Street Presbyterian Church in New York City. His monumental but strangely neglected survey contains, in a small section labelled "Chinese Literature," an overview of the influence of China in Europe, the first to be written in the Western hemisphere.

It is common knowledge that China was introduced to Western literature through the late thirteenth-century travelogue of Marco Polo, known because of his exaggerations as Marco Milione, source of the title of one of Eugene O'Neill's plays, *Marco's Millions*. Polo's narrative has been published under various titles, such as *I Viaggi (His Travels,) Il Libro (The Book,)* and *I Milione (The Million,)* the latter referring to the million wonders of China or, as some skeptics have maintained, the multitude of lies emanating from the pen of its author.

Polo had taken the overland or "silk road" route to China. When this was closed in the fifteenth century by the military prowess of the Turks, European naval powers sought an alternative direction, the passage to India around the Cape of Good Hope. The Portuguese led in this effort, eventually reaching Canton, where they sought to establish a trading post. Frustrated in this attempt by the inveterate xenophobia of the Chinese, they were allowed an enclave on the peninsula of Macao, that became in the eighteenth century the gathering place for all Western traders. The Portuguese exploits are celebrated in the epic poem *Os Lusiadas* of Camões, a work that has been condemned for its racism by Etiemble (1988:17) and for its bombast by Ezra Pound (Andrews 1988:16).

Spanish missionaries followed in the wake of the Portuguese galleons, obtaining a foothold in the Phillipine Islands from where they made several missionary expeditions to China without lasting effect. The narrative of their efforts was set forth by Juan Gonzales de Mendoza in his *Historia de las cosas mas notables, ritos y costumbres del Reyno de la China,* (*History of the most important rites and customs of the Chinese Empire*) published in 1584 in Lisbon and soon afterwards in French and English translation. This was the first of the major Western books on China in modern times and by far the most widely cited during the eighteenth century by Hispanic authors. Montaigne was delighted to find in it a practical vindication of his theory that legal justice should distribute rewards as well as punishments (Lovejoy 1948:103). In British America, however, Mendoza was practically unknown.

Matteo Ricci, an Italian Jesuit, succeeded in establishing a mission in southern China in 1583 and another in Pekin in 1601. By learning the Chinese language and studying Chinese literary classics, he penetrated the precincts of the imperial court, where he and his successors ensconced themselves for more than a century as mathematicians, astronomers, and medical experts. For the Jesuits, these activities were secondary to their mission to gain converts to the Catholic religion, and it was only because of these secular contributions that they were allowed their court privileges. Ricci wrote in Italian a circumstantial account of his mission, including a description of the geography and manners of the country, that he entrusted to his second in command, a Frenchman, Nicolas Trigault, who translated it into Latin and published it in Augsburg in 1615. Ten years later a partial English translation appeared in the third volume of the famous compilation of voyages, *Hakluyt Posthumus* or *Purchas his Pilgrimes,* from which Robert Burton learned about the Chinese system of literary examinations. In America Ricci's work was known through an edition in French under the name of the translator Trigault, *Histoire d'expédition Chrétienne,* 1616.

In 1644 the Manchus overthrew the Ming dynasty, ushering in that of the Ch'ing, which lasted until 1911. The Protestant Dutch, who had been kept out of Ming China in large measure by the influence of the Catholic missionaries, thought that the Ch'ing era offered an opportunity to gain entrance and sent an embassy to Pekin. The effort brought practically nothing in material advantage, but the secretary of the embassy, Jan Nieuhof, wrote a lengthy account of the journey published posthumously in his native language in 1665 and translated in Pinkerton's *Collection of Voyages* as *The Embassy of the Dutch East India Company to the Great Tartarian Cham, the Present Emperor of China*. Nieuhof's account was also known in America.

The two most important works on China by German authors both appeared in the seventeenth century. A Jesuit who had never been to Asia, Athanasius Kircher, edited a miscellaneous collection in Latin in 1667 that was translated by Samuel Lowndes in 1676 as *China and France*. Most notable is Kircher's theory that the Chinese are racially descended from the Egyptians. The philosopher Leibniz published his own interpretation of Chinese science and philosophy in Latin in 1697 under the title *Novissima Sinica (News from China)*, not translated until modern times. In the eighteenth century the academic philosopher Christian Wolff proclaimed the morality of Confucius as a practical standard of conduct in daily life, and the political scientist J. H. G. Justi compared European governments with those of Asia. Samuel Miller, therefore, exaggerated the Gallic influence in observing that "it is generally known that Europe is indebted to the learned men of France for almost all the knowledge of Chinese literature of which it can boast" (1803:2:83). Miller probably came to this conclusion because only Kircher among the German writers was cited in America.

French authors were the ones most readily available in the colonial and federal periods, and even modern scholarship has given them the most attention. In the seventeenth century the Jesuit influence at the Chinese court continued to prevail, giving rise to one of the most important books on the Middle Kingdom by a French national, *Nouveaux mémoires sur l'état présent de la Chine*, 1696, by Louis Le Comte, a work that was translated into English the following year as *Memoirs and observations made . . . in a late journey through the Empire of China*. Unfortunately it appeared in the midst of what is known as the rites controversy, a theological disagreement between Jesuits and other Catholic orders. The Jesuits argued that the pristine form of most concepts in the writings of Confucius could be made conformable to Christian teaching and that the ceremonies in Confucian temples for deceased ancestors were civil observances, not connected with religious worship. Opponents of the Jesuits, mainly Dominicans and Franciscans, objected to any degree of accommodation with Chinese beliefs, which they categorized as idolatrous. The Sorbonne investigated Le Comte's book along with several others and condemned them all as heretical. Despite this setback, LeComte was considered as a reliable authority both in Europe and in America, where his work was printed in Philadelphia in 1787. The Pope in 1710 forbade all publications on the China mission without express permission (Maverick 1946:21).

In 1687 a group of Jesuits, under the direction of Belgian, Philip Couplet, published the first translation of a Chinese literary work to appear in the West, a Latin edition of the writings of Confucius. This will be treated at length in the next chapter. When Couplet returned to Europe in the same year, he brought with him two native Chinese. One of these, Michel Shen Fo-tsoung, using Latin as his vehicle of communication, visited at Oxford the foremost British orientalist of the time, Thomas Hyde. Fragments of the writings in Latin of the Chinese scholar were eventually published in Hyde's collected works, *Syntagma*, 1767. A century later two other Chinese converts came to France for theological studies. The statesman Turgot wrote out fifty-two questions about science, agriculture, and politics in China that he asked them to answer in detail on their return to their native land (Maverick 1946:113). But no reply is known to have been received. As I shall show in a later chapter, five native Chinese accompanied the first American author of a book about China on his return from that country to Philadelphia in April 1796.

Samuel Miller's summary of the Jesuit influence in China reflects the probable state of knowledge concerning that relationship possessed by the average well-read American of his time.

> As early as the sixteenth century, a number of French Jesuits penetrated into China, and by their learning and address conciliated the favour of the government. These missionaries were followed by others, of various characters and talents, and, in fact, a succession of them was maintained, amidst many changes of reception and treatment, until after the middle of the century under consideration. The opportunities which they enjoyed for exploring the literature and science of that empire were diligently improved. Much of the information which they acquired was transmitted, at different periods, to Europe; and though the faithfulness of their narratives has sometimes been called in question, the works compiled from their letters and journals may be considered as, on the whole, the richest sources of instruction in this department of oriental inquiry.

After reference to Couplet's translation of Confucius, Miller treats a famous Jesuit series in thirty volumes, the *Lettres édifiantes et curieuses écrites des missions étrangères*, 1707–1773.

The greater part of this work, which was compiled from the papers of the missionaries, and which extended to more than forty [sic] volumes, was published at an early period of the eighteenth century, and contains an ample fund of instruction concerning the literature and science of China. This was followed by the *Anciennes Relations des Indes, et de la Chine* of M. Renaudot, which made an important addition to the stock of information before possessed on the subjects of which it treats. To these succeeded the great work of Father DU HALDE, entitled a *General Description of China*; and a work, under nearly the same title, by the ABBE GROSIER, both of which are considered as publications of the first class, and as containing much instructive matter relating to the learning, arts, and general condition of the wonderful country which they describe.

The general terms in which Miller describes these books indicates that he had read little more than their titles; he shows no knowledge of Renaudot's precise subject, the narrative of two Mohammedans who had allegedly penetrated into China during the ninth century, and he makes no distinction between the scope of the work of Du Halde and that of Grosier. The former is the most comprehensive and probably the most widely read book on China published in the West during the entire eighteenth century. Like Kircher and Leibniz, Du Halde had never been to China himself, but he blended a collection of texts by his fellow Jesuits into a fascinating purview of nearly all aspects of Chinese culture. His work was considered a textbook on the Middle Empire throughout most of Europe, and it was widely known in America as well. Benjamin Franklin cited it as early as 1738, only three years after its original publication in Paris. Grosier was the editor of a French history of China by Joseph Anne Marie de Moyriac de Mailla, loosely based on an actual Chinese history, *Tong-Kien-Kang-Mou*, published under the title *Histoire générale de la Chine; ou annales de cet empire* (Paris: 1777–1785) in thirteen volumes. Grosier himself wrote the thirteenth volume, consisting of a topographical description of the empire, statistics on population, and a survey of Chinese government, religion, manners, arts, and sciences. The latter volume was later published separately in several editions under the title *Description générale de la Chine* (*A General Description of China*). Both Moyriac de Mailla and Grosier were known in America, but Grosier, who had never been to the orient, was much more extensively quoted. The *Massachusetts Magazine* for April 1790 (II, 236–37) in reference to an extract from de Mailla, described as a "learned Jesuit," observed that he resided in China for forty-five years and that the emperor K'ien Long paid for his funeral. This is one of many favorable references in eighteenth-century America to the reigning emperor.

Books of universal history, a methodology introduced for the first time in the eighteenth century, tend to be overlooked in studies of influence, but they, nevertheless, had a good deal to do with shaping Western opinion concerning China. One of these that was quoted both in France and in America on Chinese affairs was the ancient history section of the *Universal History* published in London in twenty-one volumes in 1736–1765. A similar French work covering a later period was printed under the name of François Marie de Marsy, the *Histoire moderne des Chinois, des Japonnois, des Indiens, des Persans, des Turcs, des Russiens* in thirty volumes in Paris, 1755–1778.

The Jesuits praised the Chinese for the purity of their morals and the elevated state of their culture in order to portray Chinese religion as based upon the same principles of natural reason as Christianity. The deists in England admitted all the good things said about the Chinese, but drew an opposite conclusion, arguing that since Chinese religion was indeed based upon natural reason it had more in common with their own rational deism than with supernatural Christianity. Lord Bolingbroke, for example, the mentor of both Pope and Voltaire, portrayed China as "a country, into the antiquities of which we look further back than into those of any other, and where we may find examples . . . [of] the effects of natural religion, unmixed and uncorrupted, with those of artificial theology and superstition" (Aldridge, 1986:142–43). An even more notorious deist, Mathew Tindal, in his *Christianity as Old as the Creation*, insinuated the superiority of Confucius to Christ by suggesting that "the plain and simple maxims of the former, will help to illustrate the more obscure ones of the latter" (Aldridge 1986: 142–3). Milton in the seventeenth century had adopted a similar technique in regard to Confucius and Spanish Catholicism, praising the former in order to disparage the latter. In a Latin letter that was known in both England and France during the eighteenth century, the author of *Paradise Lost* gave Confucius credit for protecting China from revolution and keeping it stable, the same in his day as it had always been. This illustrious and venerable man, according to Milton, because of the wise laws he had established was the lifeblood of the people, the sustenance of its religion, and the protector of its monarchs (Etiemble 1989: 319). Confucius was well known in America throughout the eighteenth century, but only Thomas Paine attempted to place him or Chinese religion in general under the mantle of deism.

Missionaries and philosophers were not the only ones to write important books on China. The group of economists in France known as Physiocrats elevated Chinese agriculture as a model for all nations, and Americans evinced in print an equal interest in Chinese farming. International diplomacy produced even more descriptions of the Middle Kingdom. Two major embassies to the Chinese emperor taking place in the last decade of the eighteenth century inspired detailed accounts by participants in the journeys. The embassy sent by the British government gave rise to several separate reports by English members of the party, and that of the Dutch produced one narrative by the second in command, who was an American citizen, and a second one by the official translator, a French national. Most of these historical records or recollections were reprinted in America.

Two English authors were among the first to write denigrating accounts of the Chinese. Daniel Defoe in the second part of his *Farther Adventures of Robinson Crusoe* had his protagonist disparagingly "compare the miserable People of these Countries with ours, their Fabricks, their Manner of Living, their Government, their Religion, their Wealth, and their Glory as some call it." After this, Crusoe concluded, "I do not so much as think it is worth naming" (Defoe 1719: 296). Richard Walter, chaplain to the expedition of George Anson and presumed author of the latter's *A Voyage Round the World in the Years 1740–1744*, 1748, affirmed not only that Chinese theories of morality consist mainly in "recommending ridiculous attachments to certain immaterial points," but also that "their Magistrates are corrupt, their people thievish, and their tribunals crafty and venal" (Anson 1974:368–69).

Today practically nobody reads the second part of *Robinson Crusoe*, and in America of the eighteenth century it probably enjoyed no greater degree of popularity. Anson's *Voyage*, however, was not only known in colonial times, but was the first book relevant to China published on the American continent. This was not the semi-official version of 1748, but a later narrative by W. H. Dilworth, reprinted in Boston in 1760 by Benjamin Mecom, the nephew of Benjamin Franklin. This Dilworth version, unlike Walter's, has nothing disparaging to say about China or the Chinese. In France the Middle Kingdom encountered adverse criticism in the works of three major literary figures, Montesquieu, Rousseau, and Diderot, but their aspersions were not noticed in America. Among the French Sinophiles, Voltaire was the most outspoken, but much as he was cited in America on other subjects, his opinions on China drew no attention until the beginning of the nineteenth century.

Special topics debated by European writers included the powers of the Chinese emperor, the theory that the Chinese language was the primitive one spoken from the times of Adam to the flood, the possibility of developing Chinese ideograms into a universal language, the theory that the Chinese were once an Egyptian colony, and the conflict between the chronology of Chinese annals and that of the Bible. Most of these topics found expression in the New World in one form or another.

Only two Chinese literary works of importance were translated into Western languages during the eighteenth century, and both were known in America. One was a seventeenth-century Yuan drama, originally included in Du Halde, and later used as the inspiration for a famous play by Voltaire, *L'orphelin de la Chine* (*The Chinese Orphan*). The other, also from the seventeenth century, was an anonymous novel described in some detail by Samuel Miller.

> In 1761 a very singular and curious performance made its appearance in Great-Britain. This was a translation of a Chinese novel, under the title of *Hau Kiou Choan*, or the *Pleasing History*, in four volumes. The translation had been made a number of years before by Mr. JAMES WILKINSON, a British merchant, who had resided for some time at Canton, where he studied the Chinese language. The editor was Dr. THOMAS PERCY, who accompanied the publication with extensive and learned notes, which have a tendency not only to illustrate the composition immediately connected with them, but also to throw new light on the character of Chinese literature in general.

In a footnote, Miller indicates that the Scottish critic Hugh Blair "once remarked in conversation, that the *Pleasing History* contained a more authentic and interesting account of the internal state of China, than all the other publications on that subject that he had ever seen." In another section of his book, Miller remarks that Voltaire's *Chinese Orphan* along with three other European plays is "possessed of distinguished excellence," but he does not seem to realize that Voltaire's drama is based upon an authentic Chinese model (1803: 216). References to the *Pleasing History* other than Miller's may be found in eighteenth-century America, but I have seen none whatsoever to the original Chinese orphan play, despite the circumstance that Arthur Murphy's *The Orphan of China*, based on Voltaire, played in 1768 at the John Street Theatre in New York City and again in 1779 (Odell 1927:1:202,242). Between 1790 and 1795 there were several representations of "Chinese shades, a type of magic lantern displays, and in 1808 a circus advertised "The Young Chinese" as an equestrian act (Odell 1927:2:245, 305, 398).

Obviously Miller was not an expert on oriental history and culture, but it should be kept in mind that at the time he wrote his *Brief Retrospect*, he was a young man in his twenties. His work, moreover, covered all of the eighteenth century in most parts of the world, China representing only a small section of his concerns. Also he showed remarkable literary intuition in stressing the importance to Western readers of *The Pleasing History*, thereby anticipating Goethe, who saw in it a strong resemblance to eighteenth-century sentimental fiction and praised it while proclaiming the imminent arrival of the era of *Weltliteratur* (Aldridge 1986: 23).

Miller's *Brief Retrospect* does not in itself prove that the average American at the turn of the century had a vital interest in the Middle Kingdom. What it does show, however, is that considerable knowledge of China was available to those Americans who wished to take advantage of it. Two decades later every major European book about China could be found somewhere in the United States, and a number of books on China by American authors were in print and contributing to the rise of a new national literature.

CHAPTER

2

Confucius and Chinese Religion

The first person in the New World to evince an interest in Confucius, so far as I have been able to discover, was James Logan of Philadelphia, the most wealthy and eminent statesman of that city during the first half of the eighteenth century. A friend of Benjamin Franklin and a serious bibliophile, Logan in 1733 acquired for his personal library a copy of the first European printing of Confucius's philosophy, a Latin translation edited by Philip Couplet: *Confucius Sinarum Philosophus, sive Scientia Sinensis Latine Exposita. Paris: Apud Danielem Horthmels*, 1687. Since this work does not contain all of the Confucian scriptures, and since I shall repeatedly refer to these books in later chapters, some explanation is needed of the scope and nature of the writings attributed to the Chinese philosopher. The average Western reader today probably has no greater familiarity with them than had Logan and his contemporaries. These writings comprise two main bodies, the *Wu ching* (*The Five Classics*) and the *Ssu shu* (*The Four Books*). The *Wu ching* includes:

> *Shu ching* (The book of history)
> *Shih ching* (The book of poetry)
> *I ching* (The book of changes)
> *Li chi* (The book of rites)
> *Ch'un chiui* (The spring and autumn annals).

The latter is called "spring and autumn" either because the annals it contains begin in one season and finish in the other or because they represent the flowers of spring and the fruits of autumn.

The *Ssu shu* consists of four other books:

Ta hsüeh (The great science)
Chung yung (The doctrine of the mean)
Lun yü (The Analects or book of sentences)
Meng tzu (comments of Mencius, Confucius's disciple).

The only books by Confucius himself are the fifth of the *Wu ching* and the first, second and third of the *Ssu shu*. The *Confucius Sinarum Philosophus* in Logan's library contains the latter three books, comprising essentially the ethical segments of the whole. The editors and translators were all Jesuits born in the 1620s: the Sicilian Prosper Intoretta, the Austrian Christian Herdtrich, the Hollander Francis Rougemont, and the Belgian Philip Couplet.

Logan wrote to his friend Josiah Martin that he was pleased to acquire the volume, expensive as it was, but wished he could be certain "of having Confucius's own Sentiments or the true sense of the Original delivered to us, which as it Comes thro' the hands of those grand falsifiers the Jesuits is somewhat to be suspected" (Wolf 1971:4). Eventually other Americans who did not possess Confucius in their libraries came to regard him as a symbol of rectitude, comparable to Socrates as he was portrayed by some liberal thinkers in France. As I shall show in a later chapter, Thomas Paine toward the end of the century was one of these. Joel Barlow, Paine's friend, in a prose dissertation inserted in his epic poem *The Vision of Columbus* (1787) compared Confucius with both Socrates and Cicero as among the wisest philosophers of the most enlightened periods of antiquity (Aldridge 1982: 289–90). Barlow also praised Confucius for his "just idea" on the the nature and attributes of God, and his description of the deity as a "God of purity, justice and benevolence" (1976, 2: 89).

Several French authors of the eighteenth century drew parallels between Confucius and Socrates, and in the nineteenth century some Americans pointed to fancied resemblances between Confucius and Franklin. Evangelical Christians, however, almost uniformly rejected Confucius as an unbeliever and patronized Franklin as a pragmatist lacking philosophical depth. An essayist in the *Christian Examiner* of 1868 affirmed, for example, that "Confucius seems no inspired teacher—only a petty pattern of a Benjamin Franklin," who "at least had some knowledge of God" (84: [1868]: 177).

In a sense it is futile to attempt to compare Confucius and Franklin since they belong to entirely different intellectual disciplines or categories of knowledge. Confucius is a quasi-legendary figure, like Christ or Socrates, encompassing in his personality a system of ethics, a religion of diverse elements, and a national tradition. Franklin, on the other hand, is a vibrant character in modern history, whose achievements in science, states-manship, and literature are concrete and well-documented. It is true, on the other hand, that both Confucius and Franklin have achieved almost mythical status as embodiments of the national cultures they represent. The constituent elements of these myths, however, have little resemblance to each other. Confucius is considered as an inscrutable and benevolent sage, Franklin, as a self-made and resourceful entrepreneur. Both cultural heroes, nevertheless, are regarded as typical of the best qualities of their intellectual environments, as vaguely patriarchal, and as possessing great independence of character. Franklin sought information about Confucius as part of his avid quest for information about China throughout most of his life. He is already known for establishing the first fire department in America together with the first lending library and even for being the first pornographer. He was also the first and foremost American Sinophile.

An anonymous correspondent told one of Franklin's earliest editors that Franklin was "very fond of reading about China" and "that if he were a young man he should like to go to China" (Franklin 1836–40:2:241). In a later chapter I shall identify this correspondent as Benjamin Vaughan. Vastly more important, however, is the evidence that Franklin in his early years published in his weekly newspaper the *Pennsylvania Gazette* an essay with the heading "*From the Morals of* Confucius" and followed it two issues later with a "*Continuation*." He concluded the latter segment with a notice that further extracts would be given, but the promised additional material never appeared (Nos. 482 and 484, 7 and 21 March 1738). This was five years after Logan acquired his Latin version. The *Gazette* does not indicate whether Franklin's summary of the doctrines of the Chinese sage was original or reprinted from another source, a common practice among eighteenth-century newspapers. Actually, the essay is a partial copy of a London pamphlet *The Morals of Confucius, a Chinese philosopher*, published in 1691, a translation of a French work, attributed to both Jean De la Brune and to Louis Cousin, *Lettre sur la morale de Confucius, philosophe de la Chine*, (Paris, 1688) that is in turn an abridged translation of the Latin *Confucius Sinarum philosophus*. La Brune was a Protestant pastor, who wrote extensively on classical and French history. Although his edition of Confucius appeared at the height of the rites controversy, it seems that de la Brune, like his contemporary Leibniz, was more interested in spreading the true ecumenical spirit than in taking sides with or against the Jesuits' interpretation of Chinese metaphysics. La Brune also translated into French John Calvin's treatise on justification by faith. The London *Morals of Confucius* of 1691 was reprinted in 1706, 1718, 1729, and 1780. Its title is significant for both Europe and America, indicating as it does that Confucius was being considered as an ethical thinker rather than as a religious or sectarian leader. This is the way he was regarded by Franklin. One cannot be sure whether Franklin had direct access to the London pamphlet or whether he encountered extracts from it in an English periodical. The latter is the probable explanation since Logan did not own a copy of the London text nor was there one at this time in the Library Company of Philadelphia.

The derivative nature of Franklin's publication does not detract from its importance in Franklin's intellectual biography. During this period the *Pennsylvania Gazette* included for the most part, local and international news together with reprints of court documents. Literary essays such as the one on Confucius were quite uncommon. The few that were selected, including *The Morals of Confucius*, reflected a particular interest of the editor, Franklin himself. His extracts from this work are from the first book of the *Ssu shu*, that is, "the Great Learning," and they comprise 20 pages out of a total of 183 in the volume or about 11 percent of the whole. In this section Confucius treats "what we ought to do to cultivate our Mind, and regulate our Manners;" "the Method by which it is necessary to instruct and guide others;" and "the Care that every one ought to have to tend to the Sovereign Good, to adhere thereunto, and as I may say, repose himself therein."

Probably the ideology in *The Morals of Confucius* was not in itself sufficient to turn Franklin into an admirer of the Chinese sage. It is impossible fully to reconstruct his intellectual history during this period, but it is likely that he had previously encountered other printed materials concerning the Middle Kingdom during an earlier sojourn in London. At that time he read widely among the English deists and published a work of his own, *A Dissertation on Liberty and Necessity, Pleasure and Pain*, 1725, that is closer to absolute atheism than to the religion of nature.

We know from Franklin's autobiography that when he returned to Philadelphia he became greatly concerned with his private moral development. It is, therefore, likely that he published the essay on Confucius because of its relevance to his efforts to establish a personal code of behavior. Indeed significant parallels may be seen between the extracts in his newspaper and his ethical notions as revealed in his autobiography. The essayist observes that Confucius considers cultivation of the reason as "the great secret" in the acquiring of knowledge together with the preserving of reason in its utmost luster and perfection as the sovereign good of mankind. Since men "generally pursue not the the Methods that lead to the Possession of the Sovereign Good" Confucius provides relevant instructions for doing so. "After we know the End to which we must attain, it is necessary to determine, and incessantly to make towards this End, by walking in the Ways which lead thereunto, by daily conforming in his Mind the Resolution fixt on for the attaining it, and by establishing it so well that nothing may in the least shake it." Franklin in his autobiography describes a very similar process. He determines to achieve a condition of moral perfection and then establishes a method for acquiring it. This is his famous Art of Virtue, a listing in a notebook of those qualities he considers to represent the thirteen principal virtues and a scheme of checking the notebook every day to register infractions. The method envisages particular attention on successive days to each of the virtues until an unblemished book is attained after a period of daily examination for thirteen weeks. This is certainly a means of following Confucius's recommendation of the determining of an end and "daily conforming" in the mind "the Resolution fixt on for the attaining it." *The Morals of Confucius* even contains the phrase "the Art of Being Virtuous," parallel to the Art of Virtue in Franklin's autobiography.

The commentator on Confucius indicates that the great sage proposes his method to kings and princes so that their examples may spread throughout kingdoms and descend downwards to all segments of the population. A monarch's "Person being thus perfected, his Family, forming it self according to this Model, will be reform'd and amended. His Family being arriv'd at this Perfection, 'twill serve as an Example to all the Subjects of the particular Kingdoms to all those that compose the Body of the Empire. . . . These admonitions do not less regard the Subjects than the Princes." Franklin also adopted the opinion that morality may be taught to the masses by the example of the leaders, and he also conceived of extending his Art of Virtue to a society of his fellow citizens and from there to the world in general. This extended scheme is revealed in private observations he made a few years before he published the essay on Confucius.

> There seems to me at present to be great Occasion for raising an united Party for Virtue, by forming the Virtuous and good Men of all Nations into a regular Body, to be govern'd by suitable good and wise Rules, which good and wise Men may probably be more unanimous in their Obedience to, than common People are to common Laws.
> I at present think, that whoever attempts this aright, and is well qualified, cannot fail of pleasing God, and of meeting with Success. (1959–:1:193)

Franklin was fond of moral maxims and later in life spread them throughout his works, including his autobiography. The Gazette essay on Confucius has such a saying: "*Always behave thy self with the same Precaution and Discretion as you would do, if you were observ'd by Ten Eyes, and pointed at by so many Hands.*" Franklin did not reprint this maxim, perhaps because he had not yet become addicted to proverbial lore. Two sayings verbally resembling it, almost identical to each other, in his *Poor Richard's Almanac* have a completely different meaning from that of Confucius. For October, 1744, he introduced "The Eye of a Master will do more Work than his Hand," and in September, 1755, "The Master's Eye will do more Work than both his Hands."

Franklin in his own ethical system followed Confucius in recognizing the practical value of virtue. According to the Chinese sage, "whatever is honest and advantageous, is amiable; and we are obliged to love Virtue, because it includes both these Qualities." In his autobiography Franklin remarks that it is "every one's Interest to be virtuous, who wish'd to be happy even in this World." He further explains that "vicious Actions are not hurtful because they are forbidden, but forbidden because they are hurtful, the Nature of Man alone consider'd."

The last paragraph of Franklin's extracts from Confucius summarizes the character of an ideal legendary head of the Chinese empire who reigned more than two thousand years B.C.

> *Yoa* [Yao] had all the excellent Qualities desirable in a Prince; his Riches made him not Proud; his Extraction which was so noble and illustrious, puffed him not up with Arrogancy. He was Virtuous, Sincere, and Kind without Affectation. His Palace Table, Apparel and Furniture discover'd the greatest Moderation that ever was seen. He delighted in Musick; but it was a Grave, Modest and Pious Musick, he detested nothing so much as Songs wherein Modesty and Civility were blemisht. 'Twas not a Capricious Humour that made him dislike these sort of Songs, 'twas the desire he had of rendring himself in all Things pleasing unto Heaven. 'Twas not Avarice that produc'd in him that moderation which he observed in his Table, Apparel, Furniture and every Thing else. It was only the Love he bore to those that were in want, for he only design'd to relieve them. 'Twas also his great Piety, and that ardent Charity wherewith he burn'd, which made him frequently to utter these admirable Words, "The Famine of my People is my own Famine. My People's Sin is my own Sin."

Here in a nutshell we find one of the principal notions associated with China throughout the Enlightenment both in America and Europe, the emperor as the father of his people, a benevolent ruler incorporating all of the best moral qualities, particularly moderation and charity. We shall see in chapter 9 how this notion became widespread during the early years of the American republic.

In setting the type for this essay, Franklin made a spelling error in the name *Yao*, which he wrote, as we see above, *Yoa*. He made this same error elsewhere in the essay in regard to an ancient book *Camcao* that

Franklin set as *Camcoa*. The reversing of letters is a common psychological peculiarity found in many people besides Franklin. The same reversal may be found in his manuscripts, for example, writing *goal* for *gaol*, a place of incarceration (Lemay 1986:108–109).

Eleven years after Franklin published the extracts from Confucius in the *Pennsylvania Gazette*, he received a letter from the evangelist George Whitefield, describing the latter's success in spreading the Gospel among the wealthy and privileged classes of England. Franklin was thereupon reminded of Confucius, and he consequently suggested to his clerical friend that if he could persuade his converts "to a good and exemplary life, wonderful changes will follow in the manners of the lower ranks; for, *Ad Exemplum Regis* &" (Franklin 1959—:3:383). The *Morals of Confucius* gives a more amplified statement of the philosophy encapsulated in this Latin maxim, *Regis ad exemplum totus componitur orbis*. In his letter to Whitefield, Franklin added that when Confucius

> saw his country sunk in vice, and wickedness of all kinds triumphant, he applied himself first to the grandees; and having by his doctrine won them to the cause of virtue, the commons followed in multitudes. The mode has a wonderful influence on mankind; and there are numbers that perhaps fear less the being in Hell, than out of fashion. Our more western reformations began with the ignorant mob; and when numbers of them were gained, interests and party-views drew in the wise and great. Where both methods can be used, reformations are likely to be more speedy.

It is indicative of the cosmopolitanism of Franklin's religious views that he cited as his example the Chinese sage rather than Whitefield's model Christ.

Franklin seemed, however, to refute the Confucian doctrine of morality descending from the upper to the lower ranks in one of his political texts published late in life. In a letter to his daughter Sarah Bache in 1784, he affirmed that "among the Chinese, the most ancient, and from long Experience the wisest of Nations, honour does not *descend*, but *ascends*" (1905–7:9:162). Franklin made this comment in reference to the Society of Cincinnatus, an organization that had come into being at the conclusion of the American Revolution as a means of bestowing a type of hereditary nobility on all the soldiers who had fought on the American side. Franklin opposed the concept of establishing any kind of hereditary aristocracy in the United States and used the example of China to promote his argument against it. Mirabeau, who was to become one of the colorful figures of the French Revolution, translated Franklin's remarks to his daughter into French and published them in the same year, 1784, in his *Considerations sur l'ordre de Cincinnatus* (Aldridge 1957:80–82). Like his model, Mirabeau was attempting to disparage the notion of hereditary aristocracy.

Franklin told his daughter that in China when the emperor promoted a man to the rank of mandarin because of his learning, wisdom, or valor, his parents were immediately entitled to the same ceremonies of respect as those accorded to the mandarin "on the supposition that it must have been owing to the Education, Instruction, and good Example afforded him by his Parents, that he was rendered capable of serving the Publick." Franklin contrasted this *"ascending* Honour," which is useful to the state by encouraging parents to give their children a solid and virtuous education, with the harmful *"descending* Honour" of hereditary aristocracy, which is damaging to posterity "since it is apt to make them proud, disdaining to be employ'd in useful Arts, and thence falling into Poverty, and all the Meannesses, Servility, and Wretchedness attending it" (ibid.). Actually this advocacy of individual honors ascending to a single immediate family does not negate the Confucian notion of virtue descending from the higher orders of society at large to those below. It may not have occurred to Franklin, however, that his political metaphor of ascending honor would not fit the touchy relationship existing at the time between the United States and its mother country, England. That of descending honor, on the other hand, is contrary in spirit to the democratic notion widespread during the period of the American Revolution that the true origin of government is in the people and that power ascends from the people to the leaders.

In a subsequent chapter, I shall show that the emblem of the Society of Cincinnatus figured prominently in the first voyage of an American vessel to China in 1784, two years after Franklin's letter to his daughter. The supercargo on this voyage, Samuel Shaw, was one of the founding members of the society and the creator of the design for its official emblem. While in Canton, Shaw commissioned Chinese artists to decorate several pieces of porcelain with the arms of the society, and on a later visit in 1788 he ordered several sets of china bearing the design.

Six years after Franklin's reprint of the morals of Confucius, a Boston periodical, the *American Magazine and Historical Chronicle,* that was distributed in Philadelphia by Franklin, featured in its issue of November, 1744, "An Essay on the Description of China" based on Du Halde, nine years after the first edition of the latter's work. As I have already indicated, Du Halde's *Description* was probably the most important and most widely read book on China of the eighteenth century. A mine of information, it was at the same time an instrument of propaganda designed to perpetuate the Jesuits' notion that the Chinese were a noble race whose religion paralleled that of Christianity. Whatever in reality contradicted this opinion, they left out, and whatever was needed to support it, they invented (Etiemble 1989:213). Although the essay in the *American Magazine* is merely a reprint from the London *Gentleman's Magazine* (12:[1742] 320–23; 353–57), it is important for our purposes in revealing the dissemination in America of Du Halde's complimentary attitude toward Confucius and other aspects of Chinese culture. The anonymous author of the essay, after alluding to the enormous number of contradictions in the reports of travelers, affirms that the statements in which these contradictions occur are ordinarily not intended to cater to the whims of the various writers. They do not, he says, "often serve to confirm any *Opinion* favoured by the *Author,* they can neither gratify a Party, nor promote any particular Views, and therefore must be reasonably considered rather as *Errors* than *Falsehoods.*" The essayist believes that the Catholic fathers in China are to be trusted even more than other authorities, for they show fewer inconsistencies. Furthermore, they understand the language, they have absorbed native customs through their long residence in that country, and they are able to grasp the state of Chinese learning since their own function is to improve it. In commenting on the circumstance that the inhabitants of many countries, including many very distant from China, agree in their accounts of their respective national origins, he suggests that the resemblances, although astonishing, are a consequence of the "just and natural *Representations* of the early Condition of every People," an anticipation of the modern theory that there are "invariants" or universal resemblances in the various literatures and cultures of mankind.

After describing the construction of the Great Wall, the reviewer analyzes the motivations of the Emperor Chin who built it when he subsequently commanded that all books in the empire except those on medicine and architecture be burned. This he did in order to render impossible any comparisons with his forerunners. Orders such as these that vary from ancient laws, the essayist says, incite the people to discontent. In connection with education, he observes that where letters are the only means of attaining riches and preferment, the knowledge of writing characters becomes the chief science. He devotes considerable space to Confucius as a role model who sought to inculcate temperance, integrity, and purity of manners by both precepts and example. As a result, Confucius "had three Contrarieties in his Character, which scarcely any other Man has known how to reconcile, . . . all the *Graces* of *Politeness* with all the *Awefulness* of *Gravity;* uncommon *Severity* of *Countenance,* with great *Benignity of Temper;* and the most *exalted Dignity,* with the most *engaging Modesty* in his *Air.*" The commentator then presents a short summary of the Confucian Four Books, or *Ssu shu,* of which, in his words, "the first is called the *Grand Science;* the second the Immutable Medium, a Title correspondent to

Cleobulus, and to the common Maxim, *Virtus consistit* in *Medio;* and the third, *Moral and Concise Discourses;* to which is added a Fourth, of almost equal Authority, written by his scholar *Mencius."* In his conclusion the essayist affirms that the entire doctrine of Confucius "tends to the *Propagation of Virtue,* and the *Restitution* of *Human Nature* to its *original Perfection,* and it is related that his *Precepts* always received *Illustration* from his *Example,* and that in all Conditions of Life, he took Care to prove by his Conduct, that he required no more from others, than he thought it his own Duty to perform."

During the same year in which Franklin printed his excerpts from "The Morals of Confucius" in his *Pennsylvania Gazette,* he referred to "Pere Du Halde's Account of China" in the same periodical, 27 July 1738, in connection with the discovery in Pennsylvania of ginseng by the native American botanist John Bartram, a topic I shall treat in the following chapter. For the present, I shall indicate that Bartram, a self-educated pioneer of American science, was also interested in Chinese philosophy, particularly in the personality of Confucius. The Morgan Library in New York City possesses a manuscript in Bartram's hand titled "Life and Character of the Chinese Philosopher Confucius." Since many of the words in this manuscript are indecipherable, I shall give a paraphrase rather than attempt a literal transcription.

Bartram writes that the famous philosopher was born in the reign of the Emperor Ling Wang 551 years before the birth of Christ. He was justly esteemed the Prince of Chinese philosophers and was the reformer of a sect of literati and the best and wisest man that this or any other nation was ever blessed with. He applied himself to the study of moral philosophy at fifteen years of age and soon became the most learned man of the empire; he had 3,000 disciples, 500 of whom bore public offices in the state and were eminent for their learning. Ten of them were so accomplished that they were called by way of excellence the ten philosophers.

In the year 500 B.C. Confucius was appointed, for his great merit, prime minister of the kingdom of Lu in his native country. He immediately reformed the abuses which had crept into that kingdom and restored honesty in commerce. He taught all men to revere and to honor their parents, instilled into the fair sex politeness and chastity, and caused the love of virtue to be so universal that if anything happened to be lost in the high roads nobody dared meddle with it but its owner. Confucius, finding that his sovereign the King of Lu cared about nothing but a beautiful concubine who had been sent to him as a present and consequently neglected the state and ceased to administer justice, resigned his place of prime minister and left the kingdom in order that blame for the disorder in the realm not be placed upon him. He died in the seventy-fifth year of his age.

The Chinese pay the greatest veneration to the writngs of this philosopher and they are equally esteemed in Japan. Whenever any dispute arises about a doctrinal point, a citation from his works decides it at once. His posterity are still alive and enjoy the greatest privileges. He seems to have been the greatest moral as well as practical philosopher that ever lived, and he excelled Pythagoras in purity of religion and morals. He was of the most exemplary sobriety and chastity of life, was endued with every virtue and free from every vice, and showed the greatest equableness and magnanimity of temper even under the most unworthy treatment. His whole doctrine tended to restore human nature to its original dignity and that first purity and luster which it had received from heaven and which had been sullied and corrupted. He taught as means to obtain this end to honor and fear the Lord of heaven, to love our neighbor as ourselves, to subdue irregular passions and inclinations, to listen to reason in all things, and to do or say nothing contrary to it. He taught kings and princes to be fathers to their subjects, to love them as their children, and he taught subjects to reverence and obey their kings and governors with the honor and affection due to their parents.

He had the justest notions of the deity and of the spiritual worship due him alone although he conformed to the example of the best emperors of China and the orders of the theological works containing the ancient institutions of religion. He worshipped with inferior rites and sacrificed to celestial spirits who were believed according to tradition to be the ministers of divine providence appointed by the supreme God to preside over the several parts of the creation, including the planetary system, and to dispense rewards and punishments in this life. Confucius concurred with the custom of his country in paying a subordinate worship to these heavenly spirits, but he was an abhorrer of all gross idolatry and the worship of dead men or of representing the deity by images or similitudes of any creature, for his notion of God was that he was the supreme truth and reason or the fountain from whence truth and reason derived. He taught that the intelligence of the supreme being comprehended both his own nature and that of all other things and beings and, therefore, he foreknew all things. In short, he was the original ultimate end of all things and the one supremely holy, intelligent, and invisible being.

This summary of the life and character of Confucius has many verbal echoes from the edition of Du Halde's *General History*, the most important of which is the remark that "his whole doctrine tended to restore human nature to its original dignity and that first lustre and purity which it had received from heaven and which had been sullied and corrupted." This is almost identical to Du Halde's "The whole Doctrine of this Philosopher tended to restore human Nature to its former Lustre, and the first Beauty it had received from Heaven, and which had been sullied by the Darkness of Ignorance and the Contagion of Vice" (3:298). The theological implications of the two statements differ somewhat. There is nothing in Du Halde, moreover, to which Bartram's subsequent remarks on the religion of Confucius may be traced. Also Du Halde says that Confucius died at the age of seventy-three; Bartram, at seventy-five. Bartram's erratic style and errors in spelling further suggest that his essay is an original composition.

Since the writings of Confucius were known and published in Europe in the late seventeenth century, it is not strange that the earliest accounts in America of Chinese religion should be devoted to this imposing intellectual figure. The favorable treatment accorded to Confucius by Du Halde and other Jesuit writers, moreover, also helps explain why Confucius dominated early American perspectives of Chinese worship. A broader but somewhat less tolerant attitude toward religion in general was reflected in a review essay in the August, 1775, issue of the *Pennsylvania Magazine* edited at the time by Thomas Paine, who would six months later publish his fiery plea for American independence, *Common Sense*. The works under consideration comprised translations from the German by John Reinhold Foster of three Swedish accounts of China: *A Voyage to China and the East Indies*, by Peter Osbeck; *A Voyage to Suratte*, by Olaf Toreen; and an *Account of the Chinese Husbandry*, by Captain Charles Gustavus Eckeberg. The three works were published as a unit in Swedish in 1757, in J. G. Georgi's German translation in 1765, and in Foster's English translation of Georgi in 1771. In their original Swedish and in their German and English translations these works have been neglected by all the major histories of China in the European Enlightenment, making their notice in colonial America all the more significant.

The review in the *Pennsylvania Magazine* may have been extracted by Paine from a British periodical or it may even have been written by Paine himself, but whatever its origins, it reveals a vital and informed interest in China. Osbeck was a chaplain on a voyage of the Swedish East India Company, a naturalist, and a friend and disciple of Carolus Linnaeus, famous Swedish botanist and originator of taxonomic classification. Toreen was also a chaplain in the same service, and Eckeberg was the captain of one of the company's ships. Also a naturalist, he appended to his account of Chinese agriculture a catalog of the plants and animals in that country.

The first part of the essay in the *Pennsylvania Magazine* is devoted to general comments on travel literature as a means of instruction, on the importance of accuracy and honesty in reporting, and on knowledge of the subject being treated. Affirming that repetition and minuteness, even though seemingly dull and tedious, are commendable, the reviewer compliments the three authors on their credibility. He then provides extracts from Foster's preface as well as from Osbeck's descriptions of various plants and animals together with a description of Canton, including its physical features, population, language, and religion, the latter not from Osbeck or Toreen, but based to a large extent on Du Halde. The essay shows none of the stylistic peculiarities of Paine, but it has as much claim to be Paine's as some other essays now printed as his in editions of his works. All of the extracts given in the review are from Osbeck, and some are paraphrased or adorned with added comments rather than quoted verbatim. Osbeck does not devote much space to Chinese religion, but the reviewer quotes his two most interesting passages on the subject.

> Their observations on the heavens and earth, and their history are remarkable, on account of their antiquity. (According to their accounts, they go as high as the times of Noah.) Their morals are looked upon as a master-piece; their laws are considered as excellent maxims of life; their medicine and natural history are both of them founded on long experience; and their husbandry is admired for the perfection it has risen to. But the want of the true knowledge of the Supreme Being is an imperfection which outweighs all their other knowledge. . . .
> The religion in China is Pagan; but by their own accounts, there are almost as many sects as persons among them; for as soon as a Chinese expects the least advantage from it, he is without any consideration to day of one religion, and to-morrow of another, or of all together. (1771:1:297–98)

These comments are uniformly favorable except for the implied criticism of Chinese indifference to religion, which was subsequently quoted in an American encyclopedia, as I shall show later in this chapter.

An outstanding tribute to Confucius and to Chinese religion in general appeared in the *New Hampshire Magazine* for September 1793 (2, 199–203). A correspondent signing himself CONFUCII DISCIPULUS contributed "a concise History of Confucius, a famous *Chinesian* philosopher," expressing the belief that "a Character so *truly virtuous*, although born and educated in a land of Superstition and Ignorance" would be highly esteemed by readers of the magazine.

According to the American disciple of Confucius, the ancient Chinese sage was descended from an emperor of the race of Chang, but received no material inheritance. He acquired knowledge at an amazing speed, showing great precociousness in all branches of learning, particularly moral science. Before eating, he always paid adoration to the supreme Lord of the Universe, and daily rendered homage to his relatives and endeavored to imitate his grandfather, who was still living. He married at the age of nineteen and had a son, but divorced his wife after four years in order to devote himself to propagation of his philosophy. "He recommended the contempt of riches and outward pomp; he endeavoured to inspire magnanimity and greatness of soul" and to reclaim his country-men from voluptuousness to reason and sobriety. "Kings were governed by his counsels, and the people reverenced him as a saint." From time to time he accepted high offices in the magistracy, but immediately resigned them when he perceived his authority was no longer of public benefit. A great reformation, however, took place in the kingdom. He divided his disciples into four classes: those who improve the mind by meditation and purify the heart by virtuous precepts; those who cultivate the arts of reason and compose elegant and persuasive discourses; those who study the rules of good government; and those who preach to the people the doctrines of morality in a concise and polished style.

The essay concludes with remarks on contemporary religious belief:

> As Confucius is said to be the author of the present established reli-gion of the Literati in China, it may not be improper to observe that, with respect to the most essential doctrine of religion, the immortality of the soul, it appears that the followers of Confucius do not entertain uniform sentiments. The greater part of them regard the precepts of morality no farther than as they contribute to the happiness of the present life, while others, though not regarding immortality as the natural prosperity of the soul, consider it, however, as the destined reward, and just retribution of virtue. This sect use neither temples, priests, idols, sacrifices, nor any sacred rites.

Although these remarks on the immortality of the soul could perhaps be considered critical, the rest of the essay is highly commendatory. The author's pseudonym denoting him as a disciple of Confucius, moreover, represents undisguised admiration.

Jedidiah Morse in his pioneer *American Universal Geography*, 1796, cited a new French translation in 1776 of the *Ta hsüeh*, the good science, or Great Learning, and the *Chung Yung*, the exact middle way or the Doctrine of the Mean, which the French translator had attributed to the grandson of Confucius and one of his disciples. Morse praised these two pieces of morality as containing "the most excellent precepts of wisdom and virtue, expressed with the greatest eloquence, elegance and precision" (Morse 1796: 499). If they were, as the French translators maintained, composed from the lessons of the great Confucius, Morse felt that they should be regarded as "equal to the noblest philosophical remains of Greek antiq-uity, of which they bear, in several places, a very strong resemblance."

A conservative Christian minister himself, Morse compared Confu-cius to Socrates, not to Christ. Morse was particularly impressed by the following passage, which, in his words, "is very striking, and which far exceeds, in clearness, the prophecy of Socrates." "How sublime are the ways of the Holy One! His virtue shall fill the universe—shall vivify all things, and shall rise to the *Tien* or Supreme Deity. What a noble course is opening to our view! What new laws and obligations! What august rites and sacred solemnities! But how shall mortals observe them, if *He* does not first give them the example? His *coming* alone can prepare us for the performance of all ages, 'the paths of perfection shall never be frequented, until the *Holy One*, by way of eminence, shall have consecrated them by the traces of his footsteps' " (1796:2:499).

Morse may have selected this "remarkable passage" because of its millenial connotations, but he refrained from developing chiliastic elements in his commentary. His overall praise of the Chinese sage is especially significant since he wrote his *Geography* with the youth of America in mind and considered it a means of instructing students in patriotism and morality. His remarks on Confucius comprise part of an entry on China of forty-six pages, based on the best available authorities. A comparison of the objective, informed, and specific portrayal in this edition with the scant, erroneous, and general remarks on China in Morse's *American Geography* published seven years previously will reveal how one influential intellectual's attitude toward the Middle Kingdom changed dramatically in a period of less than a decade.

> The Tartar race comprehending the Chinese, and the Japanese, forms the second variety in the human species. Their countenances are broad and wrinkled, even in youth; their noses short and flat; their eyes little, sunk in the sockets, and several inches asunder; their cheek bones are high; their teeth are of a large size and separate from each other; their complexions are olive, and their hair black. These nations, in general, have no religion, no settled notions of morality, and no decency of behaviour. They are chiefly robbers; their wealth consists in horses, and their skill in the management of them. (Morse 1789:529)

About the only truthful statement in this astounding summary is that the Asiatics have black hair.

Confucius was specifically associated with millenialism in a Christian periodical *The Balance*, 13 September 1803, in comments on a "Remarkable Chinese Prediction." Quoting the identical passage that Morse had labelled "remarkable," but attributing it merely to Confucius's grandson without specifying a more precise provenance, the writer interpreted the references to "His *coming*" and the "*Holy One*" as a prophecy of the approach of the Messiah, parallel to similar auguries in Socrates and Virgil (2:392).

Name recognition of the Chinese sage was utilized in a later issue of *The Balance* in which ten maxims appeared with no other identification than the name Confucius following them (24 December 1805, 4:409). The maxims, however, have nothing whatsoever to do with Confucius or with China.

An essay in the *Columbian Magazine* for May 1788 (2, 257–263), associates Confucius with the filial piety of the Chinese. The author gives him credit for restoring to its pristine energy the respect for parents that had been recommended by ancient emperors and prints two pages of the *Li-chi*, the fourth book of the *Wu ching*, that he characterizes as a code of filial piety that has attained the status of law. An unusual story of filial piety drawn from Le Comte's *Memoirs* appeared in the *Christian's, Scholar's and Farmer's Magazine* for December–January 1789–90. After one of the emperors of China banished his mother to a distant province because she had carried on a private intrigue with one of the lords of the court, three brave mandarins protested against this unfilial behavior and were condemned to death. Subsequently many others suffered torture and death for speaking out in support of the same principle of filial duty until finally the emperor relented and restored his mother to her former dignity. Apparently both the Jesuit Le Comte and the American Christian editors believed that filial duty should take precedence over sexual continence.

Further information concerning Chinese religious beliefs and practices appeared in one of the most remarkable series of books published in America at the turn of the eighteenth century—an encyclopedia of sects and theologies—published first of all in 1784 as *An Alphabetical Compendium of the Various Sects* and reissued with extensive revisions in 1791 and 1801 under the title *A View of Religions*. A fourth edition appeared in 1817 as *A Dictionary of All Religions*. The author, Hannah Adams, was as remarkable personally as was her survey of attitudes toward divine worship throughout the world. A New England spinster, who probably derived her literary proclivities from her father's occupation of bookseller, Adams treated all faiths with a scholarly breadth and tolerance extremely liberal for the time and place. In addition to her reference works, she published in 1812 an unbiased and sympathetic *History of the Jews from the Destruction of Jerusalem to the Nineteenth Century*.

Adams's encyclopedia of belief is almost exactly parallel to an English compilation that went through many editions a century previously, Alexander Ross's *Pansebia: or, A View of All Religions in the World* (1696). Ross was famous throughout the eighteenth century not only for this comprehensive work itself, but also for a humorous reference to it in Samuel Butler's *Hudibras*, a contemporary satirical poem on Puritanism now sadly neglected. Butler begins the second canto of his satire with a couplet requiring a misplacing of accents in Ross's name.

> There was an ancient sage philosopher,
> That had read Alexander Ross over.

Out of the 450 pages of his book, Ross devotes only one, the following, to China (page 57).

[The Chinese] were always, and still are Idolaters; except a few gained to Christianity by the Jesuits, and a few Tartars that are Mahumetans. That vast Dominion is full of Temples and Monasteries, replenished with multitudes of Idols, which their cunning Priests feed with the smoak of meats, but they eat the meat themselves. The Priests here have so much power over their gods, that they may beat and whip them when they do not answer their expectation. They have one Idol with three heads, which they much reverence. These represent their three great Philosophers, *Confusius, Xequiam*, and *Tanzu*. Their chief gods are the Sun, Moon, and Stars. They worship also the Devil, not out of love, but fear that he may do them no hurt; therefore they place his picture in the Fore-castle of their ships. They are Pythagoreans in the opinion of Transanimation; therefore some of them will not kill any living thing. For this cause in *Quinsay* in a walled Park belonging to a Monastery, the Monks feed 4000 living creatures of diverse kinds, out of their charity to the souls of Noble men, which were entred [*sic*] into the bodies of these creatures. Their Monks are shaven, are bound to wear beads, to be present at burials, to maintain Celibate whilst they are Monks, to pray two hours together before day. Of these religious Orders there be four sorts, distinguished by their colours, black, white, yellow, and russet. These have their Priors, Provincials, and General; he is carried on mens shoulders in an Ivory Chair, and is cloathed in silk. Their maintenance is not only the Kings allowance, but also the benevolence of devout people, which they procure by begging and praying for them. They have their Nuns also, and Hermits, and consecrated Hills, to which the people make divers Pilgrimages. There are many Colleges for learning, which is of high esteem among them. Their Secular Priests wear long hair and black cloth, their Regulates are shaven, but neither must marry. They are bound to observe all Festival days, such as the New and full Moons, the Kings birth-day, but chiefly New-years-day, which is the first day of the New Moon in *February*. The people here are very superstitious in observing their birth-days, and in performing the Funeral Obsequies of their Parents, whom they adore, and bury in the fields, with all solemnity and excessive charges. No man is tied to any particular worship among them, but he may be of what Sect he will. They have abundance of Hospitals for the poor, and no beggars to be seen among them. But for any knowledge of heavenly joys, or hell torments, they have very little or none at all. They are very much afraid when there is an Eclipse of the Sun or Moon, which they hold to be man and wife; for then they think that these two gods are angry with them. Of their many superstitious Ceremonies and vain opinions in Divinity, see the Discourse of *China, Boterus, Ortelius, Masseus, Linschoten,* and the Jesuits Epistles.

Ross's division of the religion of China into three principal sects was not only historically correct, but based on the writings of the two major European authors available to him, the Italian Jesuit, Ricci, and the French Jesuit, Trigault. Today the three major sects are known as Confucianism, Buddhism and Taoism; these names derived from their legendary founders Confucius, Buddha, and Lao-tsu (Tanzu). Even though the Chinese then as now could pass comfortably from one sect to another and even accept all three in a day, it is extremely doubtful that an idol was ever erected bearing the effigies of all three religious luminaries.

Hannah Adams's entry on China in the first edition of her encyclopedia borrows absolutely nothing from Ross, and it is doubtful that she even knew of his existence. Considering the great amount of writing on China made available during the intervening years, one would expect her to provide a much more extensive treatment, but she presents very little new information. This economy does enable her, however, to provide a more extensive coverage of ideas rather than ceremonies.

> Besides the worship of the *Grand Lama,* the religion of *China* is divided into three sects. 1st. The followers of *Laokium,* who lived five hundred years before *Christ,* and taught that God was corporeal. They pay divine homage to the philosopher *Laokium,* and give the same worship, not only to many Emperors who have been ranked with the Gods, but also to certain Spirits under the name of *Xamte,* who preside over every element. They call this sect that of the *Magicians,* because the learned of it addict themselves to *Magic,* and are believed to have the secret of making men immortal.
>
> 2d. The worshippers of *Foe,* who flourished a thousand years before our *Saviour,* and who became a God at the age of thirty years. He is represented shining in light, with his hands hid under his robes, to shew that he does all things invisible. The Doctors of this sect teach a double law, the one *external,* the other *internal.* According to the *external law,* they say, that all the good are recompensed, and the wicked punished, in places destined for each. They enjoin all works of mercy; and forbid cheating, impurity, wine, lying and murder, and even the taking life from any creature whatever.
>
> The *interior* doctrine of this sect, which is kept secret from the

common people, teaches a pure, unmixed *atheism*, which admits neither rewards nor punishments after death,— believes not in a Providence, or the immortality of the soul,— acknowledges no other *God* but the Void or Nothing,—and which makes the supreme happiness of mankind to consist in a *total inaction*, an *intire insensibility*, and a *perfect quietude*.

3d. A sect which acknowledges the philosopher *Confucius* for its master, who lived five hundred years before *our Saviour*. This religion, which is professed by the *literati* and persons of rank in *China* and *Tonquin*, consists in a deep inward veneration for the *God* or *Kingdom of Heaven*, and in the practice of every *moral virtue*. They have neither temples nor Priests, nor any settled form of external worship; every one adores the supreme Being in the way he himself thinks best.

The entry as a whole does not differ so radically from that derived from Alexander Ross as the multiplicity of apparently contradictory names seems to indicate. The founders of the three great religions of China are Confucius, Buddha, and Lao Tsu, all three of which are indicated by both authors. Fo is identical with Buddha, and Laokium is the same as Lao Tse. Xamti is equivalent to Chamti or Chang-ti, which means Sovereign God or Emperor. I have not found other contemporary references to Xequiam or Tanzu. Adams concludes with brief references to ancestor worship, burning of incense, bowing before images, and invoking them as capable of bestowing all temporal blessings.

The entry in the later *View of Religions* is supplemented by material from a variety of sources. The opening sentence follows almost verbatim the passage from Osbeck in the review of John Reinhold Foster's translation in Paine's *Pennsylvania Magazine* of 1775: "The religion of this kingdom is Pagan: but it is said, there are almost as many sects as persons among them. For as soon as a Chinese expects the least advantage from it, he is without any consideration, to-day of one religion, to-morrow of another, or of all together." The earlier account of the followers of Laokium is supplemented with the information that their morality consists in calming the passions, living free from care, forgetting the past, and looking at the future without apprehension and that they pretend to have discovered an elixir to confer immortality. In regard to Foe, the account adds that this religion was transferred from India sixty-five years after the birth of Christ. Its members believe that human souls are transmigrated into irrational creatures, either those that they like best or those that they resemble most; for this reason they never kill these animals, but treat them with loving care. They also believe that prayers, penances, and acts of charity will win them a happy transmigration. The priests pretend to relatives of the deceased to have knowledge of the animals into which they have been transmigrated and uniformly represent these ancestors as miserable or uncomfortable in order to extort money to be used for obtaining a passage into a more favorable state. A footnote refers to the *Modern Universal History*, part of the cooperative enterprise titled *An Universal History from the Earliest Account of Time* (London, 1736–1765), considered to be the last important world history reflecting an exclusively Christian perspective. Printed by Samuel Richardson, the author of *Pamela*, the work included among its collaborators George Sale, a pioneer specialist on the Middle East, and George Salmanzar, a Frenchman who pretended to be a native of Formosa, the present Taiwan. Salmanzar published a notorious book about conditions in his alleged homeland, and almost got away with the hoax (Foley 1968:4–6).

In Hannah Adams's 1791 edition, Confucius is portrayed in a more extensive but much less accurate manner than in the earlier *Alphabetical Compendium*.

> *Confucius* did not dive into abstruse notions, but confined himself to speak with the deepest regard of the great Author of all beings, whom he represents as the most pure and perfect essence and fountain of all things; to inspire men with greater fear, veneration, gratitude and love of him; to assert his divine providence over all his creatures; and to represent him as a being of such infinite knowledge, that even our most secret thoughts are not hidden from him; and of such boundless goodness and justice, that he can let no virtue go unrewarded, or vice unpunished.

This information, attributed to the *Universal History*, is deficient because of the anthropomorphism ascribed to Confucius. Adams adds that the worship paid to Confucius and some eminent men was considered a civil matter and, therefore, complied with by the Jesuit missionaries although greatly condemned by the Dominicans. Some of her material Adams drew directly from the Roman Catholic Bishop of America, the Right Reverend Bishop John Carroll, who was appointed at the close of the War of Independence. Father Carroll had close contacts with Franklin during the conflict, and Franklin was instrumental in his being chosen as the first Roman Catholic bishop in America. Adams specifically indicates Carroll as the source of the following paragraph, printed as a note:

> From accounts from China as late as the year 1788, respecting the success of the missionaries, we are informed, that in the province of Suschuen, there had been an increase of twenty-seven thousand Christians, during the last thirty years; that it was governed by the titular bishop of Agathopolis. In the province of Nankin are thirty

thousand. A very violent storm was raised in 1785 against them and several missionaries became the victims of it. They were reduced, when the last accounts arrived, to so small a number, as to be incompetent to the services required of them.

Even more important, Adams drew verbatim from another source in her own country, the *American Museum* for April, 1790, an eyewitness account of Chinese worship in a joss house, the word *joss* a pidgin English term for *deus* or god.

In the houses which are consecrated to their idol *Joss*, there is an image of a fat laughing old man at the upper end of the room, sitting in a chair, before whom is erected a small altar, wherein tapers and sandal wood are constantly kept burning. As soon as a worshipper enters, he prostrates himself before the idol, and knocks his head three times on the ground. This done, he takes three pieces of wood that fit together in the form of a kidney; again kneels; knocks his head; holds them to *Joss*; and after bowing three times for his blessing, throws them up. If they fall with both flat or both round sides up, it is good luck; but if one of each, it is unfortunate. He renews his worship to *Joss*, and tries again. Sometimes it is repeated seven or eight times, till it is succeeded. Then he prostrates himself again, and repeats similar ceremonies. When he is satisfied, he lights his taper, and fixes it before *Joss*; then sets fire to a piece of paper washed with tin, presents it on the altar, bows three times and retires.

The account in the *American Museum* from which this paragraph is taken is titled "New observations on the religion of the Chinese, by an American traveller." Actually the author is Samuel Shaw, the supercargo on the first American vessel to visit China, and the material in the periodical is extracted without credit from his journal. In it, Shaw further indicates that in addition to the joss houses that are always open and greatly frequented, Chinese cities have larger pagodas or temples staffed by bonzes or priests and containing huge idols in the form of men and women, highly frightening in appearance. In addition every house and sampan [or house boat] has an idol of its domestic deity before whom a piece of sandal wood is constantly kept burning, which serves the double function of offering a pleasing odor for the god and lighting for the worshipper's pipe. Shaw also explains that polygamy is accepted "and a man is pleased with his favourite wife, and with his maker, in proportion to the number of sons she bears him: no account is made of daughters." Synchong, the principal porcelain merchant at Canton, told Shaw one day that joss had been very good to him by giving him three sons. In a later essay in the *New York Magazine* (1796.N.S. No.6) Shaw told of the delight

43

of another Chinese in the fecundity of his wife. *"My wife too muchey good, she have catchey four bull child mon mon* [by and by]. *I think she makey one more bull; I no likey that cow child, he makey too much bobbery* [cry too much]. *Joss love me, cause I makey he much tsin tsin* [worship]." Rich Chinese, according to Shaw, are equally concerned with procuring pleasant locations for their tombs—airy, shaded by trees, watered by running streams, located on eminences, and commanding extensive views. If a Chinese meets with some great misfortune, he believes that his father's bones are not reposing comfortably and proceeds to find a more suitable resting place and transports the remains with much ceremony. In Shaw's opinion, the most extravagant accounts of Chinese idolatry and superstition may safely be believed. "No people are more the sport of religious contingencies, or put greater faith in lucky days."

The title of Shaw's account in the *American Museum* suggests that the "American traveller" had journeyed throughout the Middle Kingdom, a completely unwarranted assumption, for all foreigners at that period, as will be pointed out in chapter 7, were strictly limited to a confined area in Canton. Shaw had been allowed to visit a Buddhist temple in the city, but must have acquired any further knowledge of Chinese religion from Synchong or other contacts in the commercial enclave.

In his journal Shaw notices an edict from the Emperor K'ien Long, 9 November 1785, relevant to the crackdown against Christians mentioned by Bishop Carroll in Hannah Adam's *View of Religion*. According to Shaw, the way in which the edict was enforced actually illustrates the emperor's humanitarianism and tolerant spirit. Twelve Catholic missionaries had been discovered secretly endeavoring to propagate their religious beliefs in five Chinese provinces, not only breaking the rule against the admission of foreigners to the empire, but furtively and secretly attempting to multiply converts to their faith. They were accordingly sentenced to life imprisonment. The emperor, reviewing the sentence, reflected that as foreigners they were not well acquainted with the laws of the empire, and his compassion led him to order their release with the option of taking up residence with other Europeans in Pekin and living according to their condition or returning to their native France (Quincy 1847: 315–16).

Extracts from a journal of a "Voyage to Canton" written in a style very much like Shaw's appeared in a New York deistical periodical, *The Correspondent*, 1 December 1827. According to this journal, a party of Western travelers visited the houses of three Chinese security merchants to observe ceremonies in honor of the devil. The houses were decorated and illuminated for the occasion "with variegated lamps, artificial flowers, and a variety of other ornaments, in honor of the DEVIL, or QUI, as he is called by the Chinese. Europeans and Americans go by the name of

FANQUI, or STRANGE DEVIL, to which they not infrequently add the term of QUISI, that means rogue, rascal, knave, or any thing bad." The journalist observes that the Chinese have no sabbath, but celebrate "the first and the few succeeding days of the new year as their only holidays." "At this time the poorest peasant makes a point of having a new suit of clothes for himself and his family, while they pay visits to their friends and relations, interchange civilities and compliments, and make and receive presents."

Adams's 1817 *Dictionary of all Religions* has a much abbreviated entry on China, dropping descriptions of the principal sects, the joss houses, and the desire for male heirs and appropriate tombs and substituting reports of Catholic attempts to proselytize and Chinese resistance to these efforts.

An American trader in China, Thomas T. Forbes, some years later confirmed the report concerning Chinese anxiety regarding an ancestor's tomb. Forbes related in March, 1839, that his business contact in Canton, Houqua, "has lately fatigued himself very much in committing to the ground his Father who died 35 years ago—it is the custom in many cases to keep the bodies of parents until a lucky spot is found to bury them in. It is said Houqua has kept a man in pay learned in such things & at last has hit on the place" (Christman 1984: 87). More about Synchong and Houqua will appear in chapter 7. In subsequent chapters, moreover, I shall introduce other references to Chinese morality and religion.

During the entire eighteenth century, American Protestants showed no interest in sending missionaries to China to supplant the Catholic priests who had been banned. Indeed the most famous Puritan of the colonies, Jonathan Edwards, argued that the people of his own country were more committed by God "to our care than the people of China, and we ought to pray more for them" (1809:3:287). Edwards made no comments at all about Confucius, moreover, nor did any other American have anything unfavorable to say about the Chinese sage until the last decade of the century. At that time when accounts of China by American travelers began to reveal unsavory aspects of worship deliberately ignored by the Jesuits, they began to associate Chinese religion with idolatry and superstition rather than with the ethical rectitude of Confucius.

Considerable scholarly attention has been given to Thoreau's publication in 1843 of the basic writings of Confucius in *The Dial*. Thoreau can hardly be considered an innovator, however, since Franklin had introduced Confucius to American readers a century earlier in a milieu dominated by Christian orthodoxy and ritual, apparently taking a chance that his subscribers would accept the philosophy of the Eastern sage in the same light in which it was viewed at its source. Thoreau merely helped to promote the image of Confucius as representative of Chinese religion as a whole and to lead American opinion back to the favorable attitude toward Chinese religion that had originated in the preceding century. He may, therefore, be given credit for attempting to stem the tide of Sinophobia, if not of contributing to the earliest wave of enthusiasm over Confucius.

The writer in the *New Hampshire Magazine* in 1793 did not hesitate to sign himself a disciple of Confucius. In 1813, moreover, the editors of the *Analectic Magazine* in Philadelphia published (I: 345–51) from the London *Analectic Magazine* "Memoirs of the Life of Confucius" based upon a translation of the Analects by James Marshman that had been printed in Bengal in 1809 at a printing press belonging to English missionaries. In the same year, the *Analectic Magazine* extracted from the *Literary Panorama* "Anecdotes of the Conduct and Maxims of Confucius, the Chinese Sage." In this highly eulogistic account, Confucius is described as an "orderly, self-governed, social and benevolent person" in contrast to Mahomet, who is portrayed as a war-crazed zealot. By the end of the eighteenth century, therefore, long before Thoreau, Confucius was not only well known, but regarded as the representative of only one of three major varieties of Chinese religion. All writers agreed that he was a wise and virtuous man whose religious practices were inspired by benevolence and exempt from superstition.

Lafitau and That Precious Root: Ginseng*

T he exporting of the medicinal root and reputed aphrodisiac ginseng from the New World to China represents an important chapter in Sino-American relations of the eighteenth century. The legendary curative powers of the plant originally became known in Europe through the reports of Jesuit missionaries long before Du Halde, some of whom even claimed that it could "revive those at death's door and provide immortality" (Appleby 1982: 3: 121). It was also, and still is, widely hailed as an aphrodisiac, perhaps because of the shape of its root, resembling, some say, a phallus and, others, the legs and waist of a man.

A Jesuit living in North America, Joseph François Lafitau, discovered the existence of the plant in Canada early in the century and used its presence as partial proof of his theory that the two Americas were once joined with China and that human physical and intellectual communication had taken place between them in prehistoric times. Very little is known about the life of this notable French-Canadian ethnologist, not even the exact date of his birth, which took place in Bordeaux toward the end of the seventeenth century. He was sent in 1712 to Sault St. Louis, an Indian village some distance from the present reserve of that name near

---

*GINSENG. s. [I suppose *Chinese*] A root brought lately into Europe. It is of a very agreeable aromatick smell, though not very strong. Its taste is acrid and aromatick, and has somewhat bitter in it. We have it from China, and there is of it in the same latitudes in America. (Samuel Johnson, *Dictionary*, 1760)

Chinese ginseng, from Mark Catesby's The Natural History of Carolina,
Florida & The Bahama Islands *(1771).*
Reproduced with permission of The Library Company of Philadelphia.

Montreal (Lafitau 1858: 9). Three years later Lafitau noticed a description of Chinese ginseng in an account by Père Pierre Jartoux of his voyage to Tartary in 1709 in Volume X of the Jesuits' *Lettres curieuses et édifiantes*. Lafitau then undertook a successful search for an American counterpart. In 1717 he returned to France, and in January of that year the Jesuit scientific periodical *Journal de Trévoux* published a preliminary account of American ginseng from his pen. Here he affirmed that the Iroquois name for the plant is *garentogen* which means, like the Chinese *ginseng*, "representation of man" or "resemblance to man." This linguistic similarity, Lafitau believed, could be accounted for only on the supposition of a communication of ideas between the two races and, therefore, of individuals as well. "D'où l'on pourroit conclure que ces Tartars orientaux, dont les moeurs ressemblent assez à celles des sauvages, ne sont pas si éloignez de Canada qu'on le pense, peut-être que quand le pais qui est au delà de la Louisiane sera habité, on ne sera pas long tems sans découvrir ces Tartares." (From this one might conclude that these oriental Tartars, whose manners resemble those of the savages, are not so distant from Canada as one might think, and perhaps when the country beyond Louisiana shall be inhabited, it will not be long before these Tartars are discovered.) Nearly two centuries later, linguists, anthropologists, and comparatists are still using the similarity in languages as evidence of pre-historic physical contact between American Indians and the Chinese (Etiemble 1989: 346).

During his period in France, Lafitau had not had the opportunity to learn whether Canadian ginseng had the same medicinal properties as the Chinese, but he affirmed from his own experience that it is an excellent febrifuge. The Indians had assured him, moreover, that it cures pleurisy, dysentery, and consumption. In 1718, Lafitau published in Paris an extension of these preliminary remarks in a formal pamphlet dedicated to the Regent of France, a notorious libertine, *Mémoire . . . concernant la précieuse plante du Ginseng de Tartarie découverte en Canada* (*Memoir . . . concerning the precious gingseng plant of Tartary discovered in America*) (Lafitau 1858). Here Lafitau answers critics who had questioned the identity of his ginseng with the Chinese variety by pointing out how his plant differed from one described by the German botanist Engelbert Kempfer, which was not true ginseng, but had been mistakenly regarded as such. Kempfer's plant had come from Japan, where the people there denied that it had healing virtue and had, therefore, prohibited its being sold as genuine ginseng. Kempfer says the Japanese plant he described also grows in China, where to distinguish it from the true Chinese *ginseng* and the Tartar *dorhata*, it is called *som* and in Tartary, *soasay*. Jartoux, moreover, had described Chinese ginseng growing in a way absolutely conforming to the Canadian plant.

Lafitau says that the Indians had told him that they used the native growth as a purge for newborn children (it was too mild for adults), to restore appetite, to reduce fever, and to combat dysentery. In connection with the Chinese variety, he quotes the affirmation of Jartoux that ginseng is a part of nearly all Chinese prescriptions. The pronouncements of Jartoux concerning its efficacy were so extraordinary that Lafitau admits that he had once wondered whether ginseng may not have been a kind of universal panacea or cure-all praised beyond its merits, but he was reassured when he heard that similar claims had been fully vindicated at Leyden by Professor Frederic Dekkers of the College of Medicine. Lafitau does, however, express at considerable length doubts concerning the conjecture that the mandragora or mandrake described by Theophrastus conforms to Chinese ginseng. At the conclusion of his memoir, Lafitau informs the Regent, who also had the title of Duke of Orleans, that he was giving the Canadian plant the botanical name *Aureliana Canadensis*, based on the Latin name for Orleans, *Aurelianum*. The name did not stick, however, for in William P. C. Barton's *Materia Medica of the United States* (Philadelphia, 1817–18), it is called *panax-quinque-folium*, the name originally given to it by Linnaeus, and by which it is still known. Modern authorities indicate, moreover, that Chinese and American ginseng are not botanically equivalent, but their "roots are virtually identical in appearance and have the same medicinal uses" (Appleby 1982–3: 137).

The only unfavorable remark concerning the Chinese in Lafitau's memoir concerns their knowledge of medicine. Sufficient information about ginseng is still not available, he affirms, "parceque nous ne la connaissons que par des sauvages, des Chinois et des Japonais, qui dans le fonds sont de mauvais médecins, peu instruits des principes de l'anatomie et des règles de l'art" (because we know it only through the savages, the Chinese and the Japanese, who are basically poor physicians, little versed in the principles of anatomy and the rules of the art) (1858: 31).

Most of what Lafitau says about Chinese ginseng was already to be found in the travels of another Jesuit, Louis Daniel Le Comte, published under the title *Nouveaux mémoires sur l'état présent de la Chine* (Paris, 1696) and translated in the next year as *Memoirs and observations . . . made by L. Le Comte in a late journey through the Empire of China*. Le Comte's remarks on the plant were reprinted in Elizabethtown, New Jersey, in the *Christian's, Scholar's, and Farmer's Magazine* for December and January 1789–90 (629–30) under the heading "*Description of* GIN-SENG." After explaining the Chinese etymology of the term, Le Comte lists some of the appellations which have been applied to it such as "the Spirituous Simple, the pure Spirit of the Earth, the Fat of the Sea, the *Panacea*, and the Remedy that dispenses Immortality." It is, according to Le Comte, commonly found under a tree called Kinchu, "little differing from the sycamore."

The Chinese make a sweet and delightful cordial from it. It "purifies the blood, fortifies the stomach, adds motion in a languid pulse, excites the natural heat, and augments the radical moisture."

Six years after his pamphlet on ginseng, Lafitau brought out his more famous treatise, *Moeurs des sauvages américains comparés aux moeurs des premiers temps [Manners of the American savages compared with those of ancient times]*, expressing his anthropological theories. The latter treatise in two large volumes is a pioneer study of East-West relations containing parallels between the Chinese and the natives of America as well as between American Indians and ancient Greeks and Romans. Lafitau's work has philosophical resemblance to that of a French free-thinker of the preceding century, *La Vertu des paiens* (1641), by François de La Mothe le Vayer. Even though the general attitudes of the two books toward Christianity are almost contrary, both proclaim the essential moral similarities of all men whether or not touched by Christianity. Among biographies of the virtuous ancients, La Mothe le Vayer inserted a panegyrical chapter on Confucius, supporting the argument of the Jesuits against their theological enemies the Jansenists that the faculty of reason brings men close to God and could aid in their salvation. In this way, he struck one blow for the Jesuits and another for the religion of nature.

In his *Manners of the American Savages*, Lafitau does not summarize his earlier memoir on ginseng. Indeed his remarks on the plant are quite brief. He merely affirms that ginseng is unlike the coca leaf of South America, which has no nutritive value and is forbidden throughout most of Peru by the Spanish Inquisition. Ginseng, to the contrary, he observes, has marvelous powers and is widely used by North American Indians. Presumably having reread Theophrastus, he surmises that the Greek author had spoken of ginseng in his *History of Plants*, Book I, chapter 13, under the name *Scythica* and adds that the Tartars are truly Scythians. Ginseng, Lafitau says, has the "virtue of sustaining, fortifying and replenishing exhausted strength. It has a slight taste of licorice" (2, 141–2).

Perhaps the most important passage in Lafitau's book, at least from the perspective of East-West relations, is that in which he joins his thesis of the parallels in character and behavior of the ancient Greeks and the American Indians with the conjecture, that he shared with several other writers, that China and the native Americans had at one time established physical contact. Lafitau and his suppositions merit a digression at this point from the theme of ginseng and its reputed virtues.

Previous scholarship has emphasized Lafitau's attention to the ancient Greeks. It is equally significant to see what he has said about the Chinese. He declares that whether the Asian and American continents in pre-historic times were contiguous or whether divided by some small bodies of water, the passage from one to the other was easy. He then offers his comparison of the manners of the American natives and those of the Asiatics and the nations comprised under the names of Thrace and Scythia as a kind of evidence "that America had been peopled by the most eastern lands of Tartary" (1, 34). The theory is considered as tenable by modern anthropologists, who support it by both ethnographic and linguistic evidence. Some of Lafitau's parallels, however, border on the trivial, for example, that of resemblances between Indian nocturnal celebrations and Chinese festivals of lanterns (1, 369). This parallel, nevertheless, later assumed considerable significance in European polemics over the relative age of the Egyptian and Chinese cultures. Those who mnaintained the priority of the Egyptians argued that since it was known that the latter had lighted candles in their ceremonies and the Chinese used lanterns extensively, China must have been colonized by the Egyptians. This argument is put forth in *Recueil d'observations curieuses* and is ridiculed in several of Voltaire's satires, published long after Lafitau (Etiemble 1989: 242).

The theory of ancient contact between China and America was resurrected by another French citizen and pioneer Sinophile,, Joseph de Guignes a few years after Lafitau. In a *Memoir upon the ancient Navigations of the Chinese to America, with some Conjecture upon the Origin of the Americans,* de Guignes affirmed that the Chinese had penetrated into America in A.D. 458 by way of Japan and the most easterly part of North Asia, landing somewhere north of California. Others, he believed, passed, not by sea, but by land, through "the most eastern extremities of *Asia,* where the two continents are only separated by a narrow strait, easy to cross." He reported instances of women who made the trip in the opposite direction, traveling from Florida and Canada to Tartary without ever seeing the ocean. Extracts from Guignes's memoir appeared in the foremost English periodical of the century, the *Gentleman's Magazine* in 1753 (23: 607–08). In chapter 12, I shall discuss some American exponents of this notion of an ethnic link between China and native Americans.

Lafitau in his *Manners of the American Savages* remarks that he had previously interpreted the fabulous reports of ancients about monsters, such as people with eyes in their trunks or those without heads, as merely figurative ways of expressing contempt for alien races—much as the Chinese of his day, believing themselves to be the wisest of all men, say that they are the only ones with two eyes—that their neighbors are blind and the Europeans have only a single eye. He changed his mind, however, on reading the account of the Papal legate to China at the height of the rites controversy, Mezzabarba, a Jesuit, but designated at the time Patriarch of Alexandria. The Chinese emperor confided to the latter that he had always been extremely reluctant to impose the death sentence in his realm and had, therefore, once refused to sanction the extreme penalty against some men who had spread a story about men without heads, whose eyes were located in the area of the breast and their mouths in that of the stomach. Shortly after his refusal to exact the death penalty, the emperor felt vindicated in his moderation when he was told that monsters of this kind actually inhabited northern Tartary (1: 54–66). Lafitau himself, therefore, had fewer doubts concerning the existence of various prodigies of nature, particularly those recounted by an Eskimo girl that there existed in the North entire nations of men who measured only three feet in stature and whose women were even smaller than this, that the tiny men were slaves of the larger ones, and that they were all very happy when given a drink of fresh water, being accustomed to drinking nothing but that containing salt.

Incidentally, Lafitau is the earliest writer I know of to quote the Chinese proverb concerning the Chinese having two eyes, their neighbors one, and the rest of the world none at all. After Lafitau, a Spanish priest, Benito Jeronimo Feijoo, quoted the saying in 1730 to counteract a Spanish one characterizing the Chinese as barbarians, affirming that he picked it up from the *Relaciones* of Giovani Botero (Aldridge 1990:3:409). The proverb also appears in Diderot's correspondence for 1760 (1957:3:113) and in Raynal's *Political and Philosophical History* (1788:2:243).

In order to support his theory that a spirit of religion is universal, Lafitau reports how the Iroquois explain the origin of the earth and of their own nation. In the beginning there were only six men, but no women and no land, merely space. Learning of the existence of a woman in the sky, the six men resolved that one of their number, Hogouaho or the Wolf, would try to find her. With the aid of the birds, who made a chair of their bodies, he ascended to the sky and waited for the woman at the foot of a tree, where she ordinarily came for her daily supply of water. The Iroquois brave made her a present of bear grease, and the woman, susceptible to gifts and easy conversation, was seduced with little effort. The master of the sky in his anger drove her over the brink of the heaven. In her fall the tortoise caught her on his back and the otter and the fish used clay from the bottom of the sea to form an island to hold her, which gradually grew into the form of the world today. From this pristine woman have descended all the generations of mankind, including the tribes of the Iroquois and Hurons, represented by the Wolf, the Bear, and the Tortoise. This narrative, now known as the Creation Myth of the Iroquois, is still repeated by American Indians (Hertzberg 1966:12–22). Its resemblance to Chinese creation myths will be noted in chapter 4.

Although describing this fable as ridiculous and worthy of pity, Lafitau finds it no more absurd than the Greek fable of Prometheus. He also recognizes in it certain similarities to the Biblical story of Genesis—both involving a woman in a terrestrial paradise, a tree of knowledge, and a temptation to which the woman succumbs. Among various resemblances to Greek mythology, he suggests a parallel between the Indian tortoise and the Greek tortoise upon which the goddess Venus Uranie rested her feet. In this Greek fable, the divine being is conceived as the creator of the harmony of the world and the tortoise the symbol of this harmony. Lafitau, therefore, draws another comparison with the Chinese fable of a tortoise, symbol of the support of the world, giving birth to a dragon, symbol of air and mountains (2, 99–100). Lafitau believes not only that the spirit of religion exists everywhere in the world, but also that all religions are hieroglyphic. He places the Chinese among the polite nations who have recognized a primordial being with their *Tien Chu*, or master of the heaven, and their *Xang Tu*, or sovereign emperor and sovereign master (1, 124). In bringing together tales and traditions, both oral and written, of these separate cultures, Lafitau was in a real sense the precursor of Etiemble and other modern experts in comparative literature, who look for invariants or fundamental esthetic resemblances in various national literatures (Etiemble 1988: 135).

Since Lafitau was a member of the Order of Jesus, it is natural that he should accept the thesis of Jesuit missionaries in China that the dominant religion of that country could be made conformable to Catholicism. In connection with various ancient fables and signs in the West, including the Virgin of the Zodiac, prefiguring the virgin birth of Christ, Lafitau cites manuscripts in his possession from missionaries to China containing extracts from the Five Chinese Classics, the *Wu ching* of Confucius. These comprise, in his words, a "complete précis of the ancient religion of the literate classes, that the Chinese respect, as we respect the Books of Moses. . . . These extracts speak of a Virgin Mother & her son in a characteristic manner in so many points that are related to that which our religion teaches that it seems that we cannot mistake them" (1, 235).

As an example of mutual esteem, Lafitau tells of the custom among American Indians of exchanging clothing and other personal items when departing for war. All persons remaining behind in the village hasten to exchange some article of wearing apparel as a token of their admiration for those going off to battle. Lafitau then quotes from Le Comte's *Memoir on China* a passage concerning the departure of a magistrate from one village to another. The inhabitants set up tables along the road where the mandarin must pass and press him to sample tea, liquors, and cakes. At the same time they exchange various articles of clothing for the purpose identical with that of the Indians—signaling respect (2, 192–3). Lafitau adds that among the Greeks the custom was extended to one's adversaries, citing as examples Glaucus and Diomede in the *Iliad* exchanging their armor.

Although it is doubtful that Lafitau's French memoir on ginseng made its way south to the English colonies, knowledge of the miraculous powers attributed to the plant existed there before the English themselves had discovered that ginseng grew in their midst. Lafitau in his memoir affirmed not only that it was to be found among the Ottawa Indians and in the vicinity of Lake Huron, but that it was said to grow in large quantities among the Five Iroquois Nations. If this were true, he assumed, the Dutch of New York would not be long before taking advantage of its commercial potentialities, for anyone seeing it sold at Montreal by the Indians would immediately ship it to England (1858:32). Lafitau's prediction was confirmed. Originally ginseng was exported from Canada to Canton in small quantities by the supercargoes or factors of ships in the French East India Company for their own profit, but in 1751 when the company realized the importance of the commodity, it entered the trade itself but without insisting upon its monopoly privilege. Greedy speculators in 1752 attempted to cut short the time needed to bring the ginseng to market. Instead of following the required procedure of harvesting it in September and allowing it to dry naturally in barns without heat for an entire year, they harvested in May and dried the plant artificially. Historians have compared the Canadian ginseng fever in the 1750s to that of the California gold rush a century later (Lafitau 1858:5). An account of the excited activity of the traders was given by the Swedish botanist Peter Kalm during his stay in Canada in 1749.

> All the merchants at Quebec and Montreal, received orders from their correspondents in France, to send over a quantity of gin-seng, there being an uncommon demand for it in this summer. The roots were accordingly collected in Canada with all possible diligence; the Indians especially travelled about the country, in order to collect as much as they could together, and to sell it to the merchants at Montreal. The Indians in the neighbourhood of this Town were likewise so much taken up with this business, that the French farmers were not able, during that time, to hire a single Indian, as they commonly do to help them in the harvest. Many people feared lest by continuing, for several successive years, to collect these plants without leaving one or two in each place to propagate their species, there would soon be very few of them left, which I think is very likely to happen, for by all accounts they formerly grew in abundance round Montreal; but at present, there is not a single plant of it to be found, so effectually have they been rooted out. This obliged the Indians, this summer, to

go far within the English boundaries, to collect these roots. After the Indians have sold the fresh roots to the merchants, the latter must take a great deal of pains with them. They are spread on the floor to dry, which commonly requires two months and upwards, according as the season is wet or dry. During that time, they must be turned over once or twice every day, lest they should putrify or moulder. The superior of the clergy here and several other people, assured me that the Chinese value the Canada gin-seng as much as the Tartarian, and that no one has ever been entirely acquainted with the Chinese method of preparing it. (Lafitau 1858:41)

As a result of the cupidity of the Canadian traders. their ginseng fell into disrepute in China. In 1754 the value of ginseng exported from Canada fell from 500,000 to 33,000 francs, giving rise to a popular Canadian saying "It will fall like ginseng" (6).

According to the Swedish naturalist Peter Osbeck, the Chinese originally forbade the importation of foreign ginseng, but the Europeans illicitly introduced the American variety from the Spanish colonies. The Chinese, however, felt that the West Indian roots were not as good as their own (1771:1:223). Osbeck also noted that in 1709 the emperor gave orders to 10,000 Tartars to go in search of the roots, to deliver two pounds of the best quality to him, and to sell the rest for silver. As a result, the emperor acquired in this year 20,000 katze, or Chinese pounds (1:224).

The plant entered American literature in a classic satirical narrative by William Byrd, *The History of the Dividing Line Betwixt Virginia and North Carolina*, written in 1728, but not published until the next century. Although Byrd had stated in a previous private letter that ginseng is not an aphrodisiac, or, as he put it, is worthless "in the Feats of Love," he eulogized it extravagantly in his narrative.

Its vertues are, that it gives an uncommon Warmth and Vigor to the Blood, and frisks the Spirit, beyond any other cordial. It chears the Heart even of a Man that has a bad Wif, and makes him look down with great Composure on the crosses of the World. It promotes insensible perspiration, dissolves all Phlegmatick and Viscous Humours, that are apt to obstruct the Narrow channels of the Nerves. It helps the Memory, and would quicken even Helvetian dulness. 'Tis friendly to the Lungs, much more than Scolding itself. It comforts the Stomach, and Strengthens the Bowels, preventing all Colicks and Fluxes. In one Word, it will make a Man live a great while, and very well while he does live. And what is more, it will even make Old Age amicable, by rendering it lively, chearful, and good-humour'd. (1966:30)

A similar narrative of American manners, Dr. Alexander Hamilton's *Itinerarium*, written in 1744, and also not published until the twentieth century, records the author's curiosity to see the ginseng plant that he described as "a thing which has been so famous." Hamilton was skeptical of its power, however, believing that "it has really no more than what may be in the common liquorice root mixed with an aromatick or spicy drug" (1948: 6).

Presumably Byrd obtained his information about ginseng from reading European books, for the presence of ginseng in the Middle Atlantic colonies was not known until 1738, when Benjamin Franklin announced in his *Pennsylvania Gazette* the discovery by the American-born botanist John Bartram of the plant growing in Pennsylvania (27 July 1738). "We have the Pleasure," Franklin wrote, "of acquainting the World, that the famous Chinese or Tartarian Plant, called *Gin Seng*, is now discovered in this Province, near Susquehannah. From whence several whole Plants with a Quantity of the Root, have been lately sent to Town, and it appears to agree most exactly with the Description given of it in Chamber's Dictionary, and Pere du Halde's Account of China. The Virtues ascrib'd to this Plant are wonderful." This announcement is significant not only for its botanical information, but also for the evidence that Franklin was then familiar with Du Halde's *Description of the Empire of China* three years after its initial publication in Paris in 1735.

In the 1750s and 1760s, as I have already indicated, the China market for American ginseng became glutted in large measure because of unscrupulous merchandizing. According to Peter Collinson, a British botanist and friend of Franklin, it had been "sold under secrecy to the great people for true Chinese Ginseng, but its great plenty soon discovered the cheat, and then it sank to nothing" (Appleby 1982–83:137). By the end of the century, however, the market revived, and ginseng constituted the chief cargo on the voyage in 1784 of the first American vessel to Canton, the *Empress of China*. The supercargo says in one place that it amounted to thirty tons (Quincy 1847:127), in another that it was just under fifteen (Shaw 1790:126). The purser, John White Swift, wrote to his father 3 December 1784, "We brought too much Ginseng. A little of the best kind will yield an immense profit, but all the European Nations trading here bring this Article, and unfortunately this year ten times as much arrived as ever did before" (Swift 1885:485).

The supercargo of the *Empress*, Samuel Shaw, however, presented a much more optimistic view of ginseng as a trading commodity in his journal, parts of which were later extracted in various American periodicals. In a passage written during his second trip to China during the years 1786 to 1789, he gloated that while Europeans were obliged to purchase Chinese tea with ready money, (chiefly Spanish silver dollars), Americans could have it on easier terms, that is, by exchanging it for ginseng. "The otherwise useless produce" of America's mountains and forests, Shaw wrote, will "in a considerable degree supply her with this elegant luxury" (Quincy 1847: 231). As proof of his assertion, he cited the success of the *Empress* in procuring a cargo of the same articles as those obtained by Europeans on equally good terms, but with the outlay of but one fifth the ready money. His countrymen

> have seen this ship again here, on her second voyage, and four others in addition. They see these ships depending, and that too, with sufficient reason, upon the productions of their own country to supply them with the merchandise of this one [China]; and, though only a small proportion of their funds consisted of specie, they see them all returning with full and valuable cargoes. Such are the advantages which America derives from her ginseng. (Quincy 1847: 231)

In November 1787, the *American Museum* published instructions on the "Mode of Curing the Ginseng Root" (2, 448). The same instructions were given verbatim in the *Massachusetts Magazine* in February, 1792 (IV, 102–03).

> Gather the root sound and good (not in the same season when the plant is in flower) and gently wash it from the earth, being careful not to break the skin; then take an iron torch (that is, a very flat kind of stew-pan used in China over a charcoal fire); boil therein water; put in the root, and let it lie three or four minutes, but not so long as to injure or break off the skin, when, on cutting the root, the inside will appear of a light straw colour: then take a clean linen cloth, and, having wiped the ginseng clean and dry, place the torch over the gentlest fire, and lay in it a row of ginseng. Here let it dry gradually, turning it leisurely till it is something elastick, but not too dry; afterwards take a damp clean cloth, in which roll up the longest pieces in parallel lines, and wrap them up very tight, binding them very hard round with thread. After being dried a day or two, by a very slow fire, unpack the same and repeat the package of the inside and moist part, until it is all like the outside, and the whole dry enough to sound like a piece of wood when dropped upon a table. The heaviest pieces of a straw, or light brown colour, are much the best.

It will be noticed that this is not the same process recommended by Peter Kalm of drying naturally rather than by artifical heat. On the same page, however, the *American Museum* presents an "Account how ginseng is cured in Tartary."

> Such as go in search of this plant, take nothing but the root, and bury in one place as many of these as they find, during ten days or a fortnight. They wash the root very carefully, and cleanse it, by rub-

bing off with a brush every thing extraneous. They afterwards dip it, for a moment, into water almost boiling, and dry it with the smoke of a kind of yellow millet, which tinges the plant a little with its colour. The millet being put into a vessel with a little water, is boiled over a slow fire, and the roots being laid on little pieces of wood, put cross-wise over the vessel, dry by degrees, under a piece of linen, or under another vessel which covers them. They also may be dried in the sun, or even by the fire: but though they then preserve their virtue, they do not keep their colour, in which the Chinese delight very much. When the roots are very dry, they are laid up in a very dry place, otherwise they would be in danger of rotting, or of falling a prey to the worms.

As I shall indicate in a later chapter on the China trade, the first shipment of American ginseng to China was not an unqualified success. A correspondent in the *American Museum*, taking note of this unfortunate situation in December, 1787 (2, 576–77), offered advice for future shipments.

Complaints have lately prevailed of ginseng arriving at the East Indies in a ruined state. This evil, if not remedied, may injure America in this important article of remittance. Should the matter be neglected, and the article continue to be badly cured, it will meet the condemnation of the Chinese mandarins.

The merchants in many instances advertise, that they want to purchase ginseng, but it must have a yellow colour. This is a mistake; as it may look yellow, and yet be very poor.

The question is, when and how it should be collected?

It ought to be collected in the driest days of October, and should have no connexion with the heat of the sun or fire, or be washed.

Ginseng is an aromatic; and its virtues are easily evaporated, after it comes out of the ground, if improperly used. I have seen the Indians laugh at the folly of the white people when they have seen them in the brooks, washing their ginseng. The reason why they wash it, is to make it look of a yellow colour, but the virtues of the root so strongly impregnate the water that it may be tasted many rods distant. After washing the root, people generally expose it to the sun or fire, which scalds the skin, and when it feels dry, it is packed up; but the watry particles left within, will soon occasion it to sweat, mould and spoil.

The root, immediately after it comes out of the ground, should be spread on boards, under a shelter where the wind can blow freely, and when dry the dust can be brushed off. When one barrel is put up so, it will fetch more than fifty barrels cured the other way.

This is the most authentic and accurate description of processing ginseng published in the American press.

The *American Museum* reported in January 1790 (51) that exports of ginseng from the port of New York alone amounted to 410 hogsheads or 65,600 pounds with a value of 13,120 pounds sterling. The same periodical published two months later anonymous "Remarks on the commerce of America with China." These remarks were in slightly revised language those of supercargo Samuel Shaw taken either from a manuscript version of his journal or from a report he wrote in Janaury, 1787, to the Secretary of State, John Jay, incorporating verbatim passages from it. Shaw's journal represents a valuable contribution to American letters that has gone largely unrecognized, and for this reason Shaw will be treated at some length in the eighth chapter. In his journal, he argues that the rest of the world had greatly underestimated the Chinese demand for American ginseng (Quincy 1847: 126–27). Until the American flag appeared in China, he wrote, " it was generally supposed that forty or fifty peculs [one pecul is equivalent to 136 pounds] were equal to the annual consumption. Experience has proved the contrary. Upwards of four hundred and forty peculs were carried there by the first American ship in 1784, which did not equal the quantity brought from Europe the same season, the greater part of which must have been previously sent thither by citizens of the united states. In 1786, more than one thousand eight hundred peculs were sold there, one half of which was carried in American vessels." After predicting that there would always be a strong demand for the American product, Shaw queried whether it would be beneficial to the United States to prohibit exports to China on any but American bottoms. He also wondered whether America should follow the European example of forming national companies for managing the trade to the East and of using for the pupose large ships, more expedient than small ones because of the large tax levied in China in an identical amount on all ships regardless of size. He concluded that time would tell. "How far," he mused, "it may be proper for America to imitate their example, and regulate the exportation of ginseng, must ultimately be determined by her own experience."

The *American Museum,* also in January 1790, published a table concerning the amount of ginseng shipped to the Chinese market in the previous season (228). Out of 2,000 peculs, 1,290 were carried in American ships, 200 in an English company ship, and 510 in other English and foreign ships.

A lengthy description of ginseng in English appeared in the *New York Magazine, or Literary Repository* for February 1795 (6, 84–85) in an account by a certain Mr. Brunel on trading in Canton, and his account was republished in full six months later in *The Rural Magazine or Vermont Repository.*

This Brunel is a shadowy figure about whom almost nothing is known. Henri Cordier's *Bibliotheca Sinica* (2175) cites as his work *Observations sur le commerce en général, et sur celui de la Chine en particulier,* 1791, but quotes Querard's *France littéraire* to the effect that the book could not be found in the Bibliothèque Nationale. I have discovered that the account in the *New York Magazine* is taken from Alexis M. Rochon's *A Voyage to Madagascar and the East Indies. . . . Translated from the French . . . To which is added a Memoir on the China Trade (by M. Brunel)* published in London in 1792. My quotations are all taken from the *New York Magazine*.

Now for Brunel on ginseng.

This oriental plant, so much celebrated, grows in the mountains of Tartary, which border on certain provinces of the Chinese empire. Its stem, which is as thick as that of wheat, and about a foot in height, bears at first red buttons, which expand each into six white leaves like those of a violet. This knotty root has almost the figure of the mandragora; but it is smaller, transparent, and interspersed with small black veins, which form two or three branches. It has a sweet taste, with a slight mixture of bitterness, and it is of an aromatic smell, which is far from being disagreeable. The root, in order that it may be preserved, is dried, and then it becomes red on the outside, and yellowish within. It is sold at a high price, especially when it is of a good quality. Those kinds which are brown and grey are much inferior to the other.

Worms sometimes get into the ginseng, and gnaw it, which would render it unfit for sale, were it not for the cunning of the Chinese, who have the patience to fill up the holes with a yellow powder which has a great resemblance to the colour of the root. They insinuate this powder into the small eyes of the plant, with so much art, that one must be a great connoisseur to avoid being deceived. The Chinese themselves, however, are sometimes dupes in their turn to the fraud of some European merchants, who mix with their oriental ginseng, a certain quantity of that of Canada, which is far inferior in value. It is deficient not only in colour, smell and transparency, but also in its virtue and properties. Notwithstanding the high idea entertained of this plant, the trials made of it in Europe never correspond with the wonders ascribed to it by the Chinese.

The immoderate use of ginseng would soon bring on death. The rich are contented with taking, in the morning, a small quantity of it, equal in weight to about a small grain of corn. When taken in small doses, either infused, or, in powder, it is salutary for old men, and those who are exhausted by excesses; but it is prejudicial to young people, and to those who are of a warm temperament. The strength and virtue of this root is so great that the same dose of it will serve twice for infusion without any addition.

The best ginseng ought to be fresh, heavy, of a strong smell, and free from caries and worm-holes. The Chinese name of it signifies *resemblance to the thighs of a man.*

Early in the next century, the New England minister and president of Yale University, Timothy Dwight, provided the information in his *Travels in New England and New York,* (1805) that Indians near Niagara Falls in New York state were cultivating the root and sending it to Philadelphia from where it was shipped to China (1969:3:125). In a satirical poem published almost two decades earlier in a different frame of mind, *The Triumph of Infidelity,* 1788, he had disparaged ginseng as an "alchymic dose."

An enormous tome entirely devoted to China published in Philadelphia in 1823 by another former supercargo, Robert Waln, Jr., contains original remarks on ginseng. He ingeniously surmises that the popularity of the root was linked to the Taoist attempt to discover a drink of immortality and that ginseng was one of the principal ingredients of the various concoctions devised throughout Chinese history to give immortal life to those who consumed it (1823: 356). A later chapter will be devoted exclusively to Waln's treatise on China.

Waln's remarks were published in 1823, and by this time the importance of ginseng in the American trade with China had greatly diminished, having been supplanted by other products. It is historically significant, however, that Europeans at the beginning of the eighteenth century were aware of ginseng growing on the North American continent, that they were also familiar with its pharmaceutical properties, and that ginseng became the major export item in the foreign trade of the United States during the first quarter of a century of the new nation's existence.

Because of the prolific nature of ginseng in the Western climate, the notion soon developed in America that tea also could be cultivated in the New World. The possibility was originally suggested in 1771 in the preface to the first volume of *Transactions* of the American Philosophical Society. The anonymous author's observation concerning the similarity of climatic conditions between China and Pennsylvania led him to "hope that, if proper enquiries were made, many more of the native plants of *China,* and very possibly the Tea, so much in use amongst us, and now become so necessary a part of our diet, might be found in *America.*" A similar proposal was made in the *Worcester Magazine* (1 [May 1786] 85).

China, like the United States, has a large territory to the West and North West; it has the same exposure to the Southern Ocean as the United States to the Atlantick; the latitudes are the same nearly; Ginseng flourishes in the back parts of both countries, and in no other country on the globe; this last circumstance proves a similarity of climate and soil, which may be deemed a sufficient inducement to make the experiment at least. The Sugar Cane, the basis of the whole trade of the West-Indies, is not a native of America—it was carried from the East-Indies to the island of Sicily, and from thence to the West Indies, and if we are not mistaken, the same is true with respect to rice.

Two months later the *New Haven Gazette* (1, 213) extracted from Le Comte's history of China "An Account of the Tea Shrub," describing the three grades in which it is classed according to quality and distinguishing the song-lo or green tea from the vai or bohea that grows in Fokien. In October 1796, *The Rural Magazine or Vermont Repository* (2, 499–502) printed "Interesting observations concerning Teas and their use," particularly on its effects on the body, medicinal or deleterious. The author, who had studied at Leyden, quotes several European authorities as well as the Chinese *Tschang Seng or the Art of Preserving Health,* that Du Halde had included in his seminal work on China.

Another agricultural staple, the soybean, regarded by Europeans of the time as equally exotic as ginseng, made its entrance in international trade during the eighteenth century. Soybeans were brought to America from China in 1765 with the hope that they would thrive in this climate, and they later developed into one of the major exports from the United States to the Far East. Franklin had apparently encountered them in England as early as 1770 when he sent from London to the native American botanist John Bartram what he called "Chinese Garavances." Garavances are chick-peas, but probably Franklin confused them with soybeans (17:22–23). In an accompanying letter, he referred to a passage in the account of China by the Spanish Jesuit missionary Domingo Fernandez Navarette concerning "the universal use of a cheese made of them in China." Here Franklin is probably not using the word *cheese* to refer to a dairy product, but rather to a paste. In modern Dutch, the product known in America as peanut butter is called "peanut cheese" or pindakase. Even today the Chinese do not have a high regard for cheese. Franklin's source Navarette was referring to bean curd or tofu, its Chinese name. Franklin admits that he is uncertain whether his garavances "are the same with these, which actually came from China, and are what the Tau-fu is made of" (17:22–23). In England throughout the eighteenth century soy beans were known as "pease or vetch" as appears from the following description in the *Gentleman's Magazine,* 1767, of the experiments of Samuel Bowen, a resident of Georgia, who had lived in China and who introduced the grain into the colony in 1765 (Hymowitz and Harlan 1983: 373).

The Chinese use these vetches for the following purposes.—From them they prepare an excellent kind of vermicelli, esteemed by some preferable to the Italian; nothing keeps better at sea, not being subject to be destroyed by the weevil.

In Canton, and other cities of China, they are used for salad, and also boiled like greens, or stewed in soup, after they have been prepared in the following manner:

They put about two quarts of the vetches into a coarse bag, or hair-cloth bag that will hold about a peck, and after steeping them in it a little time in warm water, they lay the bag on flat grating, or a wooden lattice, placed about half way down a tub, and put a cover on the tub: then every four hours they pour water on them, and in about 36 or 40 hours they will have sprouted about three inches in length; they are then taken out, and dressed with oil and vinegar, or boiled as other vegetables.

At sea, where fresh water is valuable, they place a cock in the bottom of the tub, and draw off the water that drains from them to moisten them again, so that none is lost.

Mr. Flint and Mr. Bowen having found them an excellent antiscorbutic prepared in this manner, was a principal reason for his introducing them into America, as it would be a most valuable remedy to prevent or cure the scurvy amongst the seamen on board his majesty's ships.

These vetches are also of great use in warm countries where grass is scarce, as you may soon raise most excellent fodder for your cattle, which may be given them either green, or made into hay, and not thrashed. In warm climates they yield four crops a year, each crop will ripen in six weeks; they grow erect in tufts from 18 inches to two feet high. (*Gentleman's Magazine* 37: 253)

Bowen also imported from China the use of sago as an antisorbutic. Sago is a starch powder derived from tropical palms. While in China, Bowen observed that the powder is held "in great esteem there, as an occasional diet . . . which the Mandarins never travel without" (Hymowitz and Kaplan 1983: 374).

Other Chinese agricultural products made their way to America through the efforts of British botanists. The London *Annual Register* for 1775 (18: 32) reprints from the *South Carolina and American General Gazette* of 28 December 1772 a report that

by the Indefatigable industry of a very curious gentleman at Canton, a sufficient quantity for experiment of the upland rice from Cochin China . . . so long wished for, has been sent by the Thames Indiaman, to his friend in Gray's Inn, who will take proper care that it is distributed to such persons in our southern colonies as will make a fair trial of this most useful grain. We are further indebted to this curious gentleman for a parcel of the seeds of the *croton sebiferum* of Linnaeus, or the tallow tree of china, preserved in a most excellent manner. This tree seems to afford a substance between wax and tallow, and which bids fair to be of as great use to our Southern American colonies, as it is in China.

The gentleman-benefactor of Canton was John Bradby Blake, a resident supercargo of the East India Company, and his friend at Gray's Inn was John Ellis. The notice in the *Gazette* was written by Dr. Alexander Garden, the botanist for whom the gardenia was named.

Through the efforts of men such as John Bartram, Benjamin Franklin, Samuel Bowen, and Alexander Garden, the eighteenth century saw the beginning of a mutually profitable agricultural exchange between America and China. Subsequent chapters will show that the intellectual exchanges were no less common and fruitful for the burgeoning American nation. Many Americans, moreover, regarded agricultural production as one of the marvels of Chinese society. As I shall show in chapter 9, Chinese methods of farming were associated with the political structure of the nation, and the "Chinese rural economy" was held up as a model for the United States after the attaining of independence from Great Britain.

Chinese Precursors of a Franklin Myth

So far we have been dealing with Franklin as a journalist and scientist. His purely literary work also has important links with the Middle Kingdom, even though he himself was not aware of these relationships. During his middle years while serving in London as an agent for three of the American colonies, Franklin amused himself by writing an account of an imaginary Indian trader, William Henry, that he published in 1768 in the *London Chronicle* (Franklin 1959—:15:145–157). Some time ago I identified Franklin as the author of this work in an article titled "Franklin's Deistical Indians," in which I pointed out parallels to a later work clearly established as Franklin's, his *Remarks concerning the Savages of North America* (Aldridge 1950). The latter Franklin wrote toward the end of the War for Independence while he was a commissioner at the Court of Louis XVI in Paris, and he published it in 1784 on his private printing press in Passy on the outskirts of Paris.

The centerpiece of both the *Remarks* and the "Captivity of William Henry" is an Indian legend or creation myth concerning the origin of various American agricultural products. Originally I assumed that this Indian legend was pure fiction—an ingenious fabrication on Franklin's part. I, therefore, interpreted "William Henry" as a hoax designed to disseminate some of his deistical notions in a humorous manner as well as to ridicule the assumption of orthodox Christians that their religion is the only one in existence with any claim to truth. In the course of my later readings concerning oriental culture, however, I have encountered a number of ancient Chinese myths coinciding in many ways with Franklin's legend as well as with Lafitau's portrayal of Iroquois cosmogony treated in chapter 2. The latter has elements in common with both Chinese predecessors and Franklin's adaptation. Since a writer in the *Revue de littérature comparée* has criticized one of my previous books, *The Reemergence of World Literature: A Study of Asia and the West,* precisely for not taking note of Far Eastern mythology, (72 [1988] 78), I am pleased now to be able to draw attention to resemblances between Chinese myths and those of native Americans. In so doing, I am following in the footsteps of professional anthropologists, who for many years have been studying the resemblances between myths of ancient China and those of American Indians and interpreting the parallels as evidence of actual contact between the two cultures (Erkes 1926: *passim*).

Since the Chinese myths that I shall treat are genuine reflections of the religion and folklore of Chinese culture, the presence of similar or identical motifs in Franklin's tale attributed to American Indians strongly suggests that his Indian myths are also genuine. In short, Franklin's fertile imagination was certainly at work, but his raw materials had their roots in ethnography.

The parallels between Franklin's Indian myth and a group of ancient Chinese ones may best be presented through a preliminary analysis of Franklin's *Remarks concerning the Savages of America.* In his opening sentence, he observes, "Savages we call them, because their manners differ from ours, which we think the Perfection of Civility: they think the same of theirs" (1905–7, 10:97). This observation is a close parallel to a comment he later made in his *Maritime Observations* on the different methods of rowing a boat employed by the English and the Chinese: "they see our manner, and we theirs, but neither are disposed to learn of or copy the other" (American Philosophical Society:1789:2:307). The Chinese, he regarded, on one hand, as an ancient and highly civilized nation, and the Indians, on the other, as a primitive race victimized by European conquerors, but he considered both Chinese and Indian cultures as worthy of respect and understanding.

Franklin's *Remarks* is composed of five sections, each of which is designed to illustrate a major aspect of Indian character. The opening section, based on speeches at an actual Indian treaty in 1753, concerns the Indian attitude towards European learning. When the colonial commissioners offer to educate six Indian youths at the College of William and Mary, the spokesman for the Indians thanks the commissioners for their kind proposal, but declines to accept it on the ground that the Indian notion of education is completely different from theirs. Previous experience of young Indians attending colleges in the North had shown that when they returned to their own people "they were bad Runners, ignorant of every means of living in the Woods, unable to bear either Cold or Hunger, knew neither how to build a Cabin, take Deer or kill an Enemy, spoke our Language imperfectly, were therefore neither fit for Hunters, Warriors, nor Counsellors; they were totally good for nothing" (1905–7, 10:99). After politely rejecting the invitation of the commissioners, the Indian makes a counter proposal of temporarily adopting a dozen sons of Virginia gentlemen in order to "make Men of them." Franklin's portrayal of the Indians and the Virginia gentlemen reciprocally sending their young men to be trained in each other's culture resembles a famous notion of the German philosopher Leibniz calling upon the Chinese to delegate some of their learned men to teach natural religion to the West and the Europeans to continue sending their missionaries to instruct the Chinese in the fundamentals of Christianity.

As further evidence of the extreme politeness of the natives, Franklin reports a sermon containing the fundamental articles of the Christian faith that had been delivered to a group of Susquehanna Indians with the hope of obtaining their instant conversion to Christianity. Franklin extracted the basic ingredients of this sermon from a deistical essay that had appeared in at least six newspapers in London and Pennsylvania. The sermon itself had actually been delivered to a group of Indians in Pennsylvania at the turn of the seventeenth century, and an Indian orator in reply had subjected these doctrines to critical examination and had found them deficient. This sermon and its accompanying Indian oration were reported in a Latin graduation dissertation printed in 1731 at the University of Upsala (Aldridge 1950:94:400). The enterprising deistical essayist then unearthed the Indian oration, translated it literally, and added a commentary hailing the simplicity of natural religion over the doctrinal intricacies of Christianity. This was the source from which Franklin derived the historical setting in which folklore is pitted against theology. Franklin in his own version of the proceedings greatly abbreviated the exchange. The polite Indian of his *Remarks* replies to the missionary, "What you have told me is all very good. It is indeed bad to eat apples. It is better to make them all into cyder. We are much obliged by your kindness in coming so far, to tell us those things which you have heard from your mothers. In return, I will tell you some of those we have heard from ours." That which follows is the Indian cosmogony.

> In the Beginning, our Fathers had only the Flesh of Animals to subsist on; and if their Hunting was unsuccessful, they were starving. Two of our young Hunters, having kill'd a Deer, made a Fire in the Woods to

broil some Part of it. When they were about to satisfy their Hunger, they beheld a beautiful young Woman descend from the Clouds, and seat herself on that Hill, which you see yonder among the blue Mountains. They said to each other, it is a Spirit that has smelt our broililng Venison, and wishes to eat of it; let us offer some to her. They presented her with the Tongue; she was pleas'd with the Taste of it, and said, "Your kindness shall be rewarded; come to this Place after thirteen Moons, and you shall find something that will be of great Benefit in nourishing you and your Children to the latest Generations." They did so, and, to their Surprise, found Plants they had never seen before; but which, from that ancient time, have been constantly cultivated among us, to our great Advantage. Where her right Hand had touched the Ground, they found Maize; where her left hand had touch'd it, they found Kidney-Beans; and where her Backside had sat on it, they found Tobacco. (1905–7, 10:101)

When the orator concludes, the minister rebukes him for allegedly telling idle tales, but the orator in turn reproaches the minister for not believing the legends of the Indians after they had set the example of accepting his. Franklin ended his *Remarks* by further praise of Indian politeness, which he contrasted with the greediness of Europeans, particularly those who customarily cheated the Indians in trading.

Franklin's earlier work "Extract from an Account of the Captivity of William Henry in 1755" is considerably longer and the satire more diverse. Ostensibly belonging to the genre of narratives of Indian captivity, it has many resemblances to *Gulliver's Travels* as a satire on domestic vices and idiosyncracies reported through the observations of an impartial inquirer from an alien culture. The Indian story of creation, or corn myth as it is also called, grows out of the efforts of William Henry to convince the Indians of the wisdom and goodness of European "regulation of commerce, by which one nation proposes to make advantage to itself in distressing the trade of others." A young warrior delivers the following discourse:

Nine *Oneida* Warriors passing near a certain hill, not far from the head of Sasquehanah, saw a most beautiful young Woman descend naked from the clouds, and seat herself on the ground upon that hill. Then they said, this is the great Manitta's Daughter, let us go to her, welcome her into our country, and present her some of our venison. They gave her a fawn's tongue broiled, which she eat, and thanking them, said, come to this place again after twelve moons, and you will find, where I now sit, some thing that you have never yet seen, and that will do you good. So saying she put her hands on the ground, arose, went up into the cloud, and left them. They came accordingly after twelve moons, and found growing where she had pressed the ground with her right hand, corn, where with her left hand, beans; and where her back parts had pressed it, there grew tobacco. (Aldridge 1950, 94: 403)

The only differences between the two versions are superficial. In the *London Chronicle* account there are nine Oneida Indians instead of two hungry Susquehannas, the beautiful young woman is presumably more enticing by being naked, she is identified as "the great Manitta's Daughter," and she makes the Indians wait only twelve moons instead of thirteen. The nudity of the princess gives a sexual overtone to the story reminiscent of the creation myths of other primitive cultures.

In the "Captivity" this cosmogony is not allowed to go challenged, as it is in the *Remarks*, for all the young Indians of the "Captivity" laugh heartily at the origin of tobacco described therein, and an Indian patriarch, Old Canusetego, rebukes the narrator for telling this foolish Oneida tale to their white captive. "If you tell him such tales, what can you expect but to make him laugh at our Indian stories as much as you sometimes do at his" (Aldridge 1950, 94: 405). To atone for the foolishness of the young warrior, Old Canusetego tells the true story of the beginnings of the country. In this presumably authentic account of Indian religion, the native spokesman, an actual historical Onondaga chief, indicates that there are more than a hundred gods, who love one another and live in the sun and the moon. That Indians believed in a plurality of gods may be documented from other sources. The doctrine of polytheism was also seriously accepted by Franklin, moreover, who in his private *Articles of Belief and Acts of Religion*, written in 1728, postulated "many beings or Gods, vastly superior to man," including a separate god for each sun in the universe and its system of planets. Old Canusetego describes the good Manitta strewing the fertile fields of Onondaga with five handfuls of red seeds that turned into little worms that penetrate the earth. After nine moons these worms reappear as perfect boys and girls, the origin of the Five Indian Nations. Old Canusetego further declares that the Indians believe that after their death they live as spirits under the earth until they find a suitable body back on earth as a new habitation. Franklin in a note gives further details concerning actual Indian notions of metempsychosis and preexistence, and one of the Indian treaties he had earlier printed in Philadelphia substantiates the account of spirits without bodies rambling under the earth. Although Franklin has Old Canusetego ridicule the young warrior's narrative as a foolish Oneida tale, it is the Oneida tale that is closer to actual Indian folklore than the old chief's revisionist version, the latter of which has been invested with favorite notions of Franklin himself. The story of the sky woman, moreover, is an Iroquois rather than an Oneida story (Hertzberg 1966: 12–22).

Franklin's two versions of his Indian myth are connected with Chinese mythology by the motifs of sexual contacts between supernatural and human beings and of the supernatural origins of agricultural products. The closest parallel exists in an account of a goddess-man relationship in a collection entitled the *Dynastic History of the Wei*, dated A.D. 554.

> [In the beginning,] the emperor Sheng-wu frequently led several thousand soldiers riding into the remote mountains. One day, all of a sudden, army equipment and provisions, together with some guards, descended from Heaven in the company of a beautiful girl. Being very much surprised, the emperor asked where she came from; she replied that she was the daughter of Heaven, and had received orders to be his wife. They slept together. When dawn came, she said she had to leave but instructed him to return to the same place in exactly one year. She left as swiftly as the wind and the rain. A year later, the emperor returned to the same place and found her there. She gave him a baby, saying: "This is our baby. Take good care of him. Many generations will follow his line and they will all be emperors." This baby was the founder of the Wei dynasty. (Mao 1977:31)

In both the Chinese and the Franklin stories, the beautiful daughter of the supreme god descends from heaven to a group of warriors and tells them to return to the same place a year later. When they do so, they discover a living object of great value that becomes the source of their future prosperity as a tribe or dynasty. It is the descent from heaven, moreover, that links Lafitau's Indian myth of the sky woman with Franklin's tale and with Chinese parallels.

Another Chinese myth with many variants all over East Asia combines the motif of a mortal-supernatural relationship with the gift of an agricultural product. This legend, the story of Dong Jong, originating in the thirteenth century, is also considered as a parable of filial devotion (Levi 1984:83–132). Dong Jong, a young man, is obliged to indenture himself as a slave in order to support his aged father. The Jade Emperor in heaven sends his daughter to lend a helping hand. After seducing him, the supernatural bride weaves ten rolls of marvelously beautiful silk every night, enabling Dong Jong to pay off his indenture in three months. The princess is then obliged to return to heaven even though she has become pregnant. After a heart-rending farewell, she promises to return with her child if it turns out to be a male. In the meantime Dong Jong's master takes the silk to the emperor, who summons Dong Jong to court and gives him an official post along with his daughter in marriage. Eventually the heavenly princess as promised brings her son back to Dong Jong. The child develops extraordinary intelligence, but is ridiculed by his playmates for not having a mother. Dong Jong sends him to a fortuneteller, who instructs him to seek the place where the immortals descend from the sky on the seventh day of the seventh month to look for simples. He does so and finds his mother, who gives him two flasks, one of which contains seven grains of rice. She tells him to eat them one at a time, but he disobeys by consuming them all at once. As punishment, he becomes obese and his father dies. The grieving son thereupon goes three years without eating or drinking, returns to his normal size, and is awarded a high post by the emperor.

This legend embodies disparate and even contradictory motifs, the gift from the sky of the manufacture of silk contrasting with the deprivation by celestial action of the nourishing quality of a single grain of rice. The virtue of filial duty, moreover, seems to be overlooked in the son's being punished by obesity, which anthropologists have interpreted as a rebuke against laziness, represented by his eating all of the seeds together instead of one at a time. The punishment of obesity is also interpreted as an emblem of the separation of the gods from men.

Another form of the parable, even more obvious in its message, recounts that in ancient times the sky was so low that it hindered human beings in their activities and domestic animals in their movements. Single grains of rice were as large as gourds and wheat went by itself to the villages and even entered the houses of lazy people. One day a widow who had no barn turned against the rice and grain, attacking the latter with her knife, forcing the rice back to the fields, and crying that the grain should wait until summoned to be harvested, and not disturb any of the inhabitants, not even the lazy ones. In a final burst of fury she slashed with her knife the connection with the sky, and the sky immediately rose into the firmament.

In another version, men in ancient times were completely ignorant of everything and were obliged to ascend to heaven in order to buy rice for their sustenance. The heavenly father, tired of the incessant demands of mortals for food, ordered one of the lesser deities to take some rice to the earth and plant it there so that he would no longer be bothered with importunities from below. After this, he cut off all communication. This story of the ascent into heaven resembles the Iroquois legend reported by Lafitau in which Hogouaho or the Wolf makes his way to the sky.

Franklin's Indian legend combines the foregoing motifs of the relations between a mortal and a supernatural being and the gift of agricultural products. To be sure, neither he nor any of his American contemporaries had any knowledge of Chinese myths. He either derived his own version of the motifs in question from American Indians or invented them himself. The latter is extremely unlikely since all of his other excursions into fiction or imaginative writing have recognizable precursors. I believe, therefore, that he drew the outlines of his Indian legend from native sources and added his own elements of style and other materials necessary to make the legend serve his particular ideological purpose.

Regardless of Franklin's process of literary composition, we are faced with the task of explaining the presence of strikingly similar motifs in widely separated legends of ancient China and eighteenth century America. Two major hypotheses exist. One is based on the anthropological theory that in primitive times people from Asia passed from the Eastern continent to the American either on an ice bridge in the North Atlantic or on rudimentary boats across the Pacific. According to this theory, these Chinese groups brought with them their culture and traditions, including myths and supernatural beliefs. Intermarrying with Western natives, they created a new atmosphere for the dissemination and evolution of their tales and legends. There is nothing new about this theory. It is essentially that expressed by Lafitau in 1724 in his *Manners of the American Savages*. The other theory is literary and psychological, based on the notion that the common experience of human beings in all times and parts of the globe produces identical or almost identical responses. In literature, these common reactions to the human condition are known as universal themes, and their speech formulations or structural formations are known as invariants.

As the review of Du Halde in the *American Magazine* cited in chapter 2 suggested in the middle of the eighteenth century, the amazing similarities in the accounts of the origins of various nations throughout the world stem from "just and natural *Representations* of the early Condition of People." The resemblances in Franklin's Indian mythology to much earlier Chinese precursors may be based on some form of cultural communication or they may, to the contrary, be an example of the appearance of universal themes in native American storytelling. But whatever the reason for the likenesses, they help explain Franklin's cosmopolitanism in general together with his interest in many aspects of Chinese life and manners. The significance of Franklin's retelling is that he drew mythology from anthropology and transferred it to literature.

It is obvious that a cosmogony based on a descent from the sky of the daughter of heaven has little in common with the moral teachings of Confucius that Franklin reprinted early in his career. Like a modern anthropologist, Franklin was interested in folklore, but he was not a devotee of primitive religion. The same incompatibility exists in Chinese culture. Confucius in the fifth century B.C. broke away from the notion of an anthropomorphic god. In his writings the deity becomes nature and personal attributes vanish. Yet legends and myths based on communication between the gods and human beings continued to exist in China for centuries after the death of Confucius. These myths appealed to the masses while the literati favored the more sophisticated philosophy of Confucius. Since these two radically different cosmic views persisted side by side in Chinese culture, it is not surprising that they should coexist as well in Franklin's total literary production.

Franklin's "Letter from China"

L ate in life, Franklin invented another fictional character to serve as an eyewitness and reporter of an alien culture, this time an English sailor who lives on close terms with a farming family in China. The narrative in which he appears is the most important literary work about China to originate in America in the eighteenth century. Titled by Franklin's nineteenth century editor Jared Sparks, "A Letter from China," the work deserves particular attention not only because it deals with the Middle Kingdom, but because it is one of the most imaginative or "literary" of all the writings ever attributed to the author of *Poor Richard*. As a literary genre, it belongs to the category of armchair voyages, that is, completely spurious records of travels that have taken place only in the fancy of the author. Although on a much smaller scale, the letter is a companion piece with Daniel Defoe's *The Life & Surprising Adventures of Robinson Crusoe*. It is linked to *Robinson Crusoe*, moreover, by subject matter, despite the favorable impression of China it gives in contrast to Defoe's highly denigrating one. In Franklin scholarship, the letter has been almost entirely ignored, perhaps because of its exotic subject matter or perhaps because scholars have subconsciously recognized in it characteristics not ordinarily associated with Franklin.

The letter was first attributed to Franklin by Sparks in his 1839 edition of Franklin's *Works* (2, 241). Sparks indicates that it had originally appeared in 1788 in a London periodical *The Repository* (2, 4–10), maintains that it incorporates "some of his knowledge derived from books, with fanciful descriptions of his own," and reflects "in a few passages his peculiar manner of thought and style." It is true that the letter appeared in 1788 in *The Repository*, but I have recently discovered that the letter had been printed in Philadelphia almost two years previously, in the first volume of the the *Columbian Magazine*, September 1786, with the following heading:

> For the Columbian Magazine.
> The following letter, not before published, is curious, as it contains the natural observation of an unlearned man, on the internal present state of a country seldom penetrated by Europeans, and therefore very little known to us.
>
> *Letter from a gentleman in Portugal to his friend in Paris, containing the account of an English sailor who deserted in China from Capt. Cooke's [sic] ship. Translated from the French.*

The above title is the one it bears in the original manuscript, now in the American Philosophical Society, and it is the one that logically should be used to refer to it in subsequent scholarship.

The letter is unique in Franklin's literary career, and for this reason doubts have been expressed concerning Franklin's authorship, particularly because of the nature of the work itself, imaginative fiction. Before learning that the manuscript still exists, I even published an article explaining why Franklin could not have been the author. My argument was sound, but the facts contradicted it: Franklin was capable of writing in this genre and style, but throughout his extensive literary career prior to the "Letter" he did not choose to do so. To be sure he wrote several hoaxes and bagatelles, including "The Captivity of William Henry," and his most famous example of the lighter genre, "The Speech of Polly Baker." But each of these *jeux d'esprit* like others of Franklin's fanciful pieces has some pragmatic purpose, and each is satirical or humorous. The Chinese letter is pure fiction. It may be considered a hoax, but its attempts at verisimilitude allow for few currents of humor. It is straight narrative in the vein of *Robinson Crusoe*. Apart from length, the main difference from Defoe's novel is the absence of a utilitarian purpose. Defoe had a number of objectives in his novel, for example, to defend the religious and economic values of Puritanism, but so far as I can see there are none in Franklin's anonymous letter. A passage on religion in China may have been intended for satirical effect, but this is coincidence rather than resemblance to any aspects of Franklin's private ideology.

The letter can be positively attributed to Franklin not only on the basis of his manuscript copy that is now in the American Philosophical Society, but also on a passage in a letter from Franklin to his English friend

Benjamin Vaughan of 24 July 1785. Here he writes, "I shall be glad of a line from you, acquainting me whether you ever received two pieces I sent you some months since; one on your penal laws, the other an account of the residence of an English seaman in China" (1905–7, 9:365). Vaughan had the piece published in *The Repository* and probably furnished it to Sparks along with the comment I have already quoted in chapter 2 that Franklin was "very fond of reading about China" and that "if he were a young man he should like to go to China" (Franklin 1839, 2:241). The "Letter" was probably accepted as genuine both in England and America when first published largely because of the mystery with which all aspects of the Middle Kingdom were then shrouded. This was just before the embassies to China of the British East India Company in 1793–1794 and the Dutch East India Company in 1795, both of which gave rise to a great deal of publicity about the Chinese way of life. The date of the letter is historically significant, for it appeared less than two years after the sailing of the *Empress of China*, the first vessel from the United States to enter the China trade. Considerable newspaper attention had been given to the voyage of the *Empress*, and American readers were prompted to learn as much as they could about the strange land that had been its destination.

A close reading of the Chinese letter even at that time, however, would have aroused suspicion of its authenticity. It refers, for example, to only three Chinese cities, Macao, Canton, and Pekin, those already familiar in the West, but describes none of them. The seaman mentions "a great river," but "does not remember its name;" (1905–7: 9:204) he also travels to a province in the tea country, but once again "does not recollect the name (206)." The only other geographical location is "Nooky-Bay," presumably a reference to Nootka or King George's Sound on the American West coast. Otherwise all landmarks are vague entities such as the coast, a canal, a farm, or a house. The narrator, nevertheless, remarks in his final sentence, "he gave me the names of some places, but I found them hard to remember, and cannot recollect them" (208). Despite this geographical ambiguity, the style of the author embodies enough verisimiltude for the work to have been taken seriously in both Philadelphia and England. As late as 1981, the letter was accepted by an American scholar as the true narrative of an actual English sailor (Mudge 1981:99).

The *Pennsylvania Packet* of 15 September 1785 reported that Franklin had arrived in Philadelphia in Truxtun's *London Packet* on the preceding day. Two months later (22 Nov.), the same newspaper reprinted a letter, allegedly from Truxtun, dated 10 September, indicating that he had been taken prisoner by Algerian pirates and was to be sold as a slave. According to this letter, "Poor Doctor Franklin bears the reverse of fortune with more magnanimity than I would have imagined." The *Packet* published the letter with absolutely no comment despite the fact that its pages carried almost daily accounts of celebrations during the preceding weeks of Franklin's safe return to Philadelphia. The item illustrates the mixture of truth and fiction in periodicals of the time and helps to explain why many people encountering Franklin's China letter in contemporary periodicals would have accepted it as genuine.

Franklin's purpose in writing was presumably to demonstrate his literary skill, for as I have said the letter has no ideological aim, whether political, theological, social, or philosophical. Even the passage on religion is anecdotal rather than controversial. Presumably Franklin composed the letter on the long passage back from Europe in 1785 both to experience the joys of literary composition and to while away the time. It is of considerable significance, however, that he chose China as his subject and that he wrote cogent and intriguing comments about the Middle Kingdom.

Franklin derived the inspiration for his letter from the famous explorer Captain James Cook, whom he had known in England. While still in France after the signing of the Treaty of Paris, he received a copy of Cook's *A Voyage to the Pacific Ocean* that had been sent to him by his friend Benjamin Vaughan. Cook had undertaken these voyages between 1776 and 1780. During the third, he was killed by natives in Hawaii. The printed account, therefore, had a divided authorship, that of the first and second voyages by Cook himself and the third by Captain James King (Cook: 1784). The *Voyage* was almost instantaneously known in the United States, for it was reprinted verbatim in daily installments in the *Pennsylvania Packet* during the first six months of 1785. The section on China, appearing between 26–31 May, provided American readers with information about the Middle Kingdom, including population, housing, military force, character of the people, and their manner of trading.

Franklin took a personal interest in Cook's expedition even before the appearance of the published account. In 1779 while serving as minister to France, he sent from Paris a circular letter to all captains and commanders of American vessels earnestly recommending that if they should encounter Cook at sea, they should make no effort to restrain him, but treat him with the utmost politeness. Cook met his demise three weeks before the writing of this letter, but apparently even his successor Captain James King had no knowledge of Franklin's gesture. In his narrative of the third voyage, King warmly credits the government of France for circulating instructions to allow Cook to pass unmolested and somewhat less cordially indicates that the Congress of the United States also offered Cook a free hand, but he makes no reference to Franklin (Cook 1784:4:254). The British admiralty, however, was informed of Franklin's action and sent him in June 1784 an elegantly bound copy of the *Voyage* along with a letter from Lord Richard

Howe acquainting him that the present was made "with the King's approbation" (Franklin 1945:607,773). Franklin received Lord Howe's copy in June
1784 and Vaughan's in the next month. He acknowledged the latter, adding
that "if there is a good print of Cook, I should be glad to have it, being
personally acquainted with him" (Franklin 1905–7:9:241). Presumably
Franklin did not reply to Lord Howe, but he sent an account of his circular
letter and of Howe's gift set of Cook's voyages to the *Gentleman's Magazine*,
where it was published in December 1789 (Franklin 1945:773).

Cook's third expedition was the one that reached China, and the
visits of the crew to Macao and Canton recorded in the printed account
took place after his death. His vessel, the *Resolution*, was called by the
Chinese the Ladrone or pirate ship, and this circumstance may have
inspired Franklin to incorporate the Ladrones or pirates in his own narrative. The passage from King's account that gave Franklin the basic situation for his letter concerned "two sailors belonging to the Resolution." In
January 1780, according to King, they "went off with a six-oared cutter;
and though the most diligent search was made, both that and the succeeding day, we never could gain any intelligence of her. It was imagined, that
these seamen had been seduced by the hopes of acquiring a fortune, if
they should return to the fur islands" (Cook 1784:4:251).

Franklin worked the episode of the missing seamen into a realistic
picture of Chinese life, but reduced the two sailors into a single protagonist. The narrator in the letter is not the English seaman himself, but a
gentleman in Lisbon who had interrogated him. The entire narrative,
however, concerns this enterprising sailor, with the gentleman-scribe's
contribution limited to a comment that "he appears a more intelligent
fellow than seamen in general" (1905–7: 9: 200). The mariner was persuaded by a Portuguese captain at Macao to desert and join him and his
shipmates on a trading expedition to America. As in King's account, their
destination was the fur islands of Nootka Sound. They so embarked, but
were shortly seized by Korean ladrones or pirates whom they joined in
order to save their lives. When taken in turn by Chinese vessels, the sailor
and the Portuguese crew were imprisoned and the pirates executed. The
prison was comfortable, and the British mariner was kept busy weaving
chair bottoms for which he was paid a modest sum added to his daily
allowance of rice and *chong* (tofu or bean curd). In the fall he was permitted along with other well-behaved prisoners to help farmers with the
harvest. On one day he cut his foot badly in the fields and was, therefore,
allowed to remain with the farmer's family after the harvest was over. As a
result of his skills in the manufacture of soap and leather shoes, the farmer
petitioned to have the ingenious sailor kept permanently in his care. The
captive expresses his satisfaction with the Chinese diet, including pork,

rice, and *chong*, the latter which he describes as follows: "they put kidney beans in soak for twenty-four hours, then grind them in a hand-mill, pouring in water from time to time to wash the meal from between the stones, which falls into a tub covered with a coarse cloth that lets the meal and water pass through, retaining only the skins of the beans; . . . a very small quantity of alum, or some sort of salt, put into it, makes the meal settle to the bottom, when they pour off the water" (1905–7: 9: 203–4). One of my Chinese friends has informed me that exactly the same method of producing tofu is followed today except that no salt is added. Franklin's single word *chong*, I have also been told, represents a shortened form of "I chong tofu," or a slice of tofu.

In further comments on Chinese daily life and habits, the sailor gives on the whole a balanced view, lavishing neither praise nor disparagement. His only objection to the Chinese lifestyle is "their sometimes eating dog's flesh." He affirms that there is a great deal of cheating and that there is no remedy for it. "Stealing, robbing, and house-breaking are punished severely," he adds, "but cheating is free there in every thing, as cheating in horses is among our gentlemen in England" (1905–07: 9: 205). The emperor, or as he is called, "the great father," forbids the keeping of horses since they consume great quantities of food, and he would rather have his empire filled with people than with brutes. I shall point out in a future chapter that the scarcity of horses had been noticed previously by an actual visitor to China, Pierre Poivre, who published his recollections in 1769, and the same phenomenon was confirmed by Everard Van Braam in 1795. In 1828, moreover, a Philadelphia periodical, the *Museum of Foreign Literature and Science*, published an article from an English source declaring that it was common knowledge that in China fewer animals were "employed for the purposes of draught and burthen" than anywhere else in the world (XV, 368). This may have been common knowledge in 1828, but it was a somewhat remarkable circumstance when Franklin noted it fifty years earlier.

The letter indicates that there are a considerable number of varieties of tea and that in addition to the genuine product there is a vast amount of counterfeit tea that is shipped to foreign countries. "They made ordinary tea of the leaves of sweet potatoes, which they cut into form by stamps, and had the art of giving such color and taste as they judged proper" (1905–7: 9: 206). To his objection that this amounts to fraud, the sailor's Chinese informant replies that "there was no harm in it, for strangers liked the false tea as well, or better, than the true." The letter next introduces a topic that had been somewhat widely treated in Western literature for at least two centuries, that of the use in China of sail-driven wagons. Later in this chapter, I shall treat this topic at length. The sailor maintains that "it is not true that the feet of Chinese women are less than those of English women," an observation quite contrary to the reports of genuine eyewitnesses. His subsequent comment on Chinese religion has the flavor of Jonathan Swift and is intended as a reflection on European attitudes rather than Chinese. "They have a sort of religion with priests and churches, but do not keep Sunday, nor go to church, being very heathenish." "In every house there is a little idol, to which they give thanks, make presents, and show respect in harvest time, but very little at other times." Their explanation for not going to church to pray was that "since they paid the priests to pray for them, . . . it would be a folly to pay others for praying, and then go and do the praying themselves." This also is contrary to actuality and to the report, brief as it is, in Hannah Adams's 1784 edition of *An Alphabetical Compendium of the Various Sects*.

Although I am convinced that Franklin's Chinese letter is completely fictitious, there was an American in real life who went through an experience very similar to that of Franklin's imaginary seaman. This is Samuel Bowen, who is mentioned in chapter 3 in connection with soybeans and the manufacture of tofu. His China episode illustrates the adage concerning the similarity of art and nature. In February 1758, Bowen signed as a seaman on an English vessel, the *Pitt*, bound for Canton. Seven months later he docked at Madras, India, and in June of the following year transferred to the *Success*, a smaller vessel used to guide the *Pitt* through unchartered waters. The vessel touched at Ningpo and Tientsin before reaching its final destination Canton, where its crew ran into difficulties with the Chinese authorities for violating an imperial ban against trading at ports other than Canton. Very few details are available, but Bowen claimed that he was held prisoner in China for four years, during which he was carried 2,000 miles from place to place in the interior of the country (Hymowitz and Harlan:1983, 371–72). During this period he "took notice of many things," including agricultural methods and produce, which he hoped might be of service in his native land if he ever returned there. A description of the manufacture of tofu that he published in the *Gentlemen's Magazine* in 1767 (37:253) goes through all of the steps indicated in Franklin's narrative.

One of the least conspicuous passages in Franklin's "Letter" has a number of literary precursors. In this passage the sailor affirms that "it is not true, that they have large wheel carriages . . . driven by the wind; at least he never saw or heard of any such; but that the wheel-barrow porters indeed when passing some great open countries, do sometimes, if the wind is fair, spread a thin cotton sail, supported by a light bamboo mast, which they stick up on their wheelbarrows, and it helps them along. That he once saw a fleet of near three hundred sail of those wheelbarrows, each with a double wheel." The reference to three hundred wheelbarrows with sails massed together in a "fleet" at first might seem to be an exaggeration comparable to one of Marco Polo's marvels. Chinese wind driven carts or wagons had been mentioned by a large number of Western writers, however, including Gonzales de Mendoza, Campanella, Milton, and Jonathan Swift.

In modern times the history of the sailing wagon and its renown in the West has been recounted by Joseph Needham in his monumental study *Science and Civilization in China* and by Zhouhan Yang in an article specifically devoted to literature (Yang 1986:3:29–45). My own account that follows is greatly indebted to the prior work of Needham and Yang. Gonzales de Mendoza in his *History of the Most Notable Things, Rites and Customs of the Great Empire of China* (1584) felt that the idea that land-based wagons could be propelled by the wind was so fantastic that he was obliged to present evidence of the truth of the phenomenon. He had not witnessed them himself, but believed the testimony of those who had. His history in the translation by Robert Parke in 1588, affirms that the Chinese "are great inventors of things, and that they have amongst them many coches and wagons that goe with sailes, and made with such industrie and policie that they do governe them with great ease; this is crediblie informed by many that have seene it; besides that, there be many in the Indies, and in Portugall, that have seene them painted upon clothes, and on their earthen vessell that is brought from thence to be solde: so that it is signe that their painting hath some foundation" (Yang: 1986, 30). The Renaissance philosopher, Campanella, alluded to the Chinese wagons in his *City of the Sun*, but located them in Ceylon. They appear in his utopian vision as "waggons fitted with sails, which are borne along by the wind even when it is contrary, by the marvelous contrivance of wheels within wheels." Campanella's English contemporary Ben Jonson located the wagons in outer space in his *News from the New World Discovered in the Moon* (1620). After one of the characters in this dramatic fantasy reports that there are in the moon coaches "much o' the nature of the ladies, for they go only with the wind," another replies "Pretty like China waggons."

From Jonson's masque the coaches traveled to Milton's epic poem. In the third book of *Paradise Lost*, (437–39) Milton refers to

> the barren Plains
> Of Sericana, where Chineses [sic] drive
> With Sails and Wind thir [sic] cany Waggons light.

David Masson in his edition of Milton's poem indicates that a Latin account of China accompanying an atlas of P. Bertius published at Amsterdam in 1616 reports that the Chinese "have invented chariots which they drive over the plains with spread sails without the help of cattle" and that this account is repeated in the *Microcosmography* of Milton's contemporary Heylin. Some contemporary cartographers, moreover, indicated China on the map by the portrayal of a sailing wagon. At the beginning of the eighteenth century, Swift in *A Tale of a Tub* gave the most exaggerated of all the reports. He referred to "*Chinese* Waggons, which were made so light as to sail over Mountains" (1958: 120).

Despite the extensive range of literary references to Chinese sailing carts, the pictorial record is extremely sparse. Needham reproduces several illustrations from European books of the sixteenth and seventeenth centuries, but these are all imaginary sketches, not based upon actual Chinese vehicles. The earliest Chinese representation of an authentic wagon is one by Lin Qing in *Hong Xue Yin Yuan Tu Ji* published in 1849 and the next is Liu Xinzhou's *A History of Chinese Mechanical Engineering* published in 1935. The picture in Lin Qing represents an entire rural landscape, however, and the vehicle with sails, more closely resembling a wheelbarrow than a wagon, is merely one detail among many. All of these descriptions, linguistic or pictorial, except that of Liu Xinzhou in 1935, portray a wagon or coach rather than a hand-held wheelbarrow. Franklin's letter was the first to indicate that the sail-driven vehicle was a wheelbarrow and to give what I presume is the correct description. Where Franklin obtained his information is a mystery. In chapter 8, I shall show that his account was confirmed in another Philadelphia publication in 1797, containing a full-page sketch of a wind-driven cart, drawn to scale by a skilled draftsman. Inhabitants of post-revolutionary Philadelphia, therefore, had access to more reliable knowledge concerning this aspect of Chinese life than readers anywhere else in the West.

Franklin describes in his narrative the pirates who board the Portuguese vessel as "Curry Ladrones." A footnote in both the manuscript and the *Repository* identifies Curry as "perhaps Corea." If this conjecture is correct, Franklin seems to be the first American to mention China's Western neighbor. According to *Korea; An Annotated Bibliography of Publications in Western Languages* brought out by the Library of Congress in 1950, the first book published in the United States "which referred directly to Korea" is believed to be a pirated Philadelphia edition in 1818 of Basil Hall's *Voyage of Discovery to the West Coast of Corea*.

Franklin's China letter incorporates an incredibly extensive and significant amount of information, none of which is touched upon by King's account of Cook's third voyage. King had included some cursory observations on Chinese life, but they were limited to Chinese houses taking up more space than European ones; Chinese families having more members than those in Europe; and the Chinese practicing polygamy, mandarins having five to twenty wives, merchants having three to five, tradesmen two, and most people rarely more than one (1784:4:239–241). Franklin, apart from his references to Curry ladrones and his accurate description of sailing carts, takes up the most popular topics in contemporary writing about China: the small feet of the women, the scarcity of horses, the types and qualities of tea, the cuisine, the agricultural methods and products, and the nature of religious worship.

The situation of a European in close quarters with everyday Chinese men and women presented in a style suitable to a literate sailor had not previously been exploited in Western literature except on a much smaller scale by Defoe in the second part of *Robinson Crusoe*. Franklin's protagonist is an American Crusoe, following in the footsteps of his English predecessor in order to project a more favorable image of China. The enterprising sailor, moreover, has many characteristics in common with Franklin himself, for example, mechanical dexterity, keen powers of observation, and adaptability to circumstances. In this sense, the letter reflects Franklin's personality, if not his actual experiences. At the time he was writing it on board the *London Packet* on the homeward bound voyage to Philadelphia, he also wrote observations on the Chinese method of heating houses as well as the structure of Chinese ships and the Chinese method of rowing. These observations will be treated in chapter 6. Presumably Franklin did not acquire his knowledge on these subjects from literary sources, but it is quite possible that he picked up his information on Chinese life and customs from sailors on the *Packet* who had previously made the trip to the China seas. The mariner of his letter, therefore, may be to some degree a composite of actual seamen whom Franklin had known. Whatever Franklin's sources, the letter provided the flavor of the orient in a credible and appealing manner. Franklin presumably had a high regard for the work, arranging for copies to be sent to both the *Repository* in London and the *Columbian Magazine* in Philadelphia. Although previously neglected in Franklin scholarship, it deserves to be treated as one of his most important literary creations.

6

Franklin, Paine, and Jefferson

It is not at all surprising that Franklin should have written the imaginary voyage to China described in the preceding chapter, for his correspondence and miscellaneous papers throughout his life indicate that he was familiar with various accounts of the Middle Kingdom. In a series of random notes concerning one of them, he evinced curiosity concerning the material out of which painted candles are made in China, the nature of "Vinegar of Liche," the wages of a silversmith and his apprentice, the compensation received by a physician and his expenses for chair hire, and the fees paid on a gift to the king (Franklin 1959—:10:182–3). He explained at length to one of his correspondents a manner of constructing windmills in China based on an "imperfect account" he had read. In a letter to Thomas Percival he reported from an undisclosed source, probably Marco Polo, a summary of the annual census taken in China of its population and its quantities of provision. The method consists of requiring each residence to hang outdoors a small board on which the head of the family could mark next to the appropriate headings the number of men, women, and children and quantities of various foods in the household (20:443). The material on China in this letter was first published in the *Columbian Magazine* for May 1790 (IV, 306–7).

In connection with one of his pet projects, a proposal to make English spelling completely phonetical, Franklin speculated on the development of writing in Chinese. He affirmed that "if we go on as we have done a few centuries longer, our words will gradually cease to express Sounds, they will only stand for things, as the written words do in the Chinese Language, which I suspect might originally have been a literal Writing like that of Europe, but through the Changes in Pronunciation brought on by the Course of Ages and through the obstinate Adherence of that People to old Customs, and among others to their old manner of Writing, the original Sounds of Letters and Words are lost, and no longer considered" (15:175). He was, of course, wrong about the nature of Chinese ideograms. They are neither pictorial representations nor designations of particular sounds.

A recent scholar has suggested that Franklin derived his notions of the Chinese language from an article in the *Transactions* of the Royal Society published in 1731 (Looby 1984:18:1–34). This article identified only by the intials R. A. attributes governmental corruption in China to the formation of the "Chinese Court-Language," a system of compound characters perceived as the instrument of an elite society. R. A. argues "that over the course of time the original pronunciation of the Chinese characters had been lost, because the simple characters that stood for basic units of sound had been combined to form compound characters, which then no longer corresponded to unitary-speech sounds" (18: 33). Franklin's speculation concerning the Chinese language, moreover, links him with an earlier controversy over whether Chinese was the language spoken in the world before the destruction of the Tower of Babel, according to the account in the Old Testament (Genesis XIL, 5–9). In 1669 John Webb set forth this theory in *An Historical Essay Endeavouring a Probability that the Language of China is the Primitive Language*. The hypothesis was challenged in 1686 by Robert Hook, who proclaimed in an essay "Some Observations and Conjectures concerning Chinese Characters" in the *Transactions of the Royal Society* for that year, "I conceive the present *Chinese* Language to have no affinity with the Character, the true primitive, or first Language, or pronounciation of it, having been lost" (Etiemble 1988:384). All three writers, Franklin, R. A., and Hook, however, were completely mistaken in the assumption that Chinese writing was originally phonetic rather than ideographic. Chinese characters express ideas, but they do so without attempting pictorial representations.

Like many other Americans, Franklin encouraged the manufacture of silk in the New World. During his extended residence in London, he sent to his friend Ezra Stiles of Yale some "Prints copied from Chinese Pictures concerning the Produce of Silk" (Franklin 1957—:10:389). Franklin was probably aware that Stiles was a kindred Sinophile and that he had, moreover, engaged in efforts of his own to produce silk in New England, an activity that I shall discuss in chapter 9. Franklin took an active part in marketing Pennsylvania silk in London and advocated the producing of two crops a year, citing the example of China, "where the Climate is very like that of North-America" (1959—:19:136). Back in America in 1775, Franklin wrote to Philip Mazzei, an Italian citizen who had setttled in Virginia with the support and assistance of Jefferson, encouraging him to undertake the production of silk. "We have experienc'd here," he remarked, "that Silk may be produc'd to great Advantage. While in London I had some Trunks full sent me from hence three Years successively, and it sold by Auction for about 19s. 6d. the small Pound, which was not much below the Silk from Italy" (22:308).

Franklin's reference to the similarity of climatic conditions in China and North America supports the view of some scholars that Franklin suggested to Charles Thomson a passage comparing the two in the latter's frequently-quoted preface to the first volume of the *Transactions* of the American Philosophical Society in 1771: "*Philadelphia* lies in the 40th degree of north latitude, the very same as *Pekin* in *China*, and nearly the same with *Madrid* in *Spain*." In these two cities, "which lie on the same sides of the two continents, namely, the eastern, the winters are cold, and the summers are very warm. The same winds, in both places, produce the same effects." This resemblance in weather and climate is manifest also in the soil and natural produce, for tobacco and several trees are natives of both parts of the globe. "Ginseng is gathered to the westward of *Pekin*, and as far as we know, has not been found in any other part of the world, except within the same degrees of latitude in *America*." After discussing a number of Chinese agricultural products which might possibly be introduced into America, the preface forecasts a high degree of improvement in living standards. "Could we be so fortunate as to introduce the industry of the *Chinese*, their arts of living and improvements in husbandry, as well as their native plants, *America* might in time become as populous as *China*, which is allowed to contain more inhabitants than any other country, of the same extent, in the world." This sentence, the most frequently quoted from the preface, incorporates many of the century's most favorable notions about China: the industry of its people, their high standard of living, their skill in agriculture, and their great population.

In 1744 in a pamphlet with the self-effacing title, *Account of the new-invented Pennsylvania Fire-Places*, Franklin describes a stove that he had himself devised. In this pamphlet he draws upon Du Halde's translation of "the Chinese treatise entitled *Tschang sing; i. e. The Art of Procuring Health and Long Life*" in establishing a parallel between anger as the most harmful human passion and a cold and piercing wind that comes through a narrow passage as the most dangerous of all the malignant effects of air. According to the Chinese source, an ancient proverb states that such a wind should be avoided "as carefully as the point of an arrow" (1959:

2:427). Franklin felt that his stove could be used toward the same end of eschewing harmful drafts. Half a century later, in August, 1785, on his return voyage from Paris to Philadelphia, he wrote at sea along with his fictitious account of China a long letter to the Viennese physician Johannes Ingenhausz on the causes and cure of smokey chimneys. In this letter, printed in the second volume of the American Philosophical Society's *Transactions*, Franklin remarks that Europeans may still learn something about the use of stoves "from the Chinese, whose country being greatly populous and fully cultivated, has little room left for the growth of wood, and having not much other fuel that is good, have been forced upon many inventions during a course of ages, for making a little fire go as far as possible" (American Philosophical Society 1789:2, 20). In an appendix, Franklin discusses at length an ingenious method of warming ground floors which he attributes to the "northern Chinese."

On the same sea journey back to America he wrote a letter to a scientific friend in Paris concerning various aspects of navigation. His comments were immediately published under the title *Maritime Observations to Mr Alphonsus le Roy on board the London Packet, Captain Truxton, August 1783* (1785). Here he made a number of complimentary references to Chinese ingenuity. He found worthy of notice, for example, "the well known practice of the Chinese, to divide the hold of a great ship into a number of separate chambers by partitions tightly caulked" (American Philosophical Society 1789: 2, 301). At about the same time, Franklin applied his observations concerning the division of ships into watertight sections to a proposal to institute passenger service between France and the United States. "As these vessels," he wrote, "are not to be laden with goods, their holds may without inconvenience be divided into separate apartments after the Chinese manner, and each of those apartments caulked tight so as to keep out water. In which case if a leak should happen in one apartment, that only would be affected by it, and the others would be free; so that the ship would not be so subject as others to founder and sink at sea. This being known would be a great encouragement to passengers" (Franklin 1905–7:9:148).

Referring in his *Maritime Observations* to the Chinese method of rowing boats, he remarked that "the Chinese are an enlightened people, the most anciently civilized of any existing, and their arts are ancient, a presumption in their favour" (American Philosophical Society 1789:2,307), a repetition of the judgment in his letter on the Society of the Cincinnati quoted in chapter 2 that time and long experience provide national wisdom. Ever since his boyhood, as he says in his autobiography, Franklin knew how "to manage Boats" (Franklin 1987:1314), and he consequently took an interest in the Chinese manner of rowing. According to his portrayal of the

Chinese method in his *Maritime Observations,* it differs from that customary in the West, "the oars being worked two a-stern as we scull, or on the sides with the same kind of motion, being hung parallel to the keel on a rail and always acting in the water, not perpendicular to the sides as ours are, nor lifted out at every stroke, which is a loss of time, and the boat in the interval loses motion." In conclusion, Franklin remarked, "they see our manner, and we theirs, but neither are disposed to learn of or copy the other." One may wonder where Franklin had seen the Chinese manner or whether he was thinking only in abstract terms. It has been suggested that he acquired his knowledge of Chinese navigation from Captain Truxtun, who in the following year himself made the voyage to China.

Four years before embarking on his return voyage to America, Franklin had observed that "the Compass appears to have been long known in China, before it was known in Europe" (Franklin 1987: 1034), a claim then widely cited from Jesuit writers. Franklin added his own speculation that the compass may even have been known to Homer, "who makes the Prince, that lent ships to Ulysses, boast that they had a *spirit* in them, by whose Directions they could find their way in a Cloudy Day, or the darkest Night."

It is relevant at this point to observe that one of the major criticisms directed against China by its European detractors was that it lacked scientific and technological knowledge. Franklin obviously had, to the contrary, a very favorable opinion of Chinese technology.

He had good things to say, moreover, about a reputed Chinese practice in economics. On the first day of October 1786, shortly after his return to Philadelphia, he dined with Benjamin Rush and two other physicians. During the course of the meal he spoke against the accumulation of debts as a practice adverse to the economy and cited the high interest rates in China as a salutary means of discouraging borrowing. According to Rush's notes on the occasion, 'he said interest was 3 per cent per month, for 10 months in China, or 30 per cent per ann., which promoted industry, kept down the price of land, & made freehold more common" (Rush 1905: 25).

At some point between 1765 and 1774, Franklin contributed some notes to a pamphlet on economic theory by an English friend George Whatley. The latter's title, only half of which I shall reproduce, reads *Principles of Trade, Fredom [sic] and Protection Are Its Best Suport: [sic] Industry the Only Means to Render Manufactures Cheap.* (London, 1774). The spelling in this title and throughout the work is based on a simplified system that was one of Franklin's hobbies at the time. In one of his notes, also in simplified spelling, Franklin affirms, "It was an excelent saying of a certain Chinese Emperor, *I wil if posible, have no Idlenes in my Dominions; for if there be one Man idle, some other Man must sufer Cold and Hunger.*" Even a slow-witted reader would hardly need the subsequent comment, "We take this Emperor's Meaning to be, that the Labor due to the Public by each Individual, not being perform'd by the Indolent, and necesary to furnish his Subsistence, must naturaly fal to the share of others, who must thereby sufer" (Franklin 1959—:21:173). I have not been able to discover with absolute certainty the source of Franklin's "excellent saying" attributed to a Chinese emperor, but he probably took it from the English translation of Pierre Poivre's *Voyages d'un philosophe*, that appeared in 1768, the same year as the original French edition. I shall treat this work in chapter 9. Franklin's contribution to Whatley's book was known in America and reprinted in the *Columbian Magazine* (4 [May, 1790], 308–9) as well as in *The Key* of Frederick Town, Maryland (1 [April, 1798], 102).

Like many other Enlightenment figures, Franklin held conflicting opinions concerning luxury, condemning it as morally indefensible and a deterrent to individual thrift while condoning or approving it as a stimulus to a favorable balance of trade. The *Columbian Magazine* in 1790 published two commentaries on the subject attributed to Franklin. Although these statements are not included in any edition of his works, I believe that internal evidence clearly establishes that they are from his pen. In the first of these, "Precautions to be used by those who are about to undertake a sea voyage," he refers to China voyages to obtain tea, suggesting that the beverage is a luxury, but not on that account rejecting it (4 [April, 1790] 245–8). "One is astonished," he writes, "to think on the number of vessels and men who are daily exposed in going to bring tea from China, coffee from Arabia, and sugar and tobacco from America: all commodities which our ancestors lived very well without." He seems to place his seal of approval on the tea trade by considering it in a different category from tobacco and sugar. Tobacco is useless, he affirms, and we should be willing to do without sugar in our tea if renouncing it would lead to the abolishing of the slave trade.

The other commentary in the *Columbian Magazine*, "Observations on Luxury, Idleness, and Industry, extracted from a letter written by Dr. Franklin, in 1784," repeats the sentiments concerning China trade in almost identical language. "How much labour is spent in building and fitting great ships to go to China and Arabia, for tea and coffee, to the West Indies for sugar, to America for tobacco. These things cannot be called the necessaries of life, for our ancestors lived very comfortably without them" (5 [July, 1790], 32–34). In his private life, of course, Franklin indulged himself in many luxuries, including not only tea and coffee, but also the best of French wines. Late in life, Franklin acquired a "Chinese gong," that he left in his will to his grandson William Temple Franklin (Franklin 1905–7:10:508).

At the outset of the War for Independence, when Franklin was residing in Paris as one of three commissioners seeking military and economic support for the American cause at the court of Louis XVI, he discussed with one of his fellow commissioners, Arthur Lee, their mutual admiration of the Chinese mode of government. According to the latter's journal, Lee suggested that if the Americans informed the emperor "that being a young people, desirous of adopting the wisdom of his Government, and thereby wishing to have his code of Laws, it might induce him to give it, as they would not appear, as other Nations had generally appeared, in a state to alarm the fears and excite the jealousies of that Cautious Government. Dr. Franklin was of the same opinion" (Franklin 1959—:24:15).

Franklin even used the remoteness of China to satirize the gullibility of English readers, ready to believe almost any of the tall tales of travelers. In a pseudonymous contribution to a London periodical in 1765, he reported with tongue in cheek that "Agents from the Emperor of China were at Boston in New-England treating about an Exchange of Raw-Silk for Wool, to be carried in Chinese Junks through the Straits of Magellan" (Franklin 1950: 34). At about the same time he published another letter in a London periodical satirizing newspaper exaggerations of the globe-trotting of the Duke of York. Franklin wondered why enterprising journalists had not thought of having the prince "sail for China, and go up to see the Grandeur of the Court of Pekin. This would have been a fine Subject to have enlarged upon" (Franklin 1987: 559).

Equally important from a literary perspective, Franklin drew upon Chinese art for perhaps the most striking metaphor he ever used in public life, a reference in the early years of the American Revolution to the British Empire as that "fine and noble China Vase" (Franklin 1959—:22:520). Franklin's use of this metaphor contrasts sharply with that of Emerson in the next century. In a private letter, Emerson affirmed, "But I hate China! 'Tis a tawdry vase" (1961:2:224).

Some notice should also be taken of important influences of China upon Franklin's life that were indirect and which he did not realize stemmed from China. One of these belongs in the realm of mathematics, the devising of magic squares and circles. According to Joseph Needham's encyclopedic *Science and Civilization in China* (Sec. 19, p. 57), these were first developed in China. The prototype is the *Lo Shu*, a square composed of three horizontal and three vertical figures which when added along any diagonal line or column make fifteen. In 1751 Franklin confided to Peter Collinson of the Royal Society that in his youth he had amused himself with making magic squares and had become quite adept at it. "I could fill the cells of any magic square of reasonable size, with a series of numbers as fast as I could write them, disposed in such a manner as that the sums of every row, horizontal, perpendicular, or diagonal, should be equal" (Franklin 1959—:4:394). Later, he created a square of eight horizontal and vertical figures, and eventually one of 16.

Franklin also enjoyed the game of chess throughout his life, and in his mature years he wrote a humorous sketch, "The Morals of Chess," that appeared in the *Columbian Magazine* for December, 1786. In his introduction he gives a brief history. "Playing at Chess, is the most ancient and the most universal game known among men; for its original is beyond the memory of history, and it has, for numberless ages, been the amusement of all the civilized nations of Asia, the Persians, the Indians, and the Chinese." Finally, Franklin was indebted to the Middle Empire for the invention of the kite, without which he may not have been able to make the discoveries about electricity that made him famous throughout the world.

So far as I know, no scholar has given thought to the question of whether Franklin himself may have been known to anyone in China during the eighteenth century, and the question may even appear frivolous. It appears, however, that he was known to one craftsman by name, if not by reputation. I base this affirmation on the printed catalog for a Bicentennial exhibit of Chinese export material bearing the intriguing, but greatly exaggerated, title *China's Influence in the Eighteenth and Nineteenth Centuries* (Trubner and Rathbun 1984). An export plate, dated 1780, portraying a stylishly dressed French couple in a formal dancing posture apparently "gained the identification of Benjamin Franklin at the French court." The catalog explains that although the man's costume is clearly French, it "predates the style current at the time of Franklin's presence in France. Further, Franklin who was [over] 70 and ailing at the time of his visit, cannot be recognized in this dapper young gentleman" (30). The English were guilty of a similar false identification, but in reverse. A famous early nineteenth-century Staffordshire statuette, easily recognized as Franklin, was labelled "An Old English Gentleman" on many of the copies despite their close resemblance to Franklin. Presumably the artifice was adopted because the producers had oversold the Franklin market in the United States and were trying to adapt their merchandise for home consumption.

Although Franklin, as we have seen, had a good deal to say about Confucius, he apparently never followed European deists in portraying the Chinese as advocates of the religion of nature. Franklin's friend and fellow deist Thomas Paine, however, had no hesitation about doing so. In his famous manifesto, *The Age of Reason*, 1791–1792, he joined previous advocates of the Religion of Nature in portraying Confucius and Christ as great ethical teachers. Speaking of Christ, Paine remarked, "The morality that he preached and practised was of the most benevolent kind; and though similar systems of morality had been preached by Confucius, and by some of the Greek philosophers, many years before; by the Quakers since; and by many good men in all ages, it has not been exceeded by any" (1945: 1: 465).

Paine used almost identical language in an essay in the deistical journal *The Prospect*, 31 March 1804, in which he remarked, "As a book of morals there are several parts of the New Testament that are good, but they are no other than what had been preached in the Eastern world several hundred years before Christ was born. Confucius, the Chinese philosopher, who lived five hundred years before the time of Christ, says, *acknowledge thy benefits by the return of benefits, but never revenge injuries*" (1945: 2: 805).

Earlier in Paris, Paine had associated with the members of a deistical organization known as the Theophilanthropists. In an open letter to Thomas Erskine, an attorney in charge of the prosecution of a London bookseller for publishing *The Age of Reason*, he drew upon a type of manual of worship published by the group to illustrate his principle that there do exist "religious establishments for public worship which make no profession of faith of the books called Holy Scriptures, nor admit of priests" (1945: 2:744). Paine quoted at length from this manual of worship as well as the table of contents for the volume, which includes two sections of extracts from the moral thoughts of Confucius and two other sections from the moral thoughts of other Chinese authors. In this letter to Erskine, Paine followed the technique of Voltaire in discrediting the authority of Christianity by portraying its acknowledged ancestor Judaism as contaminated by superstition and immorality in contrast to the rationality and ethical purity of Chinese philosophy. Paine argued that the Bible should be examined and scrutinized for confusion, disorder, and tales dishonorable to the Creator with the same care and precision that would be taken if it were a Chinese book. In his words, "The Chinese are a people who have all the appearance of far greater antiquity than the Jews, and in point of permanency there is no comparison. They are also a people of mild manners and of good morals, except where they have been corrupted by European commerce. Yet we take the word of a restless bloody-minded people, as the Jews of Palestine were, when we would reject the same authority from a better people" (2: 737). Franklin had used similar reasoning in regard to Chinese and Christian religion over fifty years previously. In an essay in the *Pennsylvania Gazette*, 1 June 1732, recently attributed to Franklin by Leo Lemay (1986: 69), he raises the question whether the "truly benevolent, extensive and salutary Precepts" of the Christian Gospel if "*now newly brought to us from China*" would receive the ecstatic "*Encomiums of the Wits of our Age.*"

Paine in the narrow compass of his three sentences quoted above alluded to three of what have been termed the major myths concerning China prevalent in the eighteenth century: its great antiquity, its permanency or eternal standing still, and its moral excellence. (Dawson 1967: 4,8,12,14). Even though Paine mentioned these myths in a very cursory manner, he must have had an extensive background of reading or oral information on which to base his generalizations.

A New York deistic periodical highly favorable toward Paine, *The Correspondent*, published a letter, 1 December 1827, lavishly praising China because of its rational spirit, particularly in regard to religion. Preceded by an "Extract from the *Journal of a Voyage to Canton*," presumably by Samuel Shaw, that I have already quoted in chapter 2, the letter embodies further observations on Chinese devil worship.

> It is, I believe, universally admitted by travellers in China, that its inhabitants are a very mild inoffensive people, and at least as moral, if not more so, than Christian nations; from whence it may be inferred, that it makes little or no difference which is worshipped, God or the devil. In fact by the description generally given of them, it would be difficult to decide which should have the preference. As represented by theologians, they both excite fear and horror, unaccompanied with respect; and, as the devil is considered the prime minister or executor of the Almighty in the punishment of mortals, it appears wise in the Chinese to endeavor to gain his good graces. . . . With respect to the Chinese, who practice a more pure morality than Christians, it must be attributed to the precepts of their philosophical lawgiver, Confucius, whose system of ethics is decidedly far superior to any that has ever been promulgated, either by inspiration or otherwise.

This comment embodies precisely the same view of China as Paine's. Later in the same year, an opposing periodical, the *Antidote*, designed to foster Christian doctrines against the deism of the *Correspondent*, challenged the latter periodical to produce in "the pages of Confucius, Plato, Aristotle or Mahomet" an ethical concept more sublime than "Do unto others as ye would be done by." In reply, the editor of the *Correspondent* merely asked the question, "Are not the editors aware, that the maxim do unto others &c. was borrowed or rather stolen, from the writings of that very Confucius whom they contemn, and who existed 600 years before the supposed period of their divine master?" The *Correspondent* played no favorites, however, and was just as willing to satirize Chinese superstition as that associated with Christianity. It had earlier reprinted from a Canton periodical—presumably the *Canton Register*—an advertisement offering "superior idols for public and domestic worship" together with "the most hideous monster that can be conceived, to inspire awe or reverence for religion" (1 [1827], 224).

Paine's contemporary and the future president of the United States, Thomas Jefferson, has, like Franklin, been compared to Confucius. According to a modern scholar, "they were alike in their impatience with metaphysics, in their concern for the poor as against the rich, in their insistence on basic human equality, in their belief in the essential decency of all men, (including savages), and in their appeal not to authority but to 'the head and heart of every honest man' " (Creel 1949:275). Jefferson and Franklin have also been linked to Chinese philosophy through the medium of the French Physiocrat Francois Quesnay, advocate of agriculture as the foundation of the modern state, who allegedly borrowed much of his thought from the Chinese (273–4). It has also been suggested that strong similarities exist between the Chinese examination system and Jefferson's proposal for an educational structure in the United States (9).

A highly important literary contact between Jefferson and China may be traced to Jefferson's twenty-eighth year, prior to his residence in Europe. He was asked by his brother-in-law, Robert Skipwith, to furnish him with a list of the best books on general subjects available in America at that time (Jefferson 1950—:1:76–81). As part of a bibliography of less than 200 items, Jefferson included in his answer, dated 3 August 1771, two Chinese classics, the Yuan drama *Chao-Shih-ku-erh, or The Little Orphan of the House of Chao,* and a later fictional narrative *Hau Kiou Choaan.* The first of these had been translated into English by Bishop Thomas Percy from Du Halde's collection, and it had previously been adapted by Voltaire in his very successful drama *L'Orphelin de la Chine.* The second work had also been edited by Percy, partly from an English translation by James Wilkinson and partly from a text in Portuguese that he translated himself. Percy's edition appeared under the title *The Pleasing History* only ten years before Jefferson's letter recommending it. It is significant that Jefferson stated that these literary classics were then available in America. He was obviously one of the first men in North America to acquire an acquaintanceship with Chinese belles lettres, as distinguished from works of philosophy or ethics. His recommended bibliography included, in addition to the two Chinese classics, works of fiction by Fielding, Richardson, Smollett, Cervantes, and Sterne. In explaining to his friend why he had somewhat scanted "the learned lumber of Greek and Roman reading in favor of more modern works," Jefferson argued that "the entertainments of fiction are useful as well as pleasant" by contributing "to fix us in the principles and practice of virtue" and that the moral lessons of recorded history are in comparison not sufficiently frequent. Jefferson believed that the Chinese drama and the Chinese novel that he had listed belonged in this category of practical aids to virtue and were comparable to the great Western classics. He added the novel *The Pleasing History* to his personal library in 1789 (Sowerby 1955:4:43).

While serving as ambassador to France in 1785, Jefferson was sent a full account of the involvement of the trading vessel *Empress of China* in an altercation between Western traders and Chinese officials. Details will be given in the next chapter. Apparently Jefferson approved of the Chinese policy of non-intercourse with foreign nations, for he advocated a similar attitude for his own country. Queried on the expediency of encouraging commerce in the United States, he replied, "Were I to indulge my own theory, I should wish them to practice neither commerce nor navigation, but to stand with Europe precisely on the footing of China. We should thus avoid wars, and all our citizens would be husbandmen" (1950–:8:633). If population and productivity should greatly increase so that other nations would seek to engage in commerce with America, he speculated, there would then be ample time to cultivate manufacturing or navigation. This doctrine, by no means characteristic of Jefferson alone, has elements of the system of Quesnay and the French Physiocrats as well as of the related notion of American isolationism associated with Paine and Washington.

During his own administration as president of the United States, Jefferson expressed a much more favorable attitude toward commerce, and in particular, commerce with China. This was during the period of his Embargo Act of 1807 designed to prevent attacks on American shipping by French and English vessels blockading neutral ports during the Napoleonic Wars. Jefferson had received a letter in July 1808 concerning a Chinese national, Punqua Wingchong, described as a mandarin, who needed permission to return to his homeland, "where the affairs of his family and particularly the obsequies of his grandfather require his solemn attention" (Christman 1984:39). Jefferson accordingly urged his secretary of state Albert Gallatin that Punqua be allowed to depart with all his possessions. The cultivation of "good dispositions" in this Chinese national, he remarked, "may be the means of making our nation known advantageously at the source of power in China" and "be of sensible advantage to our merchants in that country" (Jefferson 1967:1:139). Jefferson was not aware, although Gallatin had some inkling of it, that Punqua was merely a pawn in a financial scheme devised by John Jacob Astor. Gallatin, nevertheless, instructed the collector of the port of New York that "the property of Punqua Wingchong and attendants besides their baggage and personal effects, of about forty five thousand dollars, as per endorsed memorandum, may be shipped on board either in specie, or in furs, cochineal, or Ginsang" (Christman 1984: 40). The vessel on which Punqua departed on

5 August 1808 was the *Beaver*, owned by Astor. This contrived sailing aroused a letter of protest from a group of China hands, affirming that the Chinese national was no mandarin at all. "To some of us he is known as a petty shopkeeper in Canton . . . and to the remainder he is altogether unknown; which could not be the case were his character and standing in any degree respectable." The involvement of Astor in the affair became clear when it was discovered that the *Beaver* returned to America with a cargo worth "two hundred thousand dollars more than she left with" (Christman 1984:40).

Ten years after his letter to Gallatin, Jefferson wrote to Charles Jared Ingersoll, acknowledging the gift of some Chinese objects that he described as "real curiosities," offering "a better idea of the state of science in China than the relations of travelers have effected" (letter, 20 July 1818) (1903: 19: 262). Here Jefferson joined Franklin in adopting an open mind concerning Chinese technology. The *New York Literary Gazette* for 27 May 1826 published a short piece declaring "The Compass: An Original Invention of the Chinese," conjecturing that the device was brought to Europe by Marco Polo. In the same year, an American edition of a *Memoir on Acupunturation* by J. Morand was published in Philadelphia.

The "real curiosities" to which Jefferson referred in his letter to Ingersoll presumably included books or scrolls since it led him to speculate on the difficulty of intellectual progress "with characters so complicated, so voluminous and inadequate" as the Chinese ideograms (1903: 19:262). Jefferson predicted "that some fortuitous circumstance will some day call their attention to the simple alphabets of Europe, which with proper improvements may be made to express the sounds of their language as well as of others." Franklin, as I have indicated, had made quite the opposite prophecy, that the English language would evolve toward the Chinese, dropping its phonetic character in favor of the ideogrammatic. Finally, Jefferson expressed the opinion that religious missionaries would more expediently accomplish their proseletyzing goals by giving instruction in the alphabet rather than in theological doctrines for which the Chinese were at that time in no way prepared.

In the preface to this book, I quoted the statement of a recent scholar that "colonials of cosmopolitan tastes like Jefferson and Franklin . . . stumbled on the subject of China late in their careers." In actuality, as I have shown, Franklin published excerpts from Confucius at the age of thirty-two; Paine published a review essay on China at the age of thirty-eight; and Jefferson recommended the reading of two Chinese classics also at the age of twenty-eight. And, as I have shown in the present chapter, all three of these eminent colonials maintained their interest in the Middle Kingdom after the United States had won its independence.

CHAPTER

7

The China Trade

About the only branch of early American relations with the Far East that has been widely treated in print is that of the China trade—and even here the emphasis has been upon a single aspect, that of the fine arts. On the occasion of the bicentennial of the voyage of the *Empress of China* in 1784, the first American venture in the Middle Kingdom, nearly every major art museum in the United States organized a commemorative exhibition and issued an accompanying catalog, comprising illustrations and historical text. These catalogs all unavoidably repeat essentially the same information, however, and because of their main function as exhibition guides most of them do little more than portray vividly the art objects imported from China. Although one of these bears the all-embracing title *China's Influence on American Culture in the Eighteenth and Nineteenth Centuries* (Trubner and Rathbun 1984), its coverage like that of others of the kind is actually limited to the fine arts. A great deal of original biographical and historical material is to be found, however, in one or two publications of the same genre which actually do live up to the promise of their titles.

Even before 1784, China was by no means completely an unknown land among people living in North America. The English had been engaged in commerce in the Far East ever since a galley, the *Macclesfield*, had taken on a rich cargo in Canton in 1700. Crew members of various English ships, moreover, came to the American colonies as visitors or immigrants and recounted their experiences of the wonders and the inconveniences of Canton. The editor of the *Boston Magazine* in 1786, for example, published an eyewitness account of the hospitality of the Chinese over fifty years earlier, (3:220–21) introducing it with his own slightly grammatically confused comments on the contradictory reports about the Chinese people then circulating.

> Some travellers have extolled them in the highest terms, whilst others have run into the contrary extreme; those last have been of late more numerous than the former. When we hear the character of a private person loaded with reproach, founded on real or pretended facts, we have no means of contradicting, though unknown to us, it is natural, for the sake of human nature, to wish that they may be true. But if we happen to be furnished with indisputable evidence of the virtue of that person in other instances, a mind of any benevolence, will seize with pleasure an opportunity of urging them in his vindication: How much more should we be influenced by this principle of equity, when a large and populous nation is concerned?

The narrator of the episode was Alexander Weddeburn, purser on the ship *Prince Edward*, sailing in 1729 from Calcutta to Canton with a cargo valued at 60,000 pounds sterling. Running into a storm near the China coast that lasted for several days, the captain decided to run the ship ashore at Timpau. It soon stranded and fifty-two men perished, including the captain and two mates. The mandarin governing that part of the country, in Weddeburn's words, "received us with marks of humanity and kindness far exceeding our expectations, not only appointing us a guard for our protection, but also ordering out the natives to assist us in fishing upon the wreck; by which means we recovered 5000 pounds in bullion, and afterwards about 10,000 more." The mandarin furnished them in addition an escort to Canton, where those in the administration also "shewed us their benevolence by representing our situation to the Emperor, then residing at Pekin; who soon sent orders for our relief, and an order to distribute a sum of money amongst us, in order to enable us to return from whence we came." The first supercargo received 450 tales of silver, the second supercargo 350, Weddeburn himself 250, the mate 75, and each common soldier 75.

Before the War for Independence, the *New York Journal* published in its news columns an account of a group of Kalmucks (Mongolian Buddhists) who had fled from Russia, seeking refuge in China (26 October 1775). The Imperial Senate at St. Petersburg wrote to the emperor of China, asking him to refuse them admission. The ruler granted the religious emigrants permission to enter, however, and ordered that they be brought to Pekin to see the splendor of his court, where he allowed them to eat at his table and afterwards loaded them with gifts. Since they had voluntarily submitted themselves to his empire, he wanted them to be as happy there as his own subjects were.

The actual ruler between 1736 and 1796 was Ch'ien Lung, whose name during the period was uniformly spelled in the West K'ien Long. His reign, according to most historians, was as peaceful and prosperous as it was long. Western writers of the time depicted him as an idyllic ruler in a benevolent and patriarchal society, but traders and diplomats at the turn of the century, as we shall see in chapter 11, reported a somewhat less ideal state of affairs.

The voyage of the *Empress of China* was not in any sense a patriotic venture designed to reveal the presence of the United States to the rest of the world or to make an impression on the Chinese people. It was instead a purely commercial enterprise from start to finish. The moving force behind the *Empress* and the burgeoning trade with China it symbolized was Robert Morris, the financier of the American Revolution, who owned a half interest in the voyage. His attention to Chinese potentialities had been drawn by a citizen of Connecticut, John Ledyard, who had earlier sailed with Captain Cook on the latter's third voyage of discovery, during which Ledyard learned that the pelts of sea otters fetched astronomical prices at Canton (Smith 1984:24). A scheme devised by Ledyard to load up with furs on the northern Pacific coast and then sail around South America fell through, but Morris decided to carry on independently with a voyage on the usual route around Africa, substituting ginseng as the major cargo. Although Philadelphia was originally intended as port of departure, it had to be switched to New York because of ice on the Delaware River.

The *Empress* left New York harbor on Washington's birthday 1784 with John Green as captain and Samuel Shaw as supercargo. Green had served in the American navy during the Revolution and Shaw had been a major in the Continental Army and still retained his title. The supercargo, a term in use since 1682, designated the ship's officer whose major duties took place on land. He acted as purchasing agent and made decisions concerning the stowing of merchandise. He drew upon specialized knowledge of goods to be bought and sold together with diplomatic skills necessary for dealing with local officials. Although Shaw is not mentioned in any histories of American literature, he wrote a journal of his experiences in the China trade that was extensively quoted in contemporary periodicals and richly deserves attention by modern scholars.

Newspapers up and down the coast gloried in the saga of the *Empress*. The *Maryland Journal* reported, 5 March 1784: "This handsome commodious and elegant ship modelled after and built on the new invented construction of the ingenious Mr. Peck of Boston, is deemed an exceeding swift sailor. The Captain and crew, with several young American adventurers, were all happy and cheerful, in good health and high spirits; and with a becoming decency elated on being considered the first instruments, in the hands of Providence, who have undertaken to extend the commerce of the United States of America to that distant, and to us unexplored, country" (Woodhouse 1939:24). Congress, as was the custom of the times, had given the captain an official letter or international passport calling upon all persons with whom he might come into contact to treat him with consideration. Green's document read in part: "most Serene, most puissant, high illustrious, noble, honorable, venerable, wise and prudent, Emperors, Kings, Republicks, Princes, Dukes, Earls, Barons, Lords, Burgomasters, Councillors . . . who shall see these patents or hear them read . . . receive him with goodness and treat him in a becoming manner" (Dulles 1946: 2).

Philip Freneau, the major poet of the American Revolution, known for his patriotism, deism, and romantic tendencies, hailed in conventional verse the *Empress* on its departure: "On the First American Ship That Explored the Rout [*sic*] to China and the East-Indies, After the Revolution." The following text is taken from Freneau's *Poems written between the Years 1768 & 1794 (Monmouth, New Jersey, 1795)*.

> With clearance from BELLONA won
> She spreads her wings to meet the Sun,
> Those golden regions to explore
> Where George forbade to sail before.
>
> Thus, grown to strength, the bird of Jove,
> Impatient, quits his native grove,
> With eyes of fire, and lightning's force
> Through the blue aether holds his course.
>
> No foreign tars here allow'd
> To mingle with her chosen crowd,
> Who, when return'd, might, boasting, say
> They show'd our native oak the way.
>
> To that old track no more confin'd,
> By Britain's jealous court assign'd,
> She round the STORMY CAPE shall sail
> And eastward, catch the odorous gale.
>
> To countries plac'd in burning climes
> And islands of remotest times
> She now her eager course explores,
> And soon shall greet Chinesian shores.

From thence their fragrant TEAS to bring
Without the leave of Britain's king;
And PORCELAIN WARE, enchas'd in gold,
The product of that finer mould.

Thus commerce to our world conveys
All that the varying taste can please:
For us, the Indian looms are free,
And Java strips her SPICY TREE.

Great pile proceed!—and o'er the brine
May every prosperous gale be thine,
'Till, freighted deep with eastern gems,
You reach again your native streams.

The word *Chinesian* in the fourth stanza is listed in the *Oxford English Dictionary* as rare and obsolete. In 1797, Freneau republished the poem anonymously in his newspaper the *Time Piece* [1, 64], giving it a slightly different title and improving the first line of the last stanza to read:

Proceed great pile! and o'er the brine.

Freneau's superpatriotism is revealed in his references to the jealousy of the British court and to American independence from the restrictions of George III. He also probably had the British in mind in his third stanza rejecting the interference of "foreign tars." This entire stanza is quite infelicitous, however, when viewed in conjunction with the events of the voyage, for foreign navigators actually did show America's "native oak the way." When the *Empress* attained the Straits of Sunda in Indonesia, it encountered a French vessel with which it established friendly relationships. From that point until arriving at Macao, the *Empress* and the French craft sailed together, the French in the lead sending out navigational signals day and night (*Pennsylvania Packet*, 18 May 1785; Cordier 1898: 6). On the return voyage, moreover, the *Empress* sailed part of the way in company with a Dutch vessel in order to take advantage of the presumed previous experience of its officers, but the Americans later discovered to their mortification that the Dutch captain was also sailing for the first time in China seas (Quincy 1847: 201).

Not all Americans were enthusiastic about the China trade. Shortly before republishing his poem in his periodical *The Time Piece*, Freneau inserted in the same newspaper an anonymous poem (24 March 1787) "On the Too Remote Extension of American Commerce," expressing the notion that people are better off at home than seeking profit abroad—that man is designed to till the ground, not endanger his life at sea, a reflection of the political philosophy of Thomas Jefferson.

How far less wise than China's train,
Who n'er remotely strain,
But leave the world to risque the main,
And safer tribute pay.

Western vessels bound for Canton first passed the Portuguese colony of Macao, after which they obtained a permit and a pilot and entered the Pearl River. Here they proceeded to Whampoa, a "reach" ten miles below Canton. This was the place of anchorage and loading for Western ships because ocean-going vessels were unable because of shallow water to penetrate beyond this point. Whampoa island had a famous nine-story pagoda, but otherwise was dirty and undistinguished.

When the first American vessel arrived in Whampoa, a code of procedure in dealing with Chinese traditions had already been well established by European nations over a long period of years. The first compulsory contact was with a *fiador* or security agent, who guaranteed payment of the various duties and fees exacted by the government (Quincy 1847:174,346). This agent was ordinarily one of the principal merchants of Canton; he was called a *hong*, and he associated in a *cohong*, or guild with about a half dozen others. In the light of their usually good relations, the Americans called these dealers their "horse grandfathers" (Hunter 1882:36).

The name of the imperial customs officer Hai Kwan Pu is said to have been corrupted by the British to hoppo (Smith, 34), and the official boat of the collector of customs was known as the hoppo boat. A more plausible explanation is that the Chinese word for board of revenue is "Hoo-poo," and the term was applied to his local representative (Hunter 1882: 36). The hoppo himself came on board each foreign ship to measure its capacity and assess the tonnage charges. He also pocketed the cumshaw—or gratuity—a substantial amount of money which never varied, no matter the size of the ship. Morris had been warned of this novel method of peculation a year before the departure of the *Empress*. One of his acquaintances, Mathew Ridley, wrote to him from France in October 1783, "It is necessary to inform you of one Circumstance, attending these voyages, all ships large or small, pay a Certain duty of Forty Thousand Livres; and therefore no persons send any but those of 800 or 1000 Tons. If a Ship only of 300 is sent, so considerable a duty makes a great addition to the cost of the cargo" (Christman 1948:45). When the *Empress* arrived at Canton, the hoppo expected to be offered in addition some type of clockwork or mechanical gadget referred to as the "sing-song."

After the visit of the hoppo, it was necessary to secure a "chop" or license to trade (the word deriving from the Chinese "cho," meaning any kind of document) and to engage a comprador (a Portuguese word meaning "purchaser"). These words and others common to the China trade belong to what was known as pigeon or pidgin English, a corruption of business. Other words of Portuguese origin are *mandarin* from "mandar," to order; *joss* from "Deos"; *pa-te-le*, from "Padre;" and *la-le-loon* from "ladron," a thief (Hunter 1882:62). *Porcelain* came from "porzella" or "little pig" because of its resemblance to the clear pink color of mussel shells, which Portuguese merchants in the sixteenth century had used as currency (Downs 1941: 11).

The comprador was a local jack of all trades, who handled arrangements with the outside, including purchasing supplies and hiring servants, and preventing impositions from anyone other than himself (Smith 1984: 56). Thomas W. Ward, master of the *Minerva* from Salem in 1809, furnishes a sketch of one of these picaresque types: "Tom Bull . . . is like other Chinese you deal with, except in one particular: he is an honorable scoundrel, and will tell you how much, & why, & wherefore he cheats you. He is as good as any of them" (Mudge 1984:49). A linguist or interpreter was also employed not only to exercise his bilingual talents, but also to examine both arrivals and departures and to recommend duties. According to Robert B. Forbes, a contemporary American trader, he was "never expected to speak the truth on any subject" (Christman 1984: 57). Another American affirmed that the linguists were so-called "because they knew nothing of any language but their own" (Hunter 1882: 50). The linguist was absolutely necessary, however, as Samuel Shaw explains, because he transacted all business with the custom house, where no foreigners were allowed, and provided sampans for loading and unloading (Quincy 1847: 176).

Almost no foreigners knew any elements of the Chinese language, not because of laziness or lack of linguistic ability, but because the Chinese government opposed the offering of instruction in the language even going "to the length of beheading a Chinese teacher for giving lessons" (Hunter 1882:60). Foreigners were known as "fanqui" or foreign devils and were not allowed to penetrate beyond a narrow area strictly limited in territory, also known as the fanqui. The Chinese attitude toward foreigners is neatly summarized in a greatly abbreviated paraphrase of a message from the Emperor K'ien Long to the British sovereign George III delivered in 1793 through the agency of Lord Macartney, the leader of a British mission to Pekin to seek broader trading privileges for the crown: "Our Empire produces all that we ourselves need. But since our tea, rhubarb and silk seem to be necessary to the very existence of the barbarous Western peoples, we will, imitating the clemency of Heaven, Who tolerates all sorts of fools on this globe, condescend to allow a limited amount of trading through the port of Canton" (Christman 1984:53). This is the reverse side of the emperor's character and of the Chinese in general, usually portrayed as genial and benevolent, but here made to appear haughty and disdainful.

The Chinese had good reason for treating foreigners with cautious hostility, according to a Salem naval officer Amasa Delano, who several times touched at Canton. In connection with a visit in 1806, he remarked:

> When the Europeans first visited this country, they were received by the Chinese with great kindness and hospitality, granting them every indulgence in the pursuits of commerce, which was reasonable. They at first had full liberty to go where they pleased; but the strangers soon began to abuse this indulgence, and conduct themselves in such a manner, by taking liberties with their women, and other gross improprieties which a Chinese can never overlook, that the government were obliged to curtail their liberties and confine them to the port of Canton only, where they are permitted to reside for the express purpose of commerce. Foreigners are not admitted into the city of Canton; but are allowed the suburbs, to erect their factories and transact business. (Delano 1817: 531)

Ships were prohibited from entering the Canton area unless they had a cargo, a regulation designed to keep them from unloading elsewhere and seeking bargains in Canton during periods of oversupply of exportable goods. An American merchant in 1801 advised his countrymen to carry a small supply of lead and iron to be declared as cargo. This subterfuge would enable the hoppo to make peace with the security agent after accepting payment of 200 dollars, a small sum for the trader considering that it obviated the risk of a long detention (Corning 1942: 170).

The restricted area of Canton occupied by the foreign community was an enclave on the river's edge about 700 feet wide and less than a quarter mile long. It was severely regulated by eight rules, including the prohibition of women and arms of any kind as well as rowing about in the river for pleasure alone. On the eighth, eighteenth, and twenty-eighth days of the moon, the foreign devils were allowed into the city to visit the Flower Gardens and the Honam Joss house (Buddhist Temple), but not in droves of over ten at a time (Hunter 1882: 29). The reason for prohibiting women was presumably to discourage Westerners from settling down as permanent residents. For the same reason, all foreigners were required to leave Canton during the "off season," during which most of these transplanted occidentals merely went downstream to Macao. Americans were called "Flowery Flag Devils" because the stars of the stars and stripes were taken for flowers. The Chinese distinguished between Americans and English by dubbing the former "the New People."

All foreign nations in Canton were assigned "factories," which were combination offices and living quarters. The term factory was synonymous with "agency," but was also used interchangeably with "hong." A hong could be both a person and a place, the latter comprising an immense warehouse. Most Americans who wrote about the system had their list of principal merchants, along with their preferred spelling of the Chinese names. That compiled by J. F. Leaming in 1806, now in the Waln manuscript papers of the Library Company of Philadelphia, includes Paunkeiqua, Houqua, Consequa, Cheunqua, Youqua, Lyqua, Munqua, Pouqua, Neiqua and Loqua. A later list of William C. Hunter in 1825 included Houqua, Mouqua, Pwankeiqua, Pwansuylan, Chungqua, Kingqua, and Gouqua (1882:34). Pwankeiqua, the chief or head of the hong, was the security merchant for the *Empress*, on its first voyage. The suffix "qua" in a Chinese name denotes an official, but may be loosely translated as "mister," for example, Houqua and Putinqua. Three years later after Pwankeiqua had given up his connection with the Americans in order to work exclusively with the English and Spanish, he was described as possessing "immense property, great influence, and a high independent spirit. He is devoted to the English, who endeavor to engross his whole attention and influence. He will not undertake to Secure American Ships, either because it might not be agreeable to the English, or because their Concerns are not of consequence enough to merit his attention" (Smith 1984: 35).

The family of Houqua is the most famous among the hong merchants. The first of its members in business with the West, however, was given a rather poor character by Samuel Shaw. He reported that when the supercargo of the *Asia* in January 1789 entrusted his ginseng to Houqua, some English acquaintance informed him that "they might as well have thrown their property into the sea." True to this prediction, Houqua "delayed performing his contract,—absented himself almost continually from his hoang,—smoked opium,—absconded on the 24th of December,—was declared bankrupt, and his effects were seized" (Quincy 1827:301). The second Houqua, son of the former, who flourished from 1790 to 1830, became the most illustrious of the family and indeed of all the hong merchants. A painting of him attributed to the British artist resident in Canton, George Chinnery, has frequently been reproduced. Thomas W. Ward, captain of the *Minerva*, described him in 1809 as "very rich, . . . just in all his dealings, in short . . . a man of honor and veracity—has more business than any other man in the Hong and secures 12 or 14 American ships this year. Houqua is rather dear loves flattery & can be coaxed" (Mudge 1981:54).

Life on the China voyage and in the Canton factories had both its ups and downs. Jonathan Mifflin, a supercargo on the *Asia* in 1788, wrote to his brother about the "luxuries of a voyage to China," extolling the cuisine and alcoholic beverages (Smith 1984:109). Captains sometimes overindulged in expensive items for consumption on board. When one of them, Jacob Benners, was being considered by the owner of the *Susquehanna* in 1809, the latter admonished him that "some of your friends when recommending you to us thought proper to give us a hint that you were very profuse in your disbursements" (132). George Chinnery, the English painter residing in Canton, when asked how some former employees of the East India Company had passed their time replied that "they spent six months in Macao, having nothing to do, and the other six months in Canton, doing nothing" (Conner 1986: 10). Another Englishman, William Hickey, extolled a dinner at the English factory "consisting of fish, flesh and fowl, all of the best, with a variety of well-dressed made dishes, being served up in two courses, followed by a superb dessert, the wines, claret, madeira, and hock, all excellent, and made as cold as ice" (Conner 1986: 10). A later supercargo, Benjamin Rush Jr., son of the noted Philadelphia physician, however, indicated in a letter to his sister, 6 April 1823, that the structure in which he lived lacked nearly all the expected conveniences of a civilized dwelling.

> It is as large, as gloomy, and as pervious to cold wind, as any of our barns in America, and more secluded from the summer's breeze: To make an appearance of comfort, and the reality of privacy, we have had partitions erected to form rooms, which are open at the top like pews in a church, only eight feet high, because to reach the roof they would have to be about thirty: From an old rough beam in the middle of the building is suspended a lamp, which when lighted shows a place a good deal like that where Rolando took Gil Blas. All the time I have been here till within three days, the sun has only momentarily appeared twice, which is not unusual at this rainy season of the year; but it has been unseasonably cold enough for a good fire, and we have had I may almost say none; only keeping ourselves warm by redoubled clothing, and by the unwholesome heat from a chafing dish of ignited charcoal. Dining, by the light of a lamp, in the middle of this vast and gloomy building of uncouth architecture, we do surely look more like a couple of thieves in a cave, than two honest men in a comfortable place of residence. There are also other inconveniences of minor consideration, such as rats, bats, and more than our share of tormenting insects; and next July instead of a heat of 100 degrees of Fahrenheit, which I have seen in the coolest of the old factories, I expect to see the thermometer at 105 or more in our apartments. (Christman 1984: 179)

According to Shaw, the *Empress* on its first voyage made a clear profit of $30,727, or "upwards of twenty-five per cent. on one hundred and twenty thousand dollars, the capital employed" (Quincy 1847:218). Although Shaw wrote in a gloating strain, this was not a sensational return. Shaw's own share, according to his biographer, "scarcely amounted to a remuneration for his time and services" (113). The modest nature of this profit was probably due to a temporary glut on the ginseng market, although Shaw may not have made the best possible deal, as I shall indicate in the next chapter. I have already quoted the blunt remark of the purser, John White Swift, "We brought too much Ginseng." He offered advice for future voyages: "A little Tar, a little Wine, and a great many Dollars, with some &cs make the best Cargoe" (Swift 1885:485). The percentage gained by the *Experiment,* a much smaller vessel that sailed from New York in December, 1785, was considerably greater than that of the *Empress,* even though the ship weighed only eighty tons in contrast to the 360 of the *Empress* and was manned by a crew of only fifteen. After a two-way voyage of eighteen months, the venture showed a profit of over $16,000, a doubling of the initial investment in a year and a half (Howard 1984:25). Yet even this extraordinary gain apparently did not satisfy the captain, Stewart Dean. "If the Chinese duty at Canton," he wrote, "had only required a sum in proportion to the size of my boat I would have made an advantageous voyage" (Christman, 23).

The *Experiment* has received relatively little attention because of the chronological priority of the *Empress of China,* but in many ways the voyage of the smaller vessel is equally worthy of comment, considering its diminutive size and the enterprise of its owners and courage of its crew in undertaking the second adventure from America to China. A dispatch in the *New Haven Gazette* for May, 1787 (2, 84) reported its arrival at New York after a return voyage of four months and twelve days.

> It was matter of surprise to the natives to see so small a vessel from a clime so remote from China; and must have given them an exalted conception of the enterprising spirit of the United States. The successful and safe return of Captain Dean, has taught us that fancy often paints danger in higher colours than it is really found to exist, and that by maintaining a spirit of enterprize, diligence and activity, we are enabled to surmount difficulties, which on a contrary view, seem fraught with danger.—Captain Dean brought home all the hands he took out with him, having had no sickness on board.

An earlier ship, the *Pallas,* on its arrival at Baltimore, advertised the following imports in the *Pennsylvania Packet,* 17 August 1785: tea, large amounts of China, including some with the arms of the order of Cincinnati, nankeens, satins, silks, umbrellas, paper hangings, Japan work, "Sago, cinnamon, and cinnamon flowers, rhubarb, opium, gambuge, and borax."

British merchants who learned of the fall in price of American ginseng were understandably not grieved at the news. A letter on the slump from a Swedish supercargo in Canton to a friend in London, 25 February 1785, printed in the *True Briton* and reprinted in the *New Haven Gazette* (1 9 February 1786, 7), strongly suggested that the days of fast profits in ginseng were at an end.

> Trade in general wears but an unfavorable aspect, and many things that formerly yielded a large profit, will, I think, do so no more; for instance, ginseng, such a quantity has been brought by an American ship, the Empress of China, as has reduced the price lower than it has been known for these many years, and those persons who had much on hand will suffer greatly
>
> It is understood that the Americans intend sending one or more ships annually to China, with a like cargo, also with furs and other articles, and to establish themselves here and display the thirteen stripes at Canton; so that ginseng, from the immense quantity of it produced in North-America, will in all probability, never bear a better price than at present. I hope none of your friends on the way to us have speculated thereon.

American newspapers, however, uniformly reflected optimism in regard to commercial potentialities. The *Providence Gazette* for 4 August 1787 gloated that notwithstanding accounts in English journals of "the distressed situation of America, the general want of money, and the insufficiency of American credit, for the purposes of carrying on trade, &c.," there were five American ships at that time in Canton and these brought to eleven the number of vessels fitted out from various American ports for India and China since the beginning of the year 1783 (Nelson1984:11). "Beginning with the season 1795–1796, the annual number of American ships at Canton never fell below ten, with an average of between fifteen and twenty a year until 1808–1809, when only eight ships were reported" (Mudge 1981:38). Thirty ships were counted at Canton in 1815–1816, and an all-time high was reached in 1812–1819 with forty-seven (39). Some idea of the large number of Americans who actually set foot on Chinese soil—albeit in the circumscribed area of the fanqui—may be obtained from the mere naming of the American ships plying the China trade at the time. Each of the following had made at least one voyage before the end of the eighteenth century: *America, Argonaut, Asia, Astrea, Betsey, Canton, Columbia, Concord, Delaware, Eleonora, Empress of China, Experiment, General Washington, Lady Washington, Grand Turk, Jenny, Lady Louisa, Mary, Massachusetts, Nelson, Neptune, Pallas, Pigou, Sampson, Three Sisters, Union, William and Henry,* and *Woodrop Sims*. Stephen Girard, canny merchant and liberal philanthropist of Philadelphia, personally owned four ships in the Canton service, the first of which the *Rousseau* sailed in December 1802. The others were named *Voltaire, Montesquieu* and *Helvetius*, all of these names expressing Girard's free-thinking views in religion. The following additional vessels were engaged in the same waters before 1825: *Active, Addison, Adriana, Amethyst, Ann and Hope, Arthur, Bengal, Bingham, Caledonia, Caroline, Catherine, China, Clothier, Comet, Devotion, Dorothea, Eliza, Fame, George and Albert, George Washington, Glove, Governor Endicott, Harvard, Hebe, Hope, Indus, Lancaster, Manchester, Minerva, Mount Vernon, New Hazard, New Jersey, Ohio, Ophelia, Pacific, Penman, Pennsylvania, Pennsylvania Packet, Perseverance, Sally, Severen, Silenus, Susequehanna, Thalia, Thomas Scattergood, Trader, Tyre, William and John, Union,* and *William Savery.* If one considers the number of men comprising the crew of even the smallest of these vessels, one realizes that several citizens of the United States at this period possessed a firsthand acquaintance with some aspects of Chinese civilization. The *Massachusetts* in 1790, for example, carried a crew of sixty-one exclusive of officers (Delano 1817:27). In 1784 the ratio of British to American ships in Canton-Macao was 1 to 21; in 1795, 10 to 33; and in 1805, 41 to 53. In 1795, the United States became second to Great Britain in the China trade, less than ten years after the maiden voyage of the *Empress of China* (Howard 1984:59). In the season 1818–1819 the American trade exceeded that of the English East India Company by $1.5 million. (*National Gazette* 5 February 1821).

The first English-language newspaper in China, the *Canton Register,* was founded in 1827 by a citizen of Philadelphia, William Whiteman Wood, who went to Canton in 1820. Wood, son of a celebrated actor, secured a measure of literary fame by a parody of a poem he calls Byron's, "Know'st thou the land," but in reality a a paraphrase of Goethe's "Kennst du das Land." The following two stanzas of the ten of the poem give an idea of Wood's undoubted but unrecognized talent (Hunter 1882:111).

> Know'st thou the land where the nankin and tea-chest,
>   With cassia and rhubarb and camphor, abound?
> Where oft in the Hongs, by the coolies' foul feet pressed,
>   They pack their Boheas in a way to astound?
>
> Tis the land we now live in—the land that would shame
>   The world by its valour, invention, and worth;
> Where the page of her history glows with the name
>   Of her sage, [Confucius] and her warrior, [Kung-Ming], the
>   pride of the earth.

I have already made clear in chapter 2 that the principal export to China was ginseng supplemented by furs and specie (Spanish silver dollars). Wealthy Chinese used these furs to line and trim their winter garments. The ordinary exports from America for the European market had little appeal for the Chinese, and traders were forced to improvise with products such as furs and spices that could be obtained en route in Africa or Indian. Those taking the path around the Horn traded with the Indians on the Pacific coast of America. In the second decade of the nineteenth century, the least scrupulous of the American traders joined the English in carrying opium, an illegal commodity, which, as usually happens with illicit merchandise, brought the highest profits of all. According to a manuscript of 1817 by Alexander M. Neilledge, opium, although prohibited, was smuggled into the country in large quantities by means of "bribes which are paid to the public Officers which the Chinese call Smug Pigeon" (Waln manuscripts, Library Company of Philadelphia, I).

According to John K. Fairbank, the opium trade was begun by a Mr. Wilcox of Philadelphia in 1804 and after that it concentrated in Boston. An "implicit assumption became established; that the American and other Western traders in China were not responsible for the welfare of that heathen and backward kingdom. The Chinese would have to look out for themselves; and if they would persist in buying and smuggling opium, that was their problem, not the foreigners" (Fairbank 1975:15).

The major import into the United States was tea along with textiles, porcelain, furniture, and fireworks. The textiles consisted of silk and nankeen, the latter a durable fabric named after the city of Nanking, just as denim derives from the French city of Nimes (bleu de Nimes). Only porcelain and furniture have survived in measurable quantities from this period and have thus provided the substance of museum catalogues. Other recorded imports included " 'mandarin heads,' umbrellas, ciphered fans, flower seeds, bamboo washstands, sweetmeats, tea waiters, boxes of paints, ivorywork caskets" together with "sugar, cassia, clay images, paper hangings, furniture, satin, lacquerware, bamboo blinds, floor mats, fans, and whangee canes" (Smith 1984: 311).

Both the furniture and silk of Nanking were superior to those of Canton, according to the Mr. Brunel whose memoir on Chinese trade has already been quoted in connection with ginseng.

> Silk stuffs of a good quality ought to have fine borders, and to be closely woven, very soft, smooth, and bright. To judge of the goodness of a piece of silk, one must not be directed by the weight; because the more Canton silk, which is a hard kind of an inferior quality, has been employed in manufacturing it, the more it will weigh. Stuffs made of that silk do not take the die well, especially green and blue colours; and they are always hard and stiff to the

touch. The goodness of a piece of satin or damask may be known by its being soft, smooth, and even. If made of coarse silk, it will be rough and uneven. (*New York Magazine* [1785], 6:84–85)

The Chinese product that has inspired most writing since its introduction to the West is the major consumer item, tea. The English word derives from a corruption of *tay*, in the Fuh-keen dialect, the province from which it was first exported to Europe (Hunter 1882:91). In Cantonese and Mandarin, it is called *cha*, a name that has been adopted in Russian and Portuguese. The drinking of tea was praised in the seventeenth century by one of the early Western visitors to China, Jan Nieuhof, for not only producing a sense of well-being but also for counteracting an excess of alcohol, preventing gout and gallstones, and promoting the powers of memory, a roster of claims resembling those made for ginseng. Perhaps the most famous line in English verse concerning tea is William Cowper's in Book IV of *The Task*, referring to cups "That cheer but not inebriate." The American poet Philip Freneau celebrated its universal appeal in a poem "The Dish of Tea," published in his 1795 *Poems* and republished in the *Time Piece* (II [29 January 1798] No. 59). Here is the second stanza.

> From China's groves, this present brought,
> Enlivens every power of thought,
>   Riggs many a ship for sea:
> Old maids it warms, young widows charms;
> And ladies' men, not one in ten
>   But courts them for their TEA.

According to Patrick Conner, "The legendary, almost mystical status accorded to tea in the early eighteenth century was undoubtedly encouraged by its high price. In 1730 the British consumer had to pay from 6 to 36 shillings for a pound of tea, much of which was accounted for by heavy import duties on what was seen as a luxury product" (1986: 11). American consumers, who suffered the same restrictions, had not forgotten the Boston Tea Party of the Revolution. Samuel Shaw affirmed that the establishments of the Swedes and Danish in Canton were supported primarily by the smuggling trade in tea that they carried on off the British coasts. He had been told by an official of the East India Company that the annual consumption of tea in British territories was fourteen million pounds while the sales of the Company—which had the status of a monopoly—did not exceed six (Quincy 1847:171). Shaw predicted that if Parliament repealed the duty on tea that there would be no inducement for smuggling and that the tea trade would then be conducted by the consumer nations only, the British, the Americans, and the Dutch. For the American consumer after 1785, direct trade with China with its promise of lowered prices for a luxury item was a welcome development. The federal government not only limited the import of tea to American ships, but allowed a two-year delay in the payment of tea duties, a major concession to American shippers considering that the entry duty usually equalled or exceeded the original cost of the tea at Canton (Mudge 1984: 37).

Green teas were almost exclusively imported into the United States until 1828, when black tea entered the market (Hunter 1882:95). Manuscript instructions to an unidentified China trade supercargo now preserved in the Philadelphia Maritime Museum give the following advice on selecting a superior product.

> Hyson sifted, new, and of good quality, will have a fresh lively bloom, and of a deep bluish-green colour—the leaves single & closely twisted, free from dust, small broken leaves, and of Hyson Skin (which is the Chaff of Hyson) or large loose lumps. When steeped in hot Water, the leaves will spread open, and be large, fair, and unbroken, leaving the water clear, and tinged with a light Green colour, but if old, and bad, it will leave the water yellow and green." (Smith 1984 [2]: 31)

Brunel in his memoir on Chinese trade gives extensive information about tea and its cultivation.

> Tea grows on a small shrub, the leaves of which are collected twice or thrice every year. Those who collect the leaves three times a year, begin at the new moon which precedes the vernal equinox, whether it falls in the end of February or the beginning of March. At that period most of the leaves are perfectly green, and hardly fully expanded: but these small and tender leaves are accounted the best of all; they are scarce and exceedingly dear.
>
> The second crop, or the first for those who collect the leaves only twice a year, is gathered about the end of March, or the beginning of April. Part of the leaves have then attained to majority; and though the other part have acquired only half their size, they are both collected without any distinction.
>
> The third, or the second for some, and last crop, is more abundant, and is collected about the end of April, or the beginning of May, when the leaves have attained to their full growth, either in size or number. . . .
>
> The leaves of the tea shrub are oblong, sharp-pointed, indented on the edges, and of a very beautiful green colour. The flower is composed of five white petals disposed in form of a rose, and is succeeded by a pod of the size of a filberd, containing two or three small green seeds, which are wrinkled, and have a disagreeable taste. Its root is fibrous, and spreads itself out near the superficies of the ground. (*New York Magazine* [February, 1795]: 79–80)

Brunel explains that the shrub grows equally well in poor as in rich soil and is found all over China, but some regions have teas of a better quality than others. Some are exceedingly expensive and others cheap. The Chinese are very fond of good tea, however, and take as much pains to obtain good quality as Europeans do to secure fine wines. Bohea tea, which takes its name from a mountain in Fokien, has three kinds; the first or common variety grows at the bottom of the mountain; the second or *congo*, meaning "better prepared," grows at the top; and the third or *souchong*, meaning "quintessence," grows in the middle.

> Bohea tea, in general, ought to be dry and heavy in the hand; this is a sign that the leaves have been full and juicy. When infused, they ought to communicate to the water a yellow colour, inclining a little to green, which indicates that they are fresh, for old tea produces a red color. Care must be taken, above all, to avoid red leaves, and to chuse such as are large and entire. This also is a sign of freshness; for the longer tea is kept, the more it is shaken, which breaks the leaves, and mixes them with a great deal of dust. It sometimes happens, however, that the tea dust is owing to the manner in which it is put into the box, as the Chinese tread upon it with their feet to make it hold a larger quantity. (*New York Magazine* [February 1795]: 80)

Brunel describes *pekao* as "a particular kind of tea-shrub, the leaves of which are all black on the one side, and all white on the other." It is very scarce and sometimes adulterated by maintaining a preponderance of black over white leaves as well as by introducing small leaves from the bohea tree.

Ebenezer Townsend, Jr. supercargo of the *Neptune* in 1799, noted in his diary that bohea tea was exported in the same chests in which the country packers had trod upon it barefooted (Nelson 1984: 89). To protect their feet, he warned, "they are apt if not closely watched to put on their heel a sort of shoe which is injurious to the tea by grinding it to a powder. The boxes we set in tiers, and we pack two hundred a day, one man to each chest, which makes it a very unpleasant, dusty, dirty business. . . . In the weight of our teas and account of our cargo I always every night compared notes with the head Chinese clerk, or purser as they are there called, and we never differed; they are very correct."

Samuel Shaw, as usual, has something derogatory to say in a description in the *New York Magazine* (January 1796) of two or three hundred men working in a hot packing house.

> Two *naked* fellows are employed to pack one chest, and they do it by standing in the chest and stamping as the tea is supplied afresh. Here they toil and sweat; the dust from the floor (which is the natural

ground) and finer parts of the tea, form a thick fog, which, lighting continually on the packers, is again conveyed into the chest by the sweat which runs in copious streams from every part of their bodies. This should necessarily give the most insipid herb in the world a considerable odour, and an evident taste of some kind; but when connected with the delectable properties of *Thea* heightens its fragrance and sweet savour, no doubt, to that degree which the ladies so much admire.

As the major booster in America of the China trade, Shaw does not seem to realize that his remarks, if broadcast, would react against widespread consumption of tea.

Sullivan Dorr, a China merchant in 1801, wrote in his notebook that "An American can form some idea of qualities of Teas, or why they should differ in that point, by considering how various the qualities of Tobacco is, produced in the several states in America. In fact if I mistake not the harshness or strength of one kind of Tobacco is qualified by mixing that of another kind for the end intended, so it is with Teas in China, for instance one fourth Pakhoo mix'd with three fourths Souchong gives it an excellent taste or flavour" (Corning 1942: 161). Dorr added that the Chinese themselves consume no green tea whatsoever except chulon hyson. This is combined with a large amount of imlon flowers and used only for medicinal purposes. After citing the opinion of the Chinese that green tea "reduces and enervates the body," Dorr reported that a single cup of green tea would keep him awake all night; whereas a dozen cups of black had no such effect (161). Statistics show that the American consumption of tea rose sharply from an average of 2.5 million pounds annually in the period 1790–1800 to 3.8 million pounds from 1800 to 1812 (Pitkin 1817:247–48). Later in the nineteenth century, better grades were imported as well as more green over black, a trend interpreted as an increased perception of taste or quality as well as a growth in purchasing power (Latourette 1917: 76–77).

Porcelain, like tea, had been imported into the British colonies of North America long before the War of Independence. As early as 1662, settlers in Fort Orange (Albany) possessed China porcelain sent to them by relatives in Holland (Howard 1984: 61). Because of the great variety of clays in Pennsylvania, the preface to the *Transactions* of the American Philosophical Society in 1771 proposed that "a porcelain equal to that brought from China may be made here." Throughout the seventeenth and eighteenth centuries any kind of chinaware was a great luxury in the British colonies even that of the most utilitarian kind. The later porcelain products shipped to the United States after the establishing of direct trade with China were on the whole not of the first quality, the result, as Jean

McClure Mudge, the foremost authority on the subject, observes, of both economic and cultural considerations.

> The chinaware often reflected the attitude that each country had toward the other. Both nations met mainly for trade, with the aggressiveness of the Americans only increasing the restraint of the Chinese. Commerce was carried on in an atmosphere of suspicion and contempt. Understandably, then, the supercargoes ordered chinaware chiefly with Western forms and decorations, following the instructions of their patrons. Such preferences indicated not only a desire for useful objects and a certain artistic blindness due to European conditioning, but also an oblique, but definite, cultural imperialism. In return, the Chinese, regarding their nation as the unequaled Celestial kingdom, never exported any of the best-quality porcelain. All the finest pieces were reserved for imperial use, and even the second-quality porcelains were often kept at home, although a few of these entered the foreign trade. The Chinese stood aloof, looking at the Americans as they had looked at generations of foreigners—with an urbane and condescending attitude. (1981: 66)

Brunel wrote that he was unaware of who had invented porcelain, but stated that the Chinese believed that it has existed since A.D. 424. The porcelain of Kinte-ching, he affirmed, is the finest known and may easily be distinguished from that of Canton and Fokien, which is of a coarse white color without brightness and delicate tints. Brunel commented on some problems encountered by Europeans, who procured almost all their ware from Canton except that which they had made to order.

> "The Chinese merchants send models to *Kinte-Ching* to have various articles manufactured in the same manner; but it often happens that the workmen, being sure of a ready sale for their own patterns, neglect these works, and do not give themselves the trouble to correct any faults which may be in the materials or workmanship. . . . Besides this there is another inconvenience in these commissioned works. Being all made according to new models, in which it is difficult to succeed, if they have even a few imperfections, they are rejected by the Europeans, who will purchase nothing but what is thoroughly finished. They remain therefore in the hands of the manufacturers, who not being able to dispose of them to the Chinese, because they are not agreeable to their taste, lay upon the pieces they sell an additional price, in order to make up for the loss they sustain by those which are returned" (*New York Magazine* [February, 1795]: 85–86)

Brunel concluded that the difficulty of imitating models sent from the West caused the high price of commissioned porcelain. The workmen, he wrote, were not able to copy every pattern indiscriminately even though they could execute some works that others might conceive impossible. Brunel observed that the Chinese ridiculed the false notion that porcelain when buried in the earth acquires a superior degree of perfection. The idea had taken hold because some beautiful pieces had been discovered in ruins or neglected wells, but these outstanding examples did not derive their beauty from being buried, but from the artistic excellence of their original conception. They had been concealed underground by their owners for safekeeping during times of war or revolution, not for any other reason. Some Chinese connoisseurs, he added, value these pieces because they may have been used by emperors in remote ages. "All the change made in porcelain by lying long in the earth, respects its tints and colouring" (*New York Magazine* [February 1795]: 8). Exactly the same point had been previously made by Du Halde (1736: 2: 352). Brunel warned, moreover, that a method had recently been discovered of making porcelain resemble artifacts three or four hundred years old. These false antiques resembled the real in "not resounding when struck, and in producing no humming noise when applied to the ear" (*New York Magazine* [February 1795]: 87).

If the Chinese looked down upon American taste, the Americans registered in turn a deprecatory attitude toward Chinese artistic talents. Samuel Shaw observed that "there are many painters in Canton, but I was informed that not one of them possesses a genius for design. . . . It is a general remark, that the Chinese, though they can imitate most of the fine arts, do not possess any large portion of original genius" (Quincy 1847:198–9). Shaw, as the designer of the insignia of the Society of the Cincinnati, ordered a commemorative pattern of the society to be incorporated on various pieces of porcelain. His "idea was to have the American Cincinnatus, under the conduct of Minerva, regarding Fame, who, having received from them the emblem of the order, was proclaiming it to the world" (Quincy 1847: 198). To that end, he furnished a Chinese artist with two engravings of the Roman goddess, the figure of the Count d'Estaing, representing the military, and the medal of the order, hoping to have them artistically joined. He discovered to his dismay that the artist "was unable to combine the figures with the least propriety; though there was not one of them which singly he could not copy with the greatest exactness" (194). Shaw, nevertheless ordered a large quantity of blue and white dinner ware decorated with the arms of the society, but the order was not ready in time for the return voyage of the *Empress* in 1785. Only one piece of porcelain, a punch bowl, can be traced to the return voyage (Howard 1984: 73). The china decorated with the arms of the Order of Cincinnati along with other pieces was shipped on the *Pallas* a few months later and was offered for sale 12 August in the *Baltimore Advertiser* (Howard 1984:74). George Washington eventually purchased 302 pieces (Smith 1984: 61). The captain of another American ship, John E. Sword, sought to make a handsome profit from the expertise of the copyists. Having purchased from Gilbert Stuart one of his oil paintings of George Washington, he had more than 100 copies executed on glass by Chinese artists and shipped them home for sale. Stuart thereupon brought suit against Sword in 1802 at the Circuit Court of the Eastern District of the United States (Lee 1984:193; Christman 1984:77).

Robert Waln, Jr., supercargo on the *Caledonia* in 1819–20, echoed in 1820 Shaw's criticism of Cantonese artists. "The Chinese are excellent copyists," he wrote, "but possess little or no inventive faculties. In the suburbs of Canton there are many Painters chiefly depending on foreigners, by whom they are almost exclusively employed. The Chinese themselves afford little encouragement to this beautiful art." In Canton itself, however, Waln found artisans with abilities somewhat superior. He mentions three of these by name, one of whom "devotes his talents entirely to Miniature Painting" and the other two who "copy indiscriminately any originals furnished, which they often excell." Waln made these comments in an article that will be treated in Chapter 13 on "Painters of Canton" that he published in a Philadelphia newspaper, the *National Gazette* (4 August 1823).

On his return voyage to the United States in 1820, Waln wrote an essay on the commerce of the United States with China, affirming that it had become "a prolific source of emolument to our merchants and revenue to our government." Imports from China, he maintained, had become "more incorporated with the necessities than the luxuries of life" and tea was consumed upon the same scale as bread. Because of the great variety in the quality and cost of tea, it was within the means of even "the poorer classes of society" despite "the enormous import duties it carried (Waln Papers, Library Company of Philadelphia, Volume 3). Originally many nations had competed for the China market, but by this time every country had abandoned it except the United States, Britain, and Portugal. Ginseng was no longer the major item of export on America ships, but had been replaced in 1817 by iron, steel, cotton, silver, skins, furs, cochineal, quicksilver, betel nut, spices, various kinds of wood, curtlery, English cloth, porter, and ale (Waln 1).

Tea, porcelain, and art thus mingled in the American consciousness with Asian arrogance, industry, and dubious commercial ethics. The opinions concerning Chinese society expressed by Shaw and other Americans were harsh or negative in some instances, but most observers who had lived in Canton agreed that in matters of business the average Chinese was honest and trustworthy. An apparently representative American attitude by William C. Hunter, who first saw the city in 1825, reveals nostalgia and affection rather than suspicion and a feeling of superiority.

> The business transacted within their walls was incalculable, and I think I am safe in saying that from the novelty of the life, the social good feeling and unbounded hospitality always mutually existing; from the facility of all dealings with the Chinese who were assigned to transact business with us, together with their proverbial honesty, combined with a sense of perfect security to person and property, scarcely a resident of any lengthened time, in short, any "Old Canton," but finally left them with regret. (1882:26)

The China trade by bringing the United States into direct contact with Chinese people and products accounts in large measure for a drastic change in attitude toward the Middle Kingdom in all sectors of American society. By the end of the eighteenth century, Americans still considered it an exotic land, but it had lost its mythical aura. It was now known to be inhabited by people with motives and moral characteristics essentially similar to those of ordinary Americans, and it had become a nation to be exploited rather than looked upon as a source of admiration or marvel. Commercial contacts, however, did little to expand knowledge of Chinese culture except in the realm of the fine arts. They did, however, give rise to three literary works of merit, the journal of Shaw, a book of travel by Amasa Delano, and a lengthy treatise on China by Robert Waln, Jr., all of which will be treated in subsequent chapters.

CHAPTER
8

Traders and Mariners

The first literary work by an American who had actually visited China was the journal of Samuel Shaw. Although it was not published at length until long after his death, many excerpts appeared in the American press from 1785 to 1810, and it may, therefore, be considered as an effective instrument in the contemporary dissemination of knowledge concerning the Middle Kingdom in the United States and in the forming of general opinions concerning it. It also provided the substance of the first published history of Chinese-American relations by R. B. Forbes, *Remarks on China and the China Trade* (Boston:1844). Born in Boston on 2 October 1754, Shaw attended the local Latin School, where he acquired a love for classical letters extensively revealed in the writings of his mature years. On his twenty-first birthday he enrolled in the Continental Army and was almost immediately appointed by Washington as a lieutenant. For seven years he served on the staff of General Henry Knox as, respectively, adjutant, brigade-major and aide-de-camp. A warm friendship grew up between the two men, and at the close of hostilities Knox wrote that Shaw had "in every instance, evinced himself an intelligent, active, and gallant officer" (Quincy 1847: iii). Among his distinctions, Shaw served as secretary to the committee of officers who founded the Society of the Cincinnati and drafted its constitution. Having been offered the post of supercargo on the *Empress* in December 1783, he expected to sail in the next month, but the departure was delayed until Washington's birthday in February, 1784.

The record of the voyage in his journal is more than a listing of circumstances and events such as one would find in a ship's log or personal diary, but a sustained narrative in the manner, if not the style, of Samuel Johnson's *Journey to the Western Islands of Scotland*, 1775, or the more ambitious undertakings and more extensive scope of the accounts of the around-the-world voyages of George Anson and Captain Cook. Shaw pays careful attention to nuances of expression and items of general human interest and explains his personal reactions to the various scenes and situations he encounters. His journey is as much an autobiography as a travel account. This personal element probably explains why many passages from it appeared in the public prints during the author's lifetime. These I shall treat fully because of their bearing on the theme of China. Others I shall cite or paraphrase because of their revelations of the author's personality. Only three or four references to the captain of the *Empress*, John Green, appear in Shaw's narrative, a rather puzzling circumstances since it is hard to believe that in his original text, he would not have had a good deal to say about the interactions of captain and supercargo. The omission is probably the result of editing. On his second voyage to Canton, Green and Shaw had a falling out over money, and the two men became inveterate enemies. It would, therefore, appear that Shaw carefully weeded out of his narrative any passages in which Green played a major role.

While the *Empress* en route to China was anchored at the Cape Verde islands to take on supplies, Shaw paid a courtesy call on the second in command of this Portuguese colony. After describing the sallow complexion and careless attire of the official's wife, Shaw remarks that "her whole appearance was entirely different from that of the fair of our own country, and I believe she did not excite in any of us an idea that would militate with the tenth commandment, though she did not seem to be past five-and-twenty" (Quincy 1847: 138). Off the coast of Java, a number of the officers visited an uninhabited island, where they planted, presumably for symbolic or ceremonial purposes, a vegetable garden of Indian corn, oats, peas, beans, and potatoes, and afterwards drank champagne and Madeira wine (156). When the *Empress* reached its destination at Whampoa in August 1784 after a voyage of six months, Shaw recorded, "we saluted them with thirteen guns, which were returned by each nation. At eight o'clock we came to anchor, and again complimented the ships with thirteen guns. The French sent two boats to assist us in coming to anchor; the Danish sent an officer to compliment; the Dutch, a boat to assist; and the English to welcome our flag to this country" (164). The journal of another gentleman on board the *Empress* was quoted in the *Pennsylvania Packet* 18 May 1785.

On our arrival at the island of Macao, the 23d of August, [1784] the French consul for China . . . came on board to congratulate and welcome us to that part of the world; and kindly undertook the introduction of the Americans to the Portuguese governor of that place. The little time that we were there, was entirely taken up by the good offices of the consul, the gentlemen of his nation, and those of the Swedes and Imperialists, who still remained at Macao. . . . Three days later we finished our outward bound voyage. Previous to coming to anchor we saluted the shipping in the river, with thirteen guns; which were answered by the several commanders of the European nations.

All this saluting illustrates the historic importance of the advent of the *Empress*. As R. B. Forbes pointed out a generation later, "Our ships now go and come in numbers, and attract no attention; and if any vessel should fire a salute on leaving port, or on arrival in China, it would be looked upon as something extraordinary;—not an ounce of powder would be burnt in return, and the circumstance of her arrival would be forgotten in an hour, except by those who might be immediately concerned" (1844: 10). According to the gentleman's journal quoted in the *Pennsylvania Packet*, on 30 August 1784, the arrival date in Canton, and the two days following, the *Empress* was visited "by the Chinese merchants, and the chiefs and gentlemen of the several European establishments, and treated by them in all respects, as a free and independent nation; as such, during our stay, we were universally considered. The Chinese themselves were very indulgent . . . and happy in the contemplation of a new people, opening to view, a fresh source of commerce to their extensive empire." "The Chinese had never heard of us," wrote the purser of the *Empress*, John White Swift, "but we introduced ourselves as a new Nation, gave them our history, with a description of our Country, the importance and necessity of a trade here to the advantage to both, which they appear perfectly to understand and wish" (Swift 1885: 485).

While the *Empress* was in Chinese waters in November 1784, all the Westerners in the port were involved in a serious international confrontation called at the time "the war of Canton." A Chinese national was accidentally killed by a salute from the guns of an English vessel, the *Lady Hughes*, fired to honor its dinner guests. The port authorities in accordance with the Chinese custom of bloodshed in return for bloodshed, demanded that the gunner, a Philippino, be turned over to them, but the captain refused. Two days later the Chinese seized the English supercargo and clapped him in prison. All the Westerners in the port then banded together in protest and armed their launches. The Chinese replied by closing down all trade, augmenting their naval forces, and demanding to negotiate with all the nations except the British. At the negotiations in which Shaw took part, the Chinese demanded that the person responsible be handed over, but pledged that he would be judged fairly. The gunner was then surrendered, the supercargo released, and trading resumed.

On his return to America, Shaw extracted from his journal the account of this episode and incorporated it in a letter, 19 May 1785, to John Jay, Secretary of Foreign Affairs. This letter was almost immediately printed in a Philadelphia periodical, the *American Museum* (1: 194–95) as well as in the *Pennsylvania Packet*, 10 September 1785, giving the American public a sense of pride in the exploits of their countrymen as equals of the major nations of Europe. Even more important from the perspective of diplomatic history, a copy of Shaw's letter was forwarded to Thomas Jefferson, at the time American ambassador in Paris, to be delivered to the French minister of foreign affairs, Vergennes. In an accompanying letter, Jefferson conveyed the pleasure of Congress over the collaboration of the French and American vessels as a renewed proof of the friendship between the two nations (Cordier 1897–1898:11). This letter was reproduced many times in American periodicals throughout the period, even as late as 1828 (*Salem Gazette* 7 October; *National Gazette* 15 October). Shaw wrote his letter before the fate of the English sailor had been determined, but the outcome may be found in his journal. The hapless seaman was tried, found guilty and strangled. According to Shaw,

> Thus ended a very troublesome affair, which commenced in confusion, was carried on without order, and terminated disgracefully. Had that spirit of union among the Europeans taken place which the rights of humanity demanded, and could private interests have been for a moment sacrificed to the general good, the conclusion of the matter must have been honorable, and probably some additional privilege would have been obtained. But as it did terminate, we can only apply to it the observation of the Chinese themselves—"Truly, all Fanquois have much lose his face in this business."

Shaw's attitude toward the affair, reflecting the narrow interests of the foreign traders as a group, gives the impression that the Chinese were in the wrong and guilty of grave injustice to the English and ungraciousness to the Westerners as a whole. There were, however, two ways of looking at the situation. Shaw's phrases "spirit of union" and "some additional privilege" reveal a willingness to use force in order to gain concessions from Chinese weakness. In chapter 13, I shall show that another American supercargo, Robert Waln, Jr., thirty-five years later studied the episode objectively from the principle of international law and completely vindicated the Chinese.

A similar situation arose early in the nineteenth century in which a seaman under the American flag was the accused party. An Italian sailor named Francisco Terranova serving in 1821 on an American ship, the *Emily* from Baltimore, was charged with killing a Chinese woman in a small boat by throwing a jar at her from his own ship. The Americans claimed that the incident was entirely accidental, but the Canton officials, nevertheless, boarded the *Emily* and seized Terranova, who offered no resistance. At his trial no translator was present, no foreign witnesses were called, and he was summarily strangled. The Americans said to Houqua, the security merchant, "We are bound to submit to your laws while we are in your waters, be they ever so unjust. We will not resist them" (Dulles 1946: 15). The British were as much outraged by the apparent docility of the Americans as by the pertinacity of the Chinese. The Select Committee of the East India Committee declared that the American response should be held "in eternal execration by every moral, honorable and feeling mind." They had "barbarously abandoned a man serving under their flag to the sanguinary laws of this Empire without an endeavor to obtain common justice for him" (Dulles 1946: 15). The same American supercargo Robert Waln, Jr., whom I have cited on the *Lady Hughes* crisis, however, described the *Emily* affair as another example of unjustified Western bullying of the Chinese. His comments on this incident will also be treated in chapter 13.

It may be that the Chinese took into consideration in their deliberations over the fate of Terranova that the cargo of the *Emily* included opium, a commodity that had been forbidden by law. Even though the Chinese had outlawed the importation of opium, most Americans at the time apparently did not consider the drug as morally repugnant although about a dozen Philadelphia merchants refused to deal in it (Goldstein 1978: 50). A resident of Maryland, Hast (or Hastings) Handy, wrote in 1791 a dissertation on the benefits of the substance. Along with his opinion that "opium possesses stimulating powers in a healthy state of the body," Handy affirmed that it is "used by the Chinese as an agreeable cordial, and is taken by them previously to all daring and arduous exploits" (1791: 14–15). During a famine in China in 1770, he remarked, "opium was purchased at an exorbitant price, by the unhappy sufferers, to allay the craving of hunger. It not only promotes appetite, but, likewise, helps digestion" (24). A review of Handy's dissertation in the *Columbian Magazine* for July 1791 (7, 44–6) caustically observed, "Surely the Chinese, who had little to eat, did not require opium, either 'to promote appetite' or 'help digestion.'"

At the close of the *Lady Hughes* affair, the so-called Canton war, chops were issued for the shipping of all nations except the English, and Shaw was informed by his linguist that the hoppo had taken the *Empress* for an English vessel. To correct this impression, Shaw wrote to the French consul at Canton, Philippe Vieillard, asking him to make known through the French interpreter "that we are AMERICANS, a free, independent and sovereign nation, not connected with Great Britain, nor owing allegiance to her, or any power on earth" (Quincy 1847:193–4). Vieillard carried out the request and wrote a polite letter to Shaw informing him of his action. Henri Cordier, compiler of the great bibliography of Chinese-Western relations, included these letters in an article on Americans in Canton during the eighteenth century, affirming that the hoppo had been swayed by the maneuvers of the English, who sought to pass off the Americans as their compatriots (1897–1898: 4). A few days after the incident, however, Shaw learned that the real reason the *Empress* had at first been reported as English was "that the fiador, Pankekoa, knew, that had he told who we really were, he would have been obliged to accompany the information with a present" (Quincy 1847:195).

On his first interview with the hoppo, Shaw was not aware of the tradition of offering a gratuity or sing-song and was embarrassed not to have any appropriate article on board. The hoppo, after hearing his apologies based on his inexperience and provenance from a new country, generously overlooked the absence of the gadgets, but ordered him to make up for their absence on the next trip (177).

When the *Empress* docked at New York on her return voyage after an absence of scarcely more than a year, the *Pennsylvania Packet* reported (16 May 1785),

> We have the satisfaction of announcing the arrival of the ship Empress of China, captain Greene, from the EAST-INDIES, at this port, yesterday, after a voyage of 14 months and 24 days. . . . As the ship has returned with a full cargo, and of such articles as we generally import from Europe, a correspondent observes that it presages a future happy period of our being able to dispense with that burdensome and unnecessary traffick, which heretofore we have carried on with Europe—to the great prejudice of our rising empire, and future happy prospects of solid greatness.

In his letter of 19 May 1785 to John Jay, the secretary of foreign affairs, Shaw gave a glowing account of the way citizens of this "rising empire" had been received in China. "To every lover of his country," he wrote, "as well as to those more immediately concerned in commerce, it must be a pleasing reflection that a communication is thus happily opened between us and the eastern extremity of the globe" (Quincy 1847:341). Jay replied that the Congress felt "a peculiar satisfaction in the successful issue of this first effort of the citizens of America to establish a direct trade with China, which does so much honor to its undertakers and conductors." Although Shaw may not have been a great admirer of Chinese culture, he was, nevertheless, through his lobbying and newspaper publicity for many years the most effective propagandist in America for the China trade.

Through the influence of Jay, Shaw had been appointed in January, 1785, the first American consul to China, a position without salary or emoluments, but rich in respectability. The appointment was renewed in 1790 by President George Washington (Quincy 1847: 147). Shaw, nevertheless, did not return to Canton on the second voyage of the *Empress*, but accepted instead the position of first secretary in the war office of the United States under his former commander Henry Knox, who had become head of the department. By the end of 1785, however, he had already made plans for his second trip to China, not with the *Empress*, but with the *Hope* of New York. He had approached Robert Morris about returning on the *Empress*, but had been told that Captain Green had already engaged another supercargo. Undoubtedly this situation grew out of ill will between Green and Shaw that can be traced back to the disposal of the ginseng on the original voyage. The owners of the ship were also the proprietors of its cargo, but Green and the other officers were allowed to carry their own private supply. Shaw advised the interested parties that the entire cargo should be sold as a single lot, but Green, even though his own ginseng was of an inferior quality, raised difficulties. One of the owners had persuaded Shaw to sign a bill of lading indicating that the specie on board amounted to 20,000 pounds whereas it was in reality only 17,700, with both parties understanding that the deficient amount was to be made up from the profits. Unfortunately the person who had made this agreement died while the ship was at sea. Although Shaw's accounts satisfied Morris, Green kept alive the suspicion that everything had not been properly handled. In 1786, therefore, when Green and Shaw were both in Canton and passed each other in the confines of the factory square, Shaw refused to speak to Green, and Green spread the rumor that Morris had rejected Shaw for the second voyage because he could not be trusted financially and that Shaw's ineptitude had cost Green himself $5,000 in the sale of the ginseng. This story has been pieced together by Margaret C. S. Christman from Shaw's correspondence with Henry Knox (1984: 64–65). Shaw declared that he would have challenged Green to a duel, but refrained from doing so since the laws of Canton would have inexorably required that the survivor be strangled. Shaw's apparent failure to obtain the best price for the ginseng on the first voyage may have been in some measure responsible for his picturing the profits of 25 percent on the first voyage as more spectacular than they actually were.

On arrival at Whampoa on his second voyage, Shaw found four other American vessels at anchor, but a much less cordial welcome from the ships of other nations, undoubtedly because a spirit of rivalry had by then arisen. As he wrote to Henry Knox, "I think it is not difficult to account for the difference. We were then a single ship, come upon them by surprise, and as they had no instructions respecting us, they, like sensible people, made us welcome. We are now five vessels. This competition alarms them, and has created a jealousy which it is not easy for them to conceal,—and not withstanding every personal civility to us and some instances of real friendship from individuals, yet, nationally, I believe they all wish us to the d---l" (Quincy 1847: 341).

Shaw, in company with other members of the international colony, was sometimes entertained by one or another of the hong merchants, but was not favorably impressed by the cuisine.

> I had more than once an opportunity of tasting their *chow chow*, drest in the Chinese stile. At the first entertainment we had thirty-two different dishes on the table at the same time; some fine fricasee rats no doubt, as they are passionately fond of them; perhaps the hind quarters of an extraordinary tender cat, and, as a rarity, the saddle of the fattest dog in the neighborhood; for they do assuredly eat them, and esteem such fare very highly. I have often seen pedlars of live and *dead* stock too in the streets, with baskets of rats, cats, and dogs, of all sizes and ages.

In the *New York Magazine* (January 1796), Shaw added that he once asked the price of a cat, intending to use it on his ship for catching rats, but the peddler "asked more than one dollar for the animal because it was unusually large and fat." Shaw thought this too much, but admitted that for a mandarin or Chinese epicure it would be considered a bargain. William C. Hunter felt that tales of the eating of dogs were greatly exaggerated, but he, nevertheless, quoted a humorous poem on the subject. A foreign guest seeing a dish resembling duck on a festive table tried to ascertain its ingredients by using sign language.

> Still cautious grown, but, to be sure,
>   His brain he set to rack;
> At length he turned to one behind,
>   And, pointing, cried: Quack, Quack.
>
> The Chinese gravely shook his head,
>   Next made a reverend bow;
> And then expressed what dish it was
> By uttering, "Bow-wow-wow!" (1882: 42)

Spartan lodging, strange cuisine, and meager profits led Shaw eventually to maintain that overall the situation of Westerners in Canton was not enviable; "and, considering the length of time they reside in this country, the restrictions to which they must submit, the great distance they are from their connections, the want of society, and of almost every amusement, it must be allowed that they dearly earn their money" (Quincy 1847: 180).

Men from the West occasionally passed away while in Canton, and Shaw pictures the ceremonies and protocol that were followed.

> When any European dies at Canton, the chief of the nation to which he belonged sends and acquaints the different factories with the event. The flags are dropped, and remain at half-mast till the corpse is sent off to Whampoa, when they are hoisted up; the friends of the deceased, in the meanwhile, receiving visits of condolence from the other Europeans. The ships observe the same ceremony, and when the corpse appears in sight, the commodore of the nation to which it belongs begins to fire minute-guns, which are repeated by the other ships in port, and continued till the corpse is interred, on French island, when the flags are again hoisted as usual. Next day, the chief, with one or two gentlemen of his nation, returns the visits of the other Europeans, and thanks them for their attention on the occasion. (180)

In connection with his description of Chinese religious ceremonies that was extracted in the *American Museum* and in Hannah Adams's *View of Religions*, Shaw points out that the Chinese observe no special part of the week for worship, but consider every day a working day. They make feasts and perform ceremonies, however, on certain days connected with the astronomical calendar, particularly the winter solstice, observed by the Chinese as the beginning of the New Year. Two periodicals, the *Massachusetts Magazine* and the *American Magazine*, published in January 1790, Shaw's account of the Chinese custom of requiring all outstanding debts to be paid on New Year's day. On the last day of the year, the creditor goes to the debtor's house, takes a seat, while observing a total silence. "As soon as midnight is passed, he rises, congratulates the debtor on the new year, and retires. The debtor has then *lost his face*, and no person will ever trust him afterward" (Quincy 1947:197).

Shaw presumably accepted the Enlightenment doctrine of biological degeneration, that is, the view that plant and vegetable specimens from Europe decline in strength and beauty when taken to a climate for which they are not fitted. At least he includes in connection with the Dutch settlement at the Cape of Good Hope, the modern South Africa, a long quotation supporting the doctrine from Lord Kames's *Sketches of the History of Man* (207). He, nevertheless, seems to have adopted elements of the contrary notion of primitivism, judging from his favorable description of another area, Pegu.

> The inhabitants of the Car Nicobar seem to be the happiest people in the world, if a state of nature is allowed to be a state of happiness. Cocoa-nuts and yams form their principal food; in addition to which they have hogs, poultry, and fish in abundance. . . . The men have no clothing,—unless a small girdle round the waist, one end of which is drawn tight between the legs and tucked up behind, can be called such. The women wear a short petticoat, and a small piece of cotton cloth bound over their breasts. . . . The government, if they can be said to have any, is of the patriarchal kind. Though almost in the midst of the torrid zone, the air is constantly cooled by refreshing sea-breezes. . . . It is impossible for people to be more gentle than these islanders. They seem to possess much of the milk of human kindness; and though they frequently see Europeans, and have sometimes suffered by their rapacity, yet they still continue strangers to the passions attending a more civilized state. (280)

There is no passage about China in Shaw's journal equal to this one in its favorable attitude. This may be because of the complexity of Chinese culture and the narrow boundaries in which Shaw lived in Canton. He himself made this point: "In a country where the jealousy of the government confines all intercourse between its subjects and the foreigners who visit it to very narrow limits, in the suburbs of a single city, the opportunities of gaining information respecting its constitution, or the manners and customs generally of its inhabitants, can neither be frequent nor extensive" (167). One of Shaw's passages in particular portrays the Chinese as poorly organized in their attempts to relieve the poor, no matter how well intentioned their efforts may be. "At all times," he wrote, "even in the most plentiful seasons, the humanity of a foreigner is constantly shocked by the number of beggars, men, women, and children, that frequent the quay in front of the factories,—some of whom have the most loathsome appearance imaginable. The Chinese magistrates are certainly culpable in suffering such things. . . . It is not that rice is not to be had, but only that it is dear" (248). This condition and that of the great disturbances on the island of Formosa, the present Taiwan, Shaw presented as instances contradicting "the prevailing idea of the excellence of the Chinese government." In another passage he questioned whether there is a more oppressive government to be found in any civilized nation upon earth (183). Insofar as commercial relations and personal contacts are concerned, however, Shaw had good things to say.

> The knavery of the Chinese, particularly those of the trading class, has become proverbial. There is, however, no general rule without

exceptions; and though it is allowed that the small dealers, almost universally, are rogues, and require to be narrowly watched, it must at the same time be admitted that the merchants of the co-hoang are as respectable a set of men as are commonly found in other parts of the world. It was with them, principally, that we transacted our business. They are intelligent, exact accountants, punctual to their engagements, and, though not the worse for being looked after, value themselves much upon maintaining a fair character. The concurrent testimony of all the Europeans justifies this remark. (183)

Shaw's statements contradicting the received opinion of the excellence of the Chinese system of government is one of the earliest from an American placing in doubt the prevailing view of China as a land of prosperity and reason. From this time forward distrust became the predominant attitude.

The *New York Magazine* for January, 1796 (N.S.1,3–6) published extracts "from the journals of an American gentleman who lately visited the East-Indies." These extracts are definitely by Shaw since the last four paragraphs are almost verbatim with passages in Shaw's journal published by Josiah Quincy in 1847. There are some paragraphs, however, including those which I shall discuss below, that are not in Quincy. Presumably either Shaw's editor bowdlerized his manuscript or Shaw wrote an expanded spicy version for the New York periodical. Here he explains that the Chinese government allows "the Americans, English, French, Danes, Swedes, and indeed all nations trading to Canton, separate factories on the banks of the river 'Ta; and for the information of strangers, as well as for ornament perhaps, the supercargoes of the different nations have a flag constantly flying in front of their respective factories. There not being a regular trading company from America, the flag of the United States has not yet been displayed." Shaw observes that the widest street in China does not extend more than twenty feet across; the streets are not paved and are dirty in wet weather and when high tides from the canals occasionally enter. The merchants deliver salutations and invitations to purchase in a mixture of languages; they endeavor to get custom by saying they knew the prospect on a previous voyage even though this is his first visit.

The river here, and for several miles down, is so crowded with boats and shipping, that it is almost impossible for an European barge, or long-boat, with oars, to make way through. Besides this quantity, there are thousands drawn up in ranks, and anchored by stakes driven into the ground, forming streets or passages, between the stems and sterns of each rank, about twenty or thirty feet wide, and extending, in some directions near a mile. Between these ranks the boats pass and repass; and it is really surprising to see with what dexterity the Chinese manage their *sculls* in passing each other; they will push through an opening, perhaps not more than three or four inches wider than the boat, and as swift as an European barge could row in a clear river. In the smallest of these boats, or *sampans*, you will sometimes see half a dozen children, who, in summer, go quite naked, and crawling constantly about in the sun, they are so tanned and bedaubed with mud, especially in the fishing boats, that at a little distance, you could not soon determine them to be pigs or human creatures. Every child, however small, has a buoy of wood, or a gourd-shell, slung like a knapsack on its back, to keep it from sinking when it falls overboard, which is not unfrequently the case; and a father will make one scap at a fish, and a second at one of his children floating by; that is, if he is in a good humor, for ten to one if he is very poor, and the unfortunate child happens to be a female, but that he is too much engaged with a nice large fish to attend to *trifles*.

Before sailing on his second voyage, Shaw had contracted for the construction of a new ship for his future ventures in the China trade. This ship of 800 or 900 tons was to be the largest merchant vessel ever built in the United States, and the profits from Shaw's second voyage were to be used to help pay for it. Financing turned out to be amply sufficient, for the vessel was completed on schedule, named the *Massachusetts*, and launched on September, 1789 (Quincy 1847:117). In addition to being co-owner of the ship with his friend and partner on the previous voyages, Thomas Randall, Shaw himself served as captain.

The second officer, Amasa Delano, is notable for publishing in Boston in 1817 a book concerning his voyage on the *Massachusetts* and later voyages on other vessels, *A Narrative of Voyages and Travels in the Northern and Southern Hemispheres: Comprising Three Voyages Round the World; together with a Voyage of Survey and Discovery in the Pacific Ocean and Oriental Islands*. Apart from serving as a significant historical document, Delano's narrative provided Herman Melville with the inspiration for his short novel *Benito Cereno*. Delano reports with pride that an English captain had described the *Massachusetts* as being "as perfect a model as the state of the art would then permit" (1817: 25). Delano is equally complimentary in regard to Captain Shaw, describing him as "a man of fine talents and considerable cultivation; he placed so high a value upon the sentiments of honour that some of his friends thought it was carried to excess. . . . He was candid, just, and generous, faithful in his friendships, an agreeable companion, and manly in all his intercourse" (21).

Delano's narrative lacks Shaw's classical purity of style and literary embellishments, but its subject matter is perhaps even more intriguing. In addition to its revelations about China and other exotic places, it contains a chapter on Captain William Bligh and the *Bounty* mutineers based on eyewitness accounts correcting assertions about the incident published in English periodicals.

In his preface Delano apologizes for his "want of an early and academic education," but affirms that he had seized every opportunity for the improvement of his mind and the acquiring of knowledge of useful literature and science related to his profession. He had undertaken his long voyages, he says, in order to satisfy his own curiosity and particularly to discover how far he and others had been imposed upon by exaggerated accounts of the world. "The whole is written," he declares, "with a spirit of independence, without wounding the feelings, as I trust, of any good man." Later in his text he reveals that his purpose in writing is not only to give useful information about trade, navigation, and foreign ports, "but to encourage good moral sentiments, and impress the value of good examples" (44). Refuting the common view that sailors are dissolute and lacking in propriety, he emphasizes "the extensive influence which moral, domestic and religious feelings have over their hearts, their conversation, their actions and their hopes" (44).

Delano discloses that three separate crews had to be signed on the *Massachusetts* before one could be found to sail, all because of the prediction of an old woman fortuneteller in the home port of Quincy that the vessel would be lost with every man aboard. Nothing of the kind occurred, but the vessel had to be sold in Canton to the Danish East India Company in order to pay debts contracted by Randall on a previous voyage. Delano had the sad duty of hauling down the American colors. He then obtained employment as superintendent of repairs on another Danish ship. This circumstance led him to warn his readers that the port of Canton was in no way equipped for refitting Western ships and that no reliance could be placed on other ships in the port for obtaining "hard timber, iron, or copper, of the proper kind" or "mechanics qualified to do the work in a suitable manner" (111).

In regard to the size of the Chinese empire, Delano was willing to grant that it was the largest in the world even though this assumption could not be verified, but he had no doubt that it contained the greatest number of inhabitants (530). Aware of the many opinions and controversies of Western authors concerning the origin of the Chinese nation, he contented himself with the belief that his own knowledge, little as it was, amounted to as much of the truth or came as close to it as that possessed by prior writers. He had often conversed on the subject with several Chinese, "who were considered as men of information and credit," but the mixture of opinions and assertions they provided seemed "so contradictory and unreasonable" that he viewed "it all as fabulous, and set it down along with other wonderful accounts of the dark ages of the world" (531).

Contrary to Shaw, Delano considered China to be "one of the best regulated governments in the world." He affirmed that "the laws are just, and are maintained with such strict impartiality, that the guilty seldom escape punishment, or the injured fail to obtain prompt justice" (531). In regard to capital punishment, he believed no people on earth to be more scrupulous. "Under certain circumstances, if a man is accused of a crime by which his life is forfeited, he has the advantage of fifteen tribunals before he can be sentenced to death." Delano deplored, however, the law that if one person kills another, "his life should be taken as the only atonement," no matter whether the killing occurred "with premeditated malice, or by accident, or through the influence of passion" (531). This is, of course, the law that provoked the "Canton war" in 1785 and led to the strangling of Terranova in 1821. Delano added that flogging as a punishment in China is common and very severe, but that imprisonment is considered an impolitic measure; "for, say they, men are only made more wicked by confinement, and those that are free, have to work to maintain those that are in prison; and if people cannot be made to do right by flogging, let them be banished to the cold northern regions of China for life." Delano had been given to understand that the emperor rewards merit, sometimes very liberally, but he admitted that it is difficult for the ruler to ascertain when reward is due because of the jealousy existing among the officers, who do not like to see other men receive favorable notice (532).

Marriages, Delano says, are celebrated with great solemnity.

> It is the custom of the country for every man to marry one woman who is his equal in rank, and one that his parents think suitable for him. "A man can have only one lawful wife, and her rank and age must be nearly equal to his own; but he may receive into his house, on certain conditions, several concubines or wives of the second rank, who are wholly subject to the lawful spouse. Their children are considered as hers, they address her as mother, and give that title to her only." I have known some of the Chinese to have four or five wives, but it is uncommon for them to have more than one. The marriage is first contracted between the parents, when the likeness of the woman is shewn to the young man, and sometimes that of the man is sent to the woman; but the women do not have so much attention paid in this respect as the men, for there is seldom much difficulty in gaining the consent of the woman, if her parents approve of it. Neither the man or the woman ever see each other till after the marriage is consummated, and the wife is never permitted after marriage to see any man except her husband. (532)

On Delano's final voyage to China in 1806, the son of his hong merchant Conseequa was married at the age of twenty to a young woman of seventeen or eighteen, and both the son and father gave him details of the courtship. Conseequa told him that the father of the bride was a particular friend of his and that they had arranged the marriage between them. The bridegroom told him that he never saw the bride until the contract had been signed by both parties although he had previously seen her likeness and found her very attractive (533). Delano adds that it is not common for two wives to live in the same house, for they find it hard to get along together, and also that a man cannot have more than one wife unless he is able to prove that he can support two.

Delano mentions another law concerning the female sex, one that no other authors have treated, to my knowledge—the absolute forbidding of any foreign women to enter the country on any account whatsoever (540). This ordinance is related to the probibition of foreign women in the Canton factories, but is far more extensive in its application. According to Delano, death would be the penalty for any violation. He relates a story concerning the enforcement of the law, which he says he had received from good authority. An English captain had brought his wife with him to Canton disguised in masculine attire. One evening, having invited several supercargoes to dine on board his ship, he introduced the lady as an English gentleman who had come as a passenger from Macao. Suddenly a commotion occurred among the Chinese attendants when the wife affected by the heat in the cabin loosened her collar and leaned her head back while drinking. One of the attendants, after asking the captain to step outside, informed him that the gentleman was a woman and that "they were certain of the fact, for she had no protuberance in her throat, which men always have and women do not; and that there must be something done with her immediately, or the mandarins, who had already been informed of it, would cut off her head." The captain in haste passed his wife out of one of the portholes into a smaller boat and started out for Macao, which was beyond the Chinese jurisdiction. The mandarins in two boats that had been guarding the ship gave pursuit, but the Englishmen escaped because of their superior rowing ability even though they were followed forty or fifty miles down the river (540–41). Delano surmises that the cause of the interdiction of foreign women was the natural jealousy of the Chinese, leading them to believe that if foreign women were introduced into the country they would propagate and eventually become so numerous that they would be extremely troublesome or even subvert the government.

Delano refutes the accusation that is perennially leveled against the Chinese people that they practice infanticide. Some people, he says, may believe writers who assert that Chinese women are in the habit of drowning a third of their female offspring in the rivers. But he is fully convinced that the assertion is incorrect as a result of talking to respectable Chinese merchants on the subject, "who appeared to revolt at the idea, and denied it altogether." He suggests that the imputation arose from the lower class of women in the suburbs of Canton having children by European or American fathers and then exposing them in this manner to conceal their disgrace. He says that he had twice seen infants floating down the river and on viewing them was convinced that this is how they came to be there. This is a very unusual passage, for every other Western commentator that I have read implies that there was absolutely no contact between Chinese women of any class and the foreign devils. The universal prevalence of prostitution in all ages, however, suggests that Delano may have indeed been telling it how it was (533).

Other accounts confirm the accusation of infanticide. The Swedish naturalist Peter Osbeck reports that "Parents, who cannot support their female children, are allowed to cast them into the river; however, they fasten a gourd to the child, that it may float in the water" (1771:1:272). The reviewer in the *Pennsylvania Magazine* gratuitously adds the comment as though part of Osbeck's text, "and there are often compassionate people of fortune who are moved by the cries of the children to save them from death" (August 1775). A similar report is given by Olaf Toreen: "A Chinese would like better to take money for his children, [sell them] than to be oblig'd to throw them into the water for nothing. I have no reason to doubt of the fact I hint at; since I have seen several children floating in the water: but I cannot pretend to say whether they are destroyed with or without the permission of the magistrate" (Osbeck 1771:2:236–37).

Like most other foreign observers of Chinese customs, Delano has his say on the binding of women's feet. The origin of this custom, he was told by the Chinese, grew out of "its being inflicted on the women as a punishment, on account of an attempt made by them in some early period of the nation to interfere with the affairs of government. It afterwards became a mark of honour among them, and remains so to the present day" (541). I know of no other Western writer who offers this explanation. Delano adds that only Chinese of pure blood are allowed the honor of having their feet bound.

Delano's remarks on Chinese funeral ceremonies offer a number of points of comparison with the descriptions of burial ceremonies in chapter 2.

> Nothing is held more sacred with a Chinese than the death, the funeral obsequies, and the place of deposit of the remains of a parent. The mandarins that hold high offices expend large sums of money on such occasions. They make splendid feasts, and clothe a great number

of people in white, which is the colour of their mourning; they form a column of people, of half a mile in length, to attend the corpse to the grave, most of whom receive in a direct or indirect manner some present or consideration. Their tombs or places of confinement are always chosen in places that are not public, and on land that is not fit for cultivation; it being a maxim with them not to occupy for any other purpose than agriculture, land that is capable of producing any kind of verdure. The tomb is shaped according to the fancy of the owner, though they are generally round; but sometimes square, sometimes oblong, and sometimes oval. . . . They are built with a cement of stone and lime mortar, and the outside covered with a coat of handsome white chenam, which gives them a very singular appearance, and attracts the attention of travellers. One tomb serves for a family for many ages, and they are scattered singly over all the barren grounds. There are several of them on Dean's Island, which forms one side of the river below Whampoa. Some of the mandarins and wealthy people have soil placed round their tombs, and trees planted, which gives them a very pleasant appearance. (1817: 534–35)

Delano treats at some length the embassy of Lord Macartney to the Imperial Court in 1793 and that of the Dutch in the following year. His remarks on that subject I shall reserve for chapter 10. At present I shall merely indicate that he heard from both his English and his Dutch acquaintances that the northern Chinese were more athletic than those around Canton and that the northern women had more freedom. "All of their accounts were much more favourable of the northern than of the southern Chinese" (538). In regard to European efforts to force or persuade the Chinese to expand their trading activities, he offered as his own opinion that the Chinese would already have closed their ports against all Europeans and all Americans were it not for fear of their disaffected subjects. These consisted of "the Ladroons (pirates) who have thousands of vessels of different descriptions that have infested their coasts of late years at particular seasons; and the merchants and others near Canton, who have been refractory for a considerable length of time; which is probably owing to their intercourse with foreigners, and catching some of their spirit of liberty and equality" (539). Few other writers at the time make any such suggestions concerning a liberalizing influence of the West, and another American, R. B. Forbes, writing twenty years later, asserts that the hong merchants, far from showing signs of independence, were very much under the control of the imperial government (1844:14).

Delano concludes his chapter on China by remarking that the country is one of the most fertile and beautiful in the world. "It affords the fruits and vegetables of almost all climates; abounds with most of the manufactures that are useful to mankind; is favoured with the greatest conveniences by water transportation of any country; and finally, is the first for greatness, riches, and grandeur of any country ever known" (1817: 542).

Delano writes with more assurance and positive conviction than any other contemporary American observer of China and seems to have a greater store of knowledge about conditions beyond the enclave of Canton. Yet he does not seem to have spent a greater amount of time in China than most of the other Europeans or Americans who wrote about their experiences. And he gives no explanation of where he acquired his information about the Chinese hinterlands beyond his casual references to English officers and Dutch friends. In the absence of further details concerning his personal activities in the Middle Kingdom, his account should probably not be considered as completely reliable. Since his narrative was printed in book form, however, it was like Shaw's journal an instrument in the forming of American impressions of the Middle Kingdom.

An even more widely known eyewitness account of East Asia was published in Boston in 1823 under the title of *History of a Voyage to the China Sea*, and in the following year in London as *A Voyage to Cochin China*. This work has the distinction, moreover, of being reissued in London in the twentieth century under the latter title and also of being translated into French (White 1972: vi). Since the author, John White, describes only the Phillipines and Vietnam (known in the eighteenth century as Cochin China), and not the China mainland, his narrative is perhaps not entirely relevant to the present book, and for this reason I shall not give it more than a cursory treatment, despite its bibliographical importance and the opinion of its modern editor that it "ranks as a minor treasure of early nineteenth century travel literature on South-East Asia" (v).

Like Delano, White apologizes for his literary style, requesting his readers in his advertisement "to bear in mind, that this is not a book written by a professed scholar, but the production of an unlettered seaman." He is much too modest, however, for his style is refined, witty, and adorned with even more classical allusions than are to be found in the writings of Samuel Shaw. His voyage was made in the brig *Franklin*, the aim of which was to establish commercial relations with Vietnam. In his advertisement, White remarks that this nation was once considered as an El Dorado and that a previous expedition from Salem had been undertaken in 1803 under the command of Captain Josiah Briggs. The *Franklin* sailed in 1819 under White's command. He was at that time a lieutenant in the United States Navy, and the narrative is based on his journal. He is not at all complimentary to the people of Cochin China, whom he considers greatly inferior to the Chinese, primarily because of their poor government. In his opinion the Cochin Chinese "were in many respects but little removed from a state of deplorable barbarism" (36).

White was very proud of his identity as an American. After affirming that neither the French nor the Spanish had succeeded in realizing "a pure republican form of government," he made this statment.

> America presents a practical example of a free government, framed and put into operation by the inclusive wisdom and power of the nation, whose prosperity, happiness, and glory, it is so eminently calculated to promote. She, like an insulated, adamantine mountain, whose base is lashed by the impotent waves of the ocean, stands firm, fixed, and erect; aloof from the conflicts of European nations; and, with scarcely an effort, repelling the puny attacks of her enemies; a living monument of the peculiar favour of the beneficent Creator, who called her into political existence, and who, we trust, deigns to direct her councils. (139)

Among the alleged vices of the Cochin Chinese, White found their rapacity most irritating. He accused them of begging or stealing every object on board his ship they cast their eyes upon (52). He was no more flattering in his description of the inhabitants and of the physical features of Saigon.

> Toiling under a scorching sun, through a street strewed with every species of filth; beset by thousands of yelping, mangy curs; stunned alike by them and the vociferations of an immense concourse of the wondering natives, whose rude curiosity in touching and handling every part of our dress, and feeling our hands and faces, we were frequently obliged to chastise with our canes; the amusement of repelling a few of the dogs, with the swords in our canes, (which, however, made no impression of fear on the survivors,) and the various *undefinable* odours, which were in constant circulation, were among the amenities which were presented us on this our first excursion into the city. [219]
>
> During our walk we were constantly annoyed by hundreds of yelping curs, whose din was intolerable. In the bazars we were beset with beggars; many of them the most miserable, disgusting objects, some of whom were disfigured with the leprosy, and others with their toes, feet, and even legs, eaten off by vermin or disease. Nor were these the only subjects of annoyance; for, notwithstanding the efforts and expostulations of the officers who accompanied us, and our frequently chastising them with our canes, the populace would crowd round us, almost suffocate us with the fetor of their bodies, and feel every article of our dress with their dirty paws, chattering like so many baboons. (231)

Later White and his crew were advised to adopt native attire as a safety measure to keep elephants from being disturbed by their appearance

(227). This is the only example I have encountered of Americans being advised to change their manner of dress.

White included among items of miscellaneous information that all men in the land are soldiers and that commerce is carried on by women (261), that their religion is polytheistic based upon the Chinese "on which are engrafted many of the rites and superstitions of Buddhism" (277), and that their diet is "foul," including rats, mice, worms, frogs, and other vermin and reptiles (298). White adds that the Chinese have an excuse for "these dirty practices" since they have difficulty in providing wholesome food for their enormous population, but "the Onamese appear to have a predilection for filth."

White's general impression of the people as a whole may be discovered in his description of one of his hostesses, "a female of ample proportions and a smiling countenance" (207).

> She was about sixteen, and a ward of our host. Her father, who was absent, was a native of Macao, and her mother (who was dead) a Cochin Chinese. She was the most interesting object we had seen among these people; but our feelings of complacency were not a little deranged when, approaching us with her offering of tea and betel, "we nosed her atmosphere." She was dressed in black-silk trowsers, and a tunic, or robe, which descended nearly to her ancles. Her hair, glossy with cocoa-nut oil, was tastefully gathered into a knot on the top of her head, which was encircled with a turban of black crape. Her face and neck, guiltless of meretricious ornaments, were, however, decorated with variegated streaks, the accidental accumulation of extraneous matter which had come in contact with them. Her feet were naked and indurated, and the forefinger of each hand was armed with an opaque claw two inches in length.

White admits that "the young females of Cochin China are frequently handsome, and some even beautiful, before their teeth, tongues, gums, and lips, become stained with their detestable masticatory," a practice that is taken up at an early age (269). "They are by nature finely formed; their symmetrical proportions are, however, distorted and disguised by their dirty habits,—and a woman at thirty is an object of disgust, and at forty, absolutely hideous" (269).

White was disappointed both in the practical results of his voyage and in the prospects for the future. He was unable to procure a full cargo of sugar to compensate for the expense and pains of the voyage, and he was convinced that the Chochin Chinese were so dishonest and rapacious that they had already been abandoned as trading partners by the Japanese and the Portuguese of Macao.

Their total want of faith, constant eagerness to deceive and over-reach us, and their pertinacity in trying to gain by shuffling and manoeuvring, what might have been better and easier gained by openness and fair dealing; the tedious forms and ceremonies in transacting all kinds of business, carried into the most trifling transac-tions; the uncertainty of the eventual ratification of any bargain, (the least hope of wearing the patience of the purchaser out, and induc-ing him to offer a little more, being sufficient to annul any verbal stipulation,) and there being no appeal, unless there is a written contract, which is never made, till every art has been used, and every engine of extortion put in motion and exhausted to gain more; all these vexations, combined with the rapacious, faithless, despotic, and anti-commercial character of the government, will, as long as these causes exist, render Cochin China the least desirable country for mercantile adventurers. . . . The philanthropist, the man of en-terprise, and the civilised world generally, can see in the present miserable state of this naturally fine country no other than a source of deep regret and commiseration. (246–47)

Although White was disappointed in the commercial aspect of his voyage, he was gratified by the amount of new information he had col-lected during his months in Cochin China. He had originally intended his narrative to be presented as a "Memoir to be deposited in the archives of the 'East India Marine Society of Salem,' " but his friends persuaded him to allow it to be published. Throughout his travels he gathered a large number of souvenirs also destined for the marine society, of which he had been a member since 1806. The founding of this society and museum in 1799 is in itself further evidence of the vogue of China during the early years of the American republic.

Very few other captains, sailors, or merchants who visited China during this period wrote accounts of their travel for publication, but many kept journals for their own delectation. One of these that has survived concerns a voyage in 1802–1803 by a convivial entrepreneur from Ver-mont, Amos Porter, who exported a cargo of ginseng from his native state to be exchanged for Chinese goods (Porter 1984). Porter writes a vivid, racy style, not censored or tidied up for potential publication. Although he incorporates a fair share of literary allusions, his spelling and punctuation are somewhat erratic. He seems to have thoroughly enjoyed every mo-ment of his trip except seasickness, "that Tormenting malady" from which he suffered excessively.

On his first trading day, in September 1802, during which he showed several merchants samples of his ginseng, he witnessed a funeral proces-sion surpassing in grandeur any previous spectacle of the kind he had ever witnessed. Spelling and punctuation in the following passage are Porter's.

First passed 12 boys dressed in the most suburb uniform; Theatrical Manner, with spears of wood richly gilt, and dressed with ribands. Next followed a Pallanqueen, or kind of sedan Chair supported by two Men shoulders like a bier, richly Gilt and dressed in festoons around the Corecovering with the sides open, the bottom coverd with a Hog roasted whole and sweat meats etc. Next follows 6 boys with Musick, the worst in the world to a foriegn ear. Then another Pallanqueen richly furnished with daintyes the deceased was in favour of, when in life. Then 4 Men with Musick and so on in a long procession, in the center of which is supported the Deceased by 4 Men without paul bearers, or releaf. Next the Moarners in Sedan Chair, out of sight. Then 6 Men who immediately follow by hire, to Moarn, and Cry, and make the most lamentable grief for the deceased. The tail and head of the procession are somewhat similar. (Porter 1984:23)

Porter, as a hearty consumer of alcoholic beverages, combines a description of Chinese drinking habits with their manner of celebrating a national holiday on 15 August.

Their Chief amusement is in Chin-Chining Josh and burning large pieces of paper on the water, and in the air; In the evening an addition of Crackers & Skye rockets which they execute the best of any people in the world. They have innumerable quantityes of boats lying on the River Tigris and often so close together before Canton that it is difficult to pass, which are frequently illuminated in Honour of Josh and the richest daintyes offered him in hopes of obtaining favour. It is an uncommon thing to see a Chinaman intoxicated as they do not make use of much Foreign Spirits or even wine. Their Spiritous liquor is Samshou. They have it of two or three qualityes the best is very bad & an unpleasant taste. By the best calculations made here by the Security Merchant (who are the first citizens) there are 8,000 boats on the river (which are plihed for pleasure) which produce 24,000 dollars every night—Various feats are performed through the streets this day which surpass every thing in any other part of the world. (24)

Later Porter gives a detailed description of river boat activities.

Few women are seen in these crowds, except those of Charity. But the vast numbers in the San pan boats consigned to perpetual slavery, in conducting them on the waters (which they rarely leave) draws a sigh of compassion for their sufferings, at the same time arrises a just spirit of indignation to see a lazy lounging husband stretched on a matt enjoying the earnings of his two wives. Others draw out a miserable existence in boats of about 4 feet in width & 12 or 15 feet in length, covered at pleasure in the center with rattan wove together, and Mats of Grass and leaves of Bamboo. (these women have husbands to provide for) and suffer all the hardships of sickness that is alloted them by Providence. (25)

Porter has more to say about women and pleasure boats in a subsequent passage.

The Females of and about Canton . . . are Tawny or sooty com-plection small eyes look like a Monkey peeping through a key hole, small head, round faces rosy lips & black Hair. They have no need of Milliners, the only covering to their heads is their hair combed up fore and aft and twisted round two or three brass pins on top of their heads with a plate of brass for ornament. The unmarried are not allowed this privilege. their stature small and meanly dressed wareing only a course frock with large sleeves and a pair of trousers or drawers reach-ing down to the calf of the leg, and go bare footed; Speaking generally of this **sex** they want that estimable treasure (after 12 years old): (This being considered here the age of puberty) Virtue and beauty, and are equally destitute of understanding. A mans heart will not fly from its warm recess at the sight of one of these, & hover in the air like the shadow of Cupid. But falls back with a loathsome disgust, not withstanding 20,000$ every night we calculated to be expended with this order of beings, which reside on the waters of the River Tigris or Ta. (29)

Among the smattering of Chinese words Porter picked up, he reports the ones for copulation; to sleep with one's sister is "Foo Nah Achee" (36). He reveals his normal lubricity in comparing Chinese women with those of his native land (29), and in discussing Chinese cuisine he stresses the aphrodi-siac quality of birds' nest soup (28). He does not treat ginseng as an aphrodisiac, as he sets down the Chinese expression for it, Yum sum, along with a glossary of other items of Chinese food and drink. Porter is struck with the large number of foreigners in Canton and remarks that it is difficult to determine to which nation the various individuals belong. "Their dress is as widely different from American as the language in which they speak. The Chinese, the Hindoos & Lassars is such that they squat down like a young puppy to P. rest themselves, and wear large Turbans on their heads" (34).

Like nearly every other occidental visitor, Porter attempts to inter-pret Chinese religious beliefs and practices.

The Sabath is not known here by the Chinese. Mr Schynchew, a Man of the first information and who speaks good English told me the Chinese had no book containing an account of God, Christ, or Heaven. That their records were very ancient, and regular for 8 or 10 thousand years: One other Chinese of information in speaking of the flood says, if there was a great rain of 40 days & nights which drowned the world, it was not the world where the Chinese live but your own world. The Chinese have many Gods which they pay daly homage too there Gods being of wood and stuck up on some buildings side, in a narrow dirty street do not always hear the first crye of the petitioner, although bribed to their favour by Meat offerings. They have a superstitious belief that their Juncks, or Vessels of burden cannot serve them without eyes. There appears something rational in the midst of their idolatry every night on board their Juncks, SanPan boats and all other water Crafts they have a piece of paper burnt at the prow of the Craft and two lobchokes on fire at the two extreem parts which burn several hours. (24)

Porter's sprightly style may make his journal a delight to read, but since it was not printed until almost two centuries after its composition it obviously cannot be cited as contributing to the image of China in contemporary America. It is, nevertheless, a reliable indicator of the attitude toward the Middle Kingdom of an intelligent individual whose observations and opinions were based on actual experience. The topics he writes about are by and large the same ones that appear in the books of other travelers and in the popular press and because of their verisimilitude they serve as excellent points of comparison.

CHAPTER

9

The Emperor and the Plough

While Amasa Delano expatiated on the fertility of the Chinese soil and its fantastic outpouring of foodstuffs for the nourishment of its people, the *Encyclopedia Britannica* in its sixth edition in 1822 charged that Chinese agriculture was inefficient and inadequate. Although admitting that the land was fertile, the article "China" concluded that there were more famines in the Middle Kingdom than in any European nation. This condition was said to be caused by the indolence of the Tartar farmers in the north, the inability of neighboring countries to supply the deficiencies in bad years, and the great consumption of grain in the producing of wine and spiritous liquors. Most Americans who knew anything about China, however, believed that its agricultural production was immense and fully adequate for the needs of its people and that its agricultural prosperity derived from the political structure of the realm. The enormous population of the land and the Confucian teaching that the emperor is the father of his people were considered to be joint sources of the wealth and power of the nation, and the ceremony of spring planting during which the emperor guided the plough was widely accepted as a symbol of Chinese prosperity and political stability. The *Time Piece* of New York, for example, marveled at the amazing circumstance that a population of 333 million was "governed by one man; and not a murmur . . . heard in all the immense body against his authority" (2 [29 November 1797], No. 33).

In France during the first half of the century, Montesquieu and

Voltaire differed over whether this authority was based on force or on prestige. Montesquieu affirmed in *De l'esprit des lois* that the Chinese emperor was an absolute despot, but Voltaire disagreed. Among many arguments, Montesquieu maintained that since the laws of the nation required that anyone who lacked respect for the emperor would be punished by death, the broad power inherent in these laws gave the ruler a pretext to take the life of any one of his subjects or even exterminate whole families (Book 12, Chapter 7). Voltaire in the initial chapter of his *Essai sur les moeurs* cited in refutation the Chinese custom dating from the second century B.C. of allowing any person to submit in writing on a table in the palace any complaints against the government. Voltaire also cited the existence of tribunals supervising the laws and their execution. Although the emperor could promulgate the laws, he was required to consult the tribunals beforehand. In effect, as far as Voltaire was concerned, "it is impossible for the emperor to exercise an arbitrary power" (Chap 195). The notion of the emperor plowing the fields every year, moreover, familiar as it was through the description of the ceremony in Du Halde and others, was inconsistent with the concept of a tyrannical ruler. Even before Du Halde, Etienne de Silhouette in his *Idée générale du gouvernement et de la morale des Chinois*, 1729, had portrayed the emperor plowing a number of furrows in order to stimulate the farmers of the land to maximum labor (Maverick 1946: 31). And a commentator on Confucius in the *Journal des Sçavans* in 1688 affirmed that "the authority of the sovereign was not exercised by force, but by persuasion, by love, and by the knowledge that his subjects kept their eyes upon his person, and emulated his conduct" (Maverick 1946: 17). This emphasis by European commentators on the patriarchal nature of the relation between the emperor and his subjects is known as "gentling" him in contrast to later constitutional arguments maintaining that the monarch's powers were circumscribed by legal limits.

In the European Enlightenment, the locus classicus for the treatment of the political power of the emperor is a treatise, *Le despotisme de la Chine*, by François Quesnay, the leading figure of the group of French economists now classified as the Physiocrats. Although the word *despotism* in the title suggests that China is governed by an absolute tyrant, Quesnay's notion of despotism refers to the controlling force of laws—those of nature and those of the state. The ruler is as much bound by these laws as are his subjects, and both enjoy rights and privileges as well as duties. It is not the ruler, therefore, who is the despot, but the natural order of things. Franklin encountered Quesnay face to face in Paris, but he had very little understanding of the French statesman's manner of expressing himself (Aldridge 1957: 24). Despite the fact that it has become almost a commonplace in American history that the Physiocrats exercised a substantial influence on the founding fathers, I have encountered no evidence to show that Quesnay personally or his *Le despotisme de la Chine* had any effect upon American thought during the eighteenth century. This is not surprising since Quesnay's work came out serially in a comparatively obscure periodical, *Ephémérides du citoyen* in 1767 and was not published as a unit until late in the nineteenth century, when it appeared in Quesnay's *Oeuvres complètes*. Lewis A. Maverick has pointed out that most of Quesnay's material on China was copied almost verbatim from the *Mélanges intéressans et curieux . . . de l'Asie, de l'Afrique, de l'Amérique, et des terres polaires,"* 1763–65, of Jacques Philibert Rousselot de Surgy, a work that never penetrated into America.

Historical scholarship has affirmed that both Franklin and Jefferson did indeed adopt the principles of the Physiocrats, but this is true only in a limited sense. Both men agreed with Quesnay that farming represents the basis of civilized nations, that agriculture and good government are mutually dependent, and that national prosperity derives from the most successful means of cultivating the earth and the preservation of society from thieves and evildoers (Maverick 1946: 281). No evidence exists, however, that either Franklin or Jefferson accepted the opinion of Quesnay that his principles are based upon physical laws constituting part of the order of nature established by the supreme being (Maverick 1946: 280; Quesnay 1888: 642). In the sense that the term Physiocrat derives from "physical" laws, neither Franklin nor Jefferson belongs to that school of economics. It is doubtful that either would have answered affirmatively, moreover, Quesnay's question, "La durée, l'étendue et la prospérité permanente ne sont-elles pas assurées dans l'empire de la Chine par l'observation des lois naturelles?" As translated by Maverick: "Are not the continuance, the extent, and the permanent prosperity of the Empire of China assured by observance of the natural laws" (Quesnay 1888: 660; Maverick 1946: 303)?

Another of Quesnay's basic doctrines that he traces to China is that taxation should not be arbitrary, but should consist entirely of a portion of the annual production of the soil (Maverick 1946: 290). This doctrine was repeated in America, not by Franklin, and not by Jefferson, but by the Reverend Ezra Stiles, president of Yale College, in an election sermon, 8 May 1783, from which extracts were printed in the *American Museum*, in 1789 (5, 477–78) under the title "Thoughts on raising a revenue in produce." To justify his thesis that the equivalent of two or three millions in a nation's medium of exchange can be raised as revenue more easily in the form of agricultural products than in that of one million in money, Stiles appealed to the experience of China:

In one country it has been tried with success for ages, I mean in China, the wisest empire the sun hath ever shined upon. And here if I recollect aright, not a tenth of the imperial revenues have been collected in money. In rice, wheat, millet only, are collected forty millions of sacks, of one hundred and twenty pounds each: equal to eighty million bushels: in raw and wrought silk, one million pounds. The rest is taken in salt, wines, cotton, and other fruits of labour and industry, at a certain ratio per cent. and deposited in stores over all the empire. The perishable commodities are immediately sold, and the mandarins and army are paid by bills on their magazines. In no part of the world are the inhabitants less oppressed than there.

In this portrayal of China as "the wisest empire the sun hath ever shined upon," Stiles parted company from his colleague at Yale, Timothy Dwight, as he did on many other subjects.

Stiles is an important figure in American history and literature as a clergyman, patriot, and college president, but he was also an enthusiastic Sinophile and agricultural experimenter. Indeed there was probably no eighteenth century American who had made a more extensive study of China, for his manuscripts now in the Yale University Library and available on microfilm contain several hundred pages devoted to the Middle Kingdom. In miscellaneous reflections on "The Origins of Religion, Learning, and Empire," he calls China "the greatest Nation of Antiquity" and "the greatest, the richest & most populous Kingdom now known in the World" (Yale Papers: Item 130). After two pages of extracts from Voltaire on Confucius and the reception of his doctrine by the Chinese people, Stiles remarks, "This shewes that the true pure philosophic Religion may as well be introduced among the vulgar, as well as false but pompous & superstitious Mythologies." He added, apparently at a later time, "Mistake—the Doctrines of Confucius received only by the Mandarins and other Great—that of Fo is the religion of the Vulgar in China" (Yale Papers: Item 318).

Stiles's awareness of Chinese agriculture is revealed in a manuscript of 150 pages titled "Observations on Silk Worms and the Culture of Silk. A.D. 1763. Being the Journal of an Experiment made in Newport Rhode Island in the Summer of 1763 in raising about Three Thousand Silk Worms. Interspersed with Remarks selected from several Authors on the Silk Culture, particularly after the Italian or Chinese Manner." Here Stiles gives the Chinese credit for originally inventing "the Raising & Manufacture of Silk in which they bro't to perfection perhaps 2000 Years before the Art reached even India & Persia." This manuscript also includes two hand-drawn maps of China with the names of all the provinces as well as a list of Chinese emperors and a detailed history of the land by regions since the fifteenth century. A separate section treats miscellaneous topics such as revenues, famines, marital customs, and honors to the dead. I do not wish to labor the point, but Stiles is an example of an American with an extensive knowledge of China that is not apparent in his external career. If his manuscripts had not survived, we would not at this time even be aware of his intense curiosity concerning Chinese history and culture. There may have been others like him.

Whether or not later American periodicals derived their views of China from the French economists, they portrayed the same favorable image of the Chinese emperor as that conveyed by the Physiocrats. An "Anecdote of Ching Tang: One of the Emperors of China" in the *Massachusetts Magazine* for January 1793 (5, 20–21) presented the emperor as a veritable Christ figure. About 747 B.C., during a period of drought and famine, according to this narrative, the emperor was told by his astrologers that the wrath of heaven could be appeased only by human blood. Imputing the natural disaster to his own faults, the emperor decided to offer himself as the sacrificial victim. After three days of fasting, he laid aside his royal robes and ordered his grey hair to be cut, his beard shaved, and his nails pared, devoting to the welfare of his country that which "in China is considered as the greatest marks of honour." Barefooted and in the posture of a criminal, his body sprinkled with ashes, he "lifted up his hands to heaven, intreated the Supreme Being to spare his subjects, and let the whole weight of his just wrath fall on his devoted head." He had scarcely finished praying when heavy rain began to fall, and plenty was restored to the empire. "Perhaps no prince in the world ever gave a greater instance of parental love for his country; nor performed a greater act of humiliation and devotion to avert the wrath of the offended majesty of heaven." A greatly abbreviated version of this episode appears in Du Halde (1736:1:299). Anecdotes such as this were perhaps more forceful than rational arguments in projecting the image of the emperor as a father figure.

The *South Carolina Weekly Museum* published in May, 1797 (1, 567), a brief item, "Of an Empress of China," joining the benevolence of the royal family with the dedication to useful labor. According to this report, the emperors take wives from among their own subjects and pay no attention to birth or fortune if the candidates are comely and handsome, and as a consequence the monarchs often marry the daughters of artisans. "One of them was a mason's daughter, and always kept a trowel by her when she was dignified with the character of empress; and if at any time the young prince her son carried it too proudly, she humbled him with the sight of the implement with which his grandfather subsisted himself and family; which would bring him to reason."

A narrative of similar import appeared in Philip Freneau's *Time Piece*, 17 March 1797 (1, 12), under the title "Late Emperor of China." The piece is introduced by accounts from the East Indies mentioning the death of the emperor "after a long reign of more than fifty years. This Emperor was remarkable for a philosophic simplicity of appearance and demeanour, so as in that circumstance not to be distinguished from a common mandarin, or any of the higher classes of his subjects." To check useless luxury and encourage economy, the account continues, the monarch suppressed all public ceremonies on his birthday. It is true that the reigning emperor K'ien Long had recently died, but the *Time Piece* goes on mistakenly to attribute to him a famous judicial decision that had been made by a previous emperor K'ang Hai, who had died in 1722. This decision was correctly reported by Quesnay (Maverick 1946: 252–3). According to this anecdote, the essence of which appears in Du Halde (1736: 2:69), a merchant of Nanking through industry and integrity had acquired a considerable fortune, but the viceroy of the province sought to wrest it from him. The merchant divided all his possessions among his children, but the viceroy ordered them into the army. He then begged his way to Pekin and despite his poverty obtained an audience with the emperor, convincing him of the justice of his cause. The emperor then ordered the viceroy beheaded and installed the merchant in his place. Other versions of the same anecdote appear in the *Massachusetts Magazine* (5 [1793] 20–21); the *Weekly Magazine* (1 [24 February 1798] 113-15); and the *Rural Casket* (1 [19 June 1798] 43–44). I have no explanation to offer for the confusing of K'ien Long with K'ang Hai in the *Time Piece*.

Another puzzling story about the death of an emperor appeared in the *New Haven Gazette*, (1 [January 1787], 369). This one under the heading of "Foreign Intelligence. Petersburg Sept. 8" reports that "Asia has lost one of her most monarchs [*sic* "most beloved?"] by the death of the old Emperor of China, Kien Long, an account of which arrived by a courier from the frontiers of that empire." K'ien Long was indeed the reigning emperor, but he did not die until 1796, nine years later. It was common in the eighteenth century, however, for exaggerated reports of the death of famous personalities, as Mark Twain expressed it, to be circulated while they were still alive. Frederick the Great, for example, had previously written to Voltaire in March 1776, stating on the authority of the abbé De Pauw that K'ien Long had recently passed away (Voltaire 1953 & 65: 18842). The item in the *New Haven Gazette* adds that this sovereign "was remarkable for his mildness, his love of the fine arts, his well cultivated understanding for a Tartar, and for several works which he published in Chinese and Tartarean verse; he is also praised for his frugality, and particularly for his wonderful consideration for that first of all arts, Agriculture." Adding to the confusion, a quite contrary picture of the imperial structure in Asia appeared in Freneau's *Time Piece* a week after a favorable portrayal in the same newspaper elicited by an accurate report of the death of K'ien Long. According to the issue of 22 March 1797, the form of government all over Asia was immutable, an absolute despotism with no check to the ruler's power. In such a government in which the sovereign retires from public view, it was charged, "the human race appear a depressed and degraded species."

Although no single European source for all of the above portrayals of Chinese emperors may be found, it is possible to trace a large number of rhapsodic portrayals of Chinese agriculture in American periodicals to a single book. By Pierre Poivre, a French precursor of Quesnay, this book *Voyage d'un philosophe, ou observations sur les moeurs et les arts des peuples de l'Afrique, de l'Asie, et de l'Amérique* (Yverdun, 1768) was translated into English as *Travels of a Philosopher* and printed in two separate editions in the United States during the eighteenth century and in a further one in 1818. Indeed it was one of only two books about China to have more than a single edition in the United States before 1800. The other was Aeneas Anderson's *A Narrative of the British Embassy to China*, published in 1795 in both New York and Philadelphia. Anderson's narrative has been considered the first work on China printed in the United States (*China on our Shelves* 1984: 35), but it was preceded by five other works, including that of Poivre, which was the second. Whatever resemblances may be noted between French Physiocrats and American thinkers are more likely to have stemmed from Poivre than than from Quesnay. As I have already indicated, the latter's *Le despotisme de la Chine* was not reprinted in any form in the eighteenth century in either Europe or America. Although Quesnay brought out his work in the *Ephémérides du citoyen* in 1767 and Poivre's *Voyage* was not published until the following year, Poivre had originally presented the substance of his *Voyage* in two addresses given before the Royal Academy of Lyons that circulated in manuscript and are known to have influenced Quesnay (Maverick 1946: 42). Poivre's travelogue was known in America at least five years before the publication of an American edition. On 15 May 1773, Dr. Alexander Garden of Charleston wrote to John Ellis, "I have read and admired M. Poivre's book again and again. We shall have much reason to bless you and him for centuries to come" (Linnaeus 1821: 1: 598).

Because of the bibliographical significance of Poivre's work, I shall give full details of the American editions in the eighteenth century. The first of these appeared in Philadelphia during the American Revolution.

The life of David Hume, Esq; the philosopher and historian, written by himself. To which are added, the Travels of a philosopher, containing observations on the manners and arts of various nations, in Africa and Asia. From the French of M. le Poivre, late envoy to the King of Cochin-China, and now intendent of the Isles of Bourbon and Mauritius. Philadelphia: Printed and sold by Robert Bell, next door to St. Paul's Church, in Third-Street. MDCCLXXVIII.

The second American edition appeared almost twenty years later.

Travels of a philosopher; or, Observations on the manners and arts of various nations in Africa and Asia. By M. Le Poivré [sic], late envoy to the king of Cochin-China. Augusta (Kennebeck) Re-printed by Peter Edes. 1797.

Since Hume's autobiography occupies only thirteen pages, Bell, the Philadelphia printer, combined it with Poivre's travels in a joint edition in order to make up a pamphlet sizable enough to warrant separate publication. He undoubtedly gave Hume top billing because of the latter's notoriety and presumably based his justification for joining the two works on the word "philosopher" in both titles. Bell published Poivre's work in an additional composite volume entitled *Miscellany for Sentimentalists* also in 1778, containing five other pieces as well as those by Hume and Poivre. Some bibliographers would call this a separate edition, but I do not do so since the typography and pagination in both volumes are identical. Both Bell and Edes incorrectly add the article *le* to Poivre's name, and Edes by supplying an acute accent changes its meaning from *pepper* to *peppered*.

The inclusion of *l'Amérique* in the title of the Yverdun edition of *Voyage d'un philosophe* is quite misleading since Poivre did not visit the Western hemisphere. All he says about the area is that the extensive tracts of South America, covered with marshes, brambles, and woods, are hardened by the sweat of slave laborers, while the northern regions are less wretched by being free, but are ineffectual in their efforts to obtain that other happiness that derives only from good agriculture. In Poivre's address of admission to the Academy of Lyon, however, he pointed out that the discovery of America "bound Asia and Africa to Europe." According to his theory, America provided silver as the medium of commerce between Europe and Asia, and Africa furnished slaves for the cultivation of the land and the working of the mines (Maverick 1946: 40–41).

The vogue of *Travels of a Philosopher* in the United States was due to its propaganda for agriculture, considered as the basis of national prosperity both in China and elsewhere. The comforting message it beamed was that the large and happy population of China derived not from science or technology, but entirely from rational methods of cultivation and the industry of the people. The printer Edes in Maine specifically proclaimed in his preface that he had reprinted the work for the benefit of American farmers and legislators.

Bell's preface lauds the author's manner as easy and elegant, his observations as striking and judicious, and his sentiments as philanthropic and benevolent. According to this preface, "the genuine happiness of every nation must depend on agriculture, and agriculture must ever be influenced by established laws and modes of government: nature indulgently smiles on the labour of a free-born people, but shrinks with horror from the tyrant and the slave." The preface also warns the reader to bear in mind that many of the author's comments on agriculture apply to Europe, but not to Great Britain, a rather odd sentiment to appear at that time in Philadelphia, which was then in the process of breaking away from Britain in the midst of the War for Independence. More apposite would have been a reference to the similarity of climatic conditions in Pekin and Philadelphia that had already been noticed in the *Transactions* of the American Philosophical Society.

Edes's preface repeats the above compliments on Poivre's style and then observes that the author's "principal idea appears to be to prove that the genuine happiness of every nation depends upon the improvement of Agriculture; and that for this end the property of the industrious ought to be permanently secured by laws and modes of government that should be subject to no violation." This principle amounts to the application of Montesquieu's theory of the spirit of laws to agricultural production. Poivre in his text specifically affirms that "in every country, in every quarter of the world, the state of agriculture depends entirely on the established laws, and, consequently, on the manners, customs, and prejudices from which these laws derived their origin" (1797: 56). A vigorous opponent of slavery, Poivre stresses that in Cochin China all labor is free and suggests that the sugar produced there can be sold at a lower price than that "cultivated and prepared by the wretched slaves of our European colonies" (1797: 63).

Like many of his predecessors, Poivre celebrates the emperor of China engaging in ritual plowing, but he has the advantage of having seen a viceroy opening the ground at Canton. He affirms that he "never remembers to have beheld any of the ceremonies invented by men, with half the pleasure and satisfaction with which I observed this" (1797: 85). The secret of the agricultural prosperity of the Chinese people he attributes to their "manuring their fields judiciously, ploughing them to a considerable depth, sowing them in the proper season, turning to advantage every inch of ground which can produce the most inconsiderable crop and preferring to every other species of culture that of grain" (1797: 75). He adds that this system except for the emphasis on grain is the one recommended by all the best authors, ancient and modern. Unlike Western farmers, however, the Chinese never allow their land to remain fallow, and they keep no land for meadows or grazing. Even without meadows they have all the horses and buffalo necessary for labor, but fewer horses and horned cattle than people possess in the West. They do not maintain large numbers of horses for carriages and chariots, as is customary in European cities. Nor do they use hills for the cultivation of wine. "They would imagine it is a sin against humanity, to endeavour to procure, by cultivation, an agreeable liquor, whilst from the want of the grain which this vineyard might have produced, some individual perhaps might be in danger of perishing of hunger." In the same spirit, "an ancient emperor of China in a public instruction, exhorting the people to labor, observed that if in one corner of the empire there was one man who did nothing, there must, in some other quarter, be another who suffers on that account, deprived of the necessaries of life" (75). I have indicated in chapter 6 that Franklin repeated this sentiment and that he probably derived it from Poivre. It is also possible that his Chinese letter is indebted to Poivre for the assertion that the emperor opposed the breeding of large numbers of horses. Poivre also introduces the notion, later adopted by Quesnay, that the annual tax necessary for the state should be limited to a portion of the annual produce of the soil. Stiles in his sermon on raising a revenue in produce, cited earlier in this chapter, could also have been inspired by Poivre.

At the close of his discourse, Poivre adds liberty to good management as the source of national prosperity, another reason for the appeal of his work to federal America. In his words, "it is liberty, it is their undisturbed right of property that has established a cultivation so flourishing, under the auspices of which this people have increased as the grain which covers the fields" (93). For all these reasons, the emperor is the happiest of men; he does not command, but instructs. His words are maxims of justice and wisdom. In these panegyrical terms, Poivre as much as any author established in America the concept of the benevolent Chinese emperor.

As would be expected, Poivre's ideas were widely summarized and extracted in American periodicals, and with one exception all references were to the Chinese part of his book. The single exception consists of a paragraph in the *Rural Magazine* (Newark No. 21) titled "Hospitality," but with no indication of the author or source of the excerpt. The paragraph reports that in Cochin China, when a traveler has no money, he goes to the first house he sees, enters, modestly approaches the table as soon as the rice is served, takes his portion, drinks, and departs without a word being said on either side.

The *Worcester Magazine* in September 1787 (3, 300–302), under the heading "From the TRAVELS OF A PHILOSOPHER," reprints the first half of Poivre's section on China (corresponding to pages 71–79 of the later Edes's edition). Here Poivre describes the environs of Canton, the system of manuring, the use of every available inch of land, the declining to set aside fallow lands or meadows, and the rejection of horse-drawn carriages for human transportation. In April, 1792, the *Massachusetts Magazine* (4, 223–24) reprinted the subsequent part of Poivre's work, consisting of the spring ceremony of ground breaking (corresponding to pages 84–85 of the Edes's edition) with no indication of the source or author. In February, 1795, the *Rural Magazine: or Vermont Repository* (1, 57) reprinted the same material along with an additional paragraph, presumably by the editor, suggesting an ethnic link between the Chinese and American Indians.

> There seems to have been a similar custom in South America. The emperors of Peru, named Incas, as an example to the people, began the cultivation of the earth in the spring with their own hands, with ceremonies and festivals of a similar nature; and a field was reserved every year to be cultivated by the royal family, called the children of the sun. This custom was derived from Manco Capac, the first emperor of Peru. It was designed, like the Chinese ceremonies, to teach the people the superior importance and dignity of agriculture to all other professions. As this custom was altogether arbitrary, there can be but little doubt that Manco Capac learned it of the Chinese.

Extraneous material was joined to Poivre in another periodical, the *New York Magazine* in November 1795 (6, 643–46). In an article titled "Some Account of the Chinese Agriculture, and Ceremonies, in honor thereof (From the Chinese Traveller)," eight paragraphs from Poivre, including those in the Vermont *Rural Magazine*, are followed by seven paragraphs not in Poivre on Chinese gardens, the two texts appearing as one. The article is continued in the December issue (6, 713–15) with nine more paragraphs on Chinese gardens. The actual author of this gardening material was William Chambers, who had printed it originally under the modest title *Design of Chinese buildings . . . from the originals drawn in China by Mr. Chambers . . . To which is annexed a description of their temples, houses, gardens, etc.* (London, 1757). The section on gardening was reprinted in Thomas Percy's *Miscellaneous Pieces relating to the Chinese* (London, 1762), from where it may have been taken by the American editor. Another possibility, however, is that the editor saw it in the *Columbian Magazine* for December 1790 (5, 389–92) under the title "Of the Art of Laying out Gardens among the Chinese" but without an author's name. This is the title in Percy's miscellany. Chambers's esthetics of gardening is important in its own right, but its influence was felt in England rather than America, as A. O. Lovejoy has explained in a classic article "The Chinese Origin of a Romanticism" (1948: 99–135). Poivre not only says nothing about gardening, but his utilitarian emphasis on the maximum use of land for agriculture suggests that ornamental gardens are a superfluous luxury. The combining of the somewhat incompatible notions of Poivre and Chambers in the *Rural Magazine* is one additional paradox revealed in the American reaction to China.

The essence of Poivre was summarized in the *Massachusetts Magazine* for November, 1793 (5, 679–80), under the title "Rural Economy of the Chinese." Without mentioning Poivre by name, the article indicates that the sentiments it contains stem from "a philosopher, whom the spirit of observation has led into their empire." After describing the ceremony of the spring plowing, the American essayist comments, "The Europeans, who have been present at this solemnity at Canton, never speak of it without emotion; and make us regret that this festival, whose political aim is the encouragement of labor, is not established in Europe, instead of that number of religious feasts, which seem to be invented by idleness, to make the country a barren waste," an emphasis that would have been appropriate to a deistical periodical like the later *Correspondent*, but seems out of place in a conservative family magazine in New England.

Another essay combining Chinese agriculture and government appeared in the *New Haven Gazette* for 21 June 1787 (2, 142), essentiallly a précis of Poivre, skillfully incorporating some of his most striking phrases. Although containing no original ideas and in part taken verbatim from Poivre, the essay deserves to be ranked as a notable example of American writing on the subject of China. For this reason, I shall print it in entirety.

> Turn your eyes, to the eastern extremity of the Asiatic continent inhabited by the Chinese, and there you will conceive a ravishing idea of the happiness the world might enjoy, were the laws of this empire the model of other countries. This great nation unites under the shade of agriculture, founded on liberty and reason, all the advantages possessed by whatever nation, civilized or savage. The blessing pronounced on man, at the moment of his creation, seems not to have had its full effect, but in favour of this people, who have multiplied as the sands on the shore.
>
> Princes, who rule over nations! arbiters of their fate! view well this perspective: it is worthy your attention. Would you wish abundance to flourish in your dominions, would you favor population, and make your people happy; behold those innumerable multitudes which cover the territories of China, who leave not a shred of ground uncultivated; it is liberty, it is their undisturbed right of property that has established a cultivation so flourishing, under the auspices of

which this people have increased as the grains which cover their fields.

Does the glory of being the most powerful, the richest, and the happiest of sovereigns touch your ambition, turn your eyes towards Pekin, and behold the most powerful of mortal beings seated on a throne of reason; he does not command, he instructs; his words are not decrees, they are maxims of justice and wisdom; his people obey him, because his orders are dictated by equity alone.

He is the most powerful of men, reigning over the hearts of the most numerous society in the world. He is the richest of sovereigns, drawing from an extent of territory six hundred leagues square cultivated even to the summits of the mountains, the tenth of those abundant harvests it incessantly produces: this he considers as the wealth of his children, and he husbands it with care.

Sentiments such as this represent the pinnacle of Chinese prestige in the United States. Going to a further extreme than Thomas Paine, who had proclaimed in *Common Sense* that "Europe, and not England, is the parent country of America," the author in the New Haven periodical urges his countrymen to look beyond Europe and to take China as a model in agriculture, in government, and in personal liberty.

As I have already indicated, Jefferson has traditionally been associated with the Physiocrats. No specific reference to the *Travels of a Philosopher* appears in his papers although evidence of his acquaintance with Poivre's work may be found in his correspondence. On 26 March 1789, Benjamin Vaughan wrote to him from London inquiring whether a collection of "le Poivre's" works had been published or was likely to appear. He had read in a *Notice sur la vie de M. le Poivre* two or three years previously that Poivre had been captured by Commodore Barnet [sic] and his papers with him. This was a reference to Commodore Curtis Barnett of the British navy, who had taken Poivre prisoner in the Straits of Banca on 20 January 1745. He was soon released, and after his death in 1780, his widow married another prominent Physiocrat, Dupont de Nemours. Vaughan had applied for further information about Poivre's papers to Barnett's son, who was then a banker in London, but the latter could discover no traces of such a prisoner or such papers (Jefferson 1950—:14:707–78). Jefferson, who was then in Paris, replied, 17 March 1789, "The collection of the works of M. de Poivre has not, as I believe, been ever published. It could hardly have escaped my knowledge if they had been announced" (15: 133). Both Vaughan and Jefferson seem to be referring to a French edition of hitherto unpublished works, not to an American version of the *Travels*, and both seem to be well acquainted with the nature of Poivre's life and intellectual interests.

The influential Physiocrat was noticed also by John White in his 1823 *History of a Voyage to the China Sea*. He based two pages in his book concerning diplomatic relations between Onam, the country now known as Vietnam, and the West on Poivre and cited the latter's prediction that due to the decline of agriculture that had already set in, the entire nation would revert to a primitive condition (White 1972: 86–87).

Although Poivre' raptures over Chinese agriculture enjoyed enormous success in the United States, the Swedish work by Charles Gustavus Eckeberg, *Account of the Chinese Husbandry*, seems to have been completely ignored except for the notable review in Paine's *Pennsylvania Magazine* that I have mentioned in chapter 3. Eckeberg actually gives much more information about agricultural products and methods than does Poivre, but his style incorporates more fact and less rapture. He, nevertheless, preaches the same gospel. He affirms that "the empire of nature is found in the greatest perfection in China" and that favorable natural advantages exist in both North and South. In asserting the enormous population of China, he maintains that a country can never have too many inhabitants. "Rather, it is the number of industrious men, that contributes to the riches of the country, and to the comfortable subsistence of its inhabitants; for every industrious labourer, especially a husbandman, always produces more from the grateful soil, than he wants for himself" (Osbeck 1771:2:270– 275). As an example of the respect in which farming is held in China, Eckeberg naturally cites the emperor's annual ceremonial plowing of the fields.

In the next chapter I shall show that the dedication of a book by A. E. Van Braam published in Philadelphia in 1797 compares the Chinese system of government "that makes its Chief the Father of the National Family" with the newly established government of the United States "in which everything bespeaks the love of the First Magistrate for the People." George Washington is the patriarchal figure to whom the book is dedicated. One could hardly have more convincing proof of the respectable position of China in American public opinion than this pairing of Washington with the Chinese emperor. In the dedication in which this occurs, the emperor is not referred to by his name K'ien Long, but by the phrase "Father of the National Family." The custom of alluding to the emperor as a functionary or figurehead rather than as an individual was practically universal throughout the eighteenth century. K'ien Long was not introduced to the West as a personality until 1773–1774, when a description of the personal encounters of a Jesuit priest, Michel Benoît, with the monarch appeared in the collection *Lettres édifiantes et curieuses*, but even here the emperor is not referred to by name, but consistently by title alone. The name K'ien Long, however, had been made known in the

Portrait of Emperor Ch'ien Lung, from Memoires concernant l'historie, les sciences, les arts . . . *(1776–1791).*
Reproduced with permission of The Library Company of Philadelphia.

West three years earlier by means of a volume of translations of the emperor's poems, edited by another Jesuit, Joseph Marie Amiot (1770). Voltaire became instantly intrigued by the notion of a great monarch doubling as a poet, a parallel to Frederick of Prussia. He thereupon composed the first of a series of poems and letters in French, ostensibly written by or addressed to the Chinese emperor, and Frederick himself, Diderot, and others joined in the game. In 1773, the English architect William Chambers included a translation of one of K'ien Long's poems in the second edition of his *A Dissertation on Oriental Gardening*, which a rival landscape architect, William Mason immediately ridiculed in a lengthy verse satire, *The English Garden* in which he associated Chinese gardens with the emperor's poetry. Shortly after Lord Macartney's dismal mission to Pekin, another satirist Thomas James Mathias, basing his knowledge of K'ien Long on Chambers, penned a satire on Anglo-Chinese relations, *The Imperial Epistle from K'ien Long, Emperor of China, to George the Third, King of Great Britain* (1795).

When the latter was published in Philadelphia in a separate edition in 1800, it became the medium through which the name and some aspects of the personality of K'ien Long traveled to America. In *The Prospect*, 17 November 1804, an American deist followed the example of the French and English satirists by directing a putative epistle to the Chinese emperor, designed to expose various anomalies of Western civilization (395–96; continued 24 Nov. [405–60], 2 Dec. [410–13]). The primary target of the author, E. Church, about whom nothing else is known, was the Christian religion and the ruin and desolation it has caused through efforts to spread its influence throughout the world. Church remarks in his introduction that he had originally intended to dedicate some verses to a Christian monarch, but finding none sufficiently virtuous had decided to dedicate his work to the Chinese emperor because of the latter's poetical achievements. Obviously not aware that K'ien Long had died eight years previously, Church describes him as "the greatest sovereign of the greatest empire on earth, who is the greatest philosopher, historian, and poet in all his vast dominions." He is at the same time "equally distinguished for his good as his great qualities, and, . . . happily for his people, unites the talents and disposition to make them happy."

Church congratulates the Chinese nation for having escaped Christian invasions and depredations, but recognizes that some of his fellow citizens consider it a misfortune that the Chinese do not share the felicity of the Mexicans and Peruvians who have "succumbed under the violent religious operations of the ghostly Christian fathers to save them." He advises the emperor to study the history of European religious wars and crusades before admitting into his realm either missionaries or soldiers from the West.

Church concludes his epistle with a dedication in which he says he has avoided the conventional European style of fulsome flattery.

> With truly cordial and fraternal affection I salute your Majesty, and when these my feeble essays shall be laid at your feet, I pray you to receive them with brotherly kindness and indulgence; and to be pleased to recollect, that the Author is a Citizen of a country whose laws and constitution are as free from religious prejudices as those of China, and the people as little disposed to invade the peace, happiness, or territory of other nations, either for the purpose of possession, or conversion, being content with the abundant portion of blessings which bounteous Heaven has already lavished on them.

These are certainly the sentiments of one who admires what he knows about Chinese culture.

The Embassy of
Van Braam Houckgeest

Themepere came from the Far East published in the Western
hemisphere came from the press in 1797-1798. Written by a naturalized American citizen and dedicated to George Washington, it
describes among other things, the author's formal presentation to the
emperor K'ien Long in 1794, fifty years prior to the official establishment
of relations between China and the United States. This book has a fascinating history. The manuscript on which it is based was written in Dutch,
and it was then translated into French for its first edition in two volumes in
Philadelphia under the title *Voyage de l'ambassade de la Compagnie des Indes
Orientales hollandaises, vers l'empereur de la Chine, dans les années 1794 &
1795* (*Voyage of the Embassy of the Dutch East India Company to the Emperor of
China in the Years 1794 & 1795*). A pirated edition of the first volume soon
appeared in Paris, and later translations of this pirated edition were issued
in English, German, and Dutch, the latter representing two removes from
the Dutch of the original manuscript! The Paris edition was a pirated one
in a double sense. Five hundred copies of volume one of the Philadelphia
printing while being shipped across the Atlantic to London booksellers
were seized by a French privateer, and one of these copies was used as the
basis of the unauthorized Paris edition, which carefully excised all references to a second volume. Only the Philadelphia edition has both volumes. The London edition in English is a translation from the pirated
edition of Paris. No edition in the English language was ever published in
the United States.

The author of this significant cultural document is Andrew Everard Van Braam Houckgeest, who was born in 1739 in Utrecht Province, Holland. After a brief period in the Dutch navy, Van Braam in 1758 sailed to China in the service of the Dutch East India Company, residing in Macao and Canton on and off for fifteen years. He revealed an interest in America as early as 1777, when he wrote to Franklin supporting the application of three lieutenants in the Dutch service for appointments in the United States Army. In his letter, he assured Franklin that he was "entirely devoted" to the American cause (Van Braam 1797–98: 1: viii). In 1783, when the independence of the new nation had finally been recognized, Van Braam emigrated to South Carolina, where he was appointed Dutch consul to Georgia and the two Carolinas. Settling as a rice planter, he became a naturalized citizen in March or April, 1784. In September of the same year, his four youngest children died of diphtheria. He then accepted the post of factor of the Dutch East India Company in Canton. In 1794 he was chosen to accompany the ambassador of the company, Isaac Titsingh, as second in command on a mission to the Chinese emperor, K'ien Long, ostensibly to congratulate him on the sixtieth anniversary of his accession to the throne. The stimulus for the expedition came from Van Braam, who was also its driving force. Titsingh's previous Asian experience had been mainly in Japan, not China. He wrote his own journal of the expedition, but it has never been printed (Boxer 1939: 19).

Only nine or ten of the twenty-seven non-Europeans on the mission were Hollanders by birth. One of its French nationals was the orientalist, Chrétien-Louis-Joseph de Guignes, who served as translator and later wrote his own account of the embassy. The British East India Company had in the preceding year sent a mission under the leadership of a distinguished diplomat, Earl Macartney, for the undisguised purpose of establishing official commercial relations. This expedition had not accomplished its objective, and the Dutch hoped to succeed where the British had failed. The British voyage gave rise to one of the most popular contemporary descriptions of China in English, Sir George Staunton's *An Authentic Account of an Embassy from the King of Great Britain to the Emperor of China*, published in London in 1797, the same year as Van Braam's, but it was not printed in Philadelphia until two years later. Probably the great publicity accorded to Staunton's work together with the circumstance that Van Braam's was printed originally in Philadelphia rather than in London or Paris and in French in an Anglophone milieu explains why Van Braam's narrative has been greatly neglected by scholars and historians.

Several other books on the Macartney embassy came out about the same time. The first of these was William Winterbotham's *An Historical View of the Chinese Empire to which is added a copious account of Lord*

Macartney's Embassy, 1795. The "copious account," however, is a fraud. Winterbotham, a Baptist minister, was incarcerated at Newgate prison for sedition during the period of the mission and wrote his book during his imprisonment. The work was republished in Philadelphia in 1796. I have already referred to Aeneas Anderson's *Account of the Embassy of Lord Macartney,* a satirical backstairs recital, two editions of which were printed in the United States in addition to British ones. Sketches made on the voyage by the official illustrator, William Alexander, were reproduced in book form in 1805 under the title *Costume of China.* Finally, a popularized account of all aspects of the mission by John Barrow, *Travels in China,* was published in London in 1804 and in Philadelphia the following year. This work was extensively quoted by periodicals in the United States. Macartney's own daily record was also published by John Barrow in the second volume of his *Some Account of the Public Life of Earl Macartney,* 1807. Many other works have been published on the Macartney embassy, and a separate bibliography devoted entirely to this subject has been published in *Notes and Queries* (154 [1958]: 201–204). Since it would require another book for me to do justice to the British mission, I shall treat it only incidentally while concentrating on the event of primary American interest, the Dutch expedition as recorded in Van Braam's *Voyage.*

After Van Braam left Canton to return to the United States in December, 1795, his advanced age together with the ties of friendship led him to consider passing the rest of his life in his adopted country. The announcement of his arrival in Claypole's *American Daily Advertiser,* 25 April 1796, indicated that he was the owner of the vessel, the *Lady Louise,* on which he sailed and that he was accompanied by five native Chinese. This is the first mention I have encountered of Chinese on American soil, and these five doughty souls may have been the first to set foot in the United States and perhaps to settle there. It is known that they remained as servants in Van Braam's employ. Other sources indicate that a single Chinese came to the United States in 1800 for the purpose of learning English; another in 1819 was reported to have been residing in Boston for two or three years; and a Cantonese named Atit, who had lived in the same city for eight years, became a citizen in 1845 (Latourette 1917: 123). An American publication, *The National Era,* reported in its issue of 7 June 1855 that the Chinese population in New York at that time totaled 1,500, only two of which were female.

Van Braam brought back with him an extensive collection of Chinese works of art, which was later exhibited in Philadelphia. According to his editor and translator, "It was even impossible to avoid fancying ourselves in China, while surrounded at once by living Chinese, and by representations of their manners, their usages, their monuments, and

Reception of the Dutch Embassy by the Chinese Viceroy, from A. E. Van
Braam Houckgeest's Voyage de l'ambassade . . . *(1797–1798).*
Reproduced with permission of The Library Company of Philadelphia.

their art" (Van Braam 1797–98: 1, xiii). Van Braam built for himself a fine house on the Delaware River not far from Philadelphia "in the Adam style surmounted by a Chinese pagoda from which were suspended silver bells. This he called 'Chinese Retreat.' " (Kent 1931: 167). A Polish member of the American Philosophical Society, Julian Ursyn Niemcewicz, described Van Braam as "at once a Dutch Baron and a Chinese Mandarin" and charged that in his buildings he sought "to flaunt an Asiatic luxury" instead of "conforming to the simplicity of the country" (1965: 62). There was so much Chinese porcelain in the house and premises that Niemcewicz thought for a moment that Van Braam's wife, aged eighteen, the niece of a previous wife whom he had recently divorced, "was made of the same material, she was so pale and still" (92).

Van Braam's Dutch manuscript was edited, translated, and published by a Philadelphia printer, M. L. E. Moreau de Saint-Méry, a French creole recently emigrated from Santo Domingo and a prolific translator and author in his own right. Van Braam asked and was given permission to dedicate his work to George Washington (Loehr 1954: 184). In his dedication, he drew a parallel between the Chinese patriarchal system of government "that makes its Chief the Father of the National Family" and the government of the new nation elected by universal suffrage "in which everything bespeaks the love of the First Magistrate for the People." In expressing his veneration for the virtues exemplified in Washington's character, he thereby provided a striking analogy between China and America.

Moreau in his introductory notes presents a rather extensive commentary on Chinese religion, but does not indicate his sources. He affirms that the primitive religion of the Chinese was that of the ancient patriarchs such as Abraham and Melchizedek and that the emperor's title of Grand Priest of the All-Powerful derives from ancient times. The second form of religion in China, adopted much later when a recognizable national tradition had evolved, consisted, according to Moreau, of idolatry pushed to such extremes that each person could manufacture a deity after his own notions; consequently every head of a family possessed one of his own creation. This plurality of deities effectively excluded the possibility of uniting large numbers of believers into single sects, and as a result there were no religious enthusiasts in China except possibly the bonzes and bonzesses. Moreau adds that certain principal divinities were nearly universally accorded reverence and were thought to possess powers relative to particular objects and circumstances. Both men and women, Moreau says, offer homage to these divinities in temples erected in their honor, but the emperor never goes to these temples. He joins only in the cult of the All Powerful, God of the Sky, God of the Earth, and he offers sacrifices only to his ancestors and to Confucius.

Because of the great length of Van Braam's narrative, comprising two huge volumes of more than 400 pages each, I am unable to cover all of its contents. Instead I shall concentrate on passages relative to the other texts I have treated in previous pages together with those on literary topics. In general he portrays the life and culture of China as primitive, but appreciates the hospitality accorded him.

He remarks that he was frustrated in his desire to examine in detail a temple dedicated to Confucius that he visited early in his journey because of the large number of people who gathered around him, eager to see a visitor from the West with their own eyes (1, 58). Although deprived of the Confucian temple, Van Braam was able to examine twenty-five grandiose memorial arches erected in various localities through which he passed. As an indication of the moral attitudes of the people, he categorizes the classes of worthy people to whom these impressive arches had been erected: children who have offered notable examples of filial love; women remarkable for their chastity; mandarins who have governed with fidelity and justice; men who have served the state with distinction or invented things of great utility; and centenarians, it being theoretically impossible to reach the age of 100 years without practicing lifelong sobriety and virtue (1, 85).

As might be expected, Van Braam shows great interest in the emperor's participation in the spring rites of plowing and planting. Equally enthusiastic as Pierre Poivre over Chinese agricultural methods, he refers to several books on agriculture worthy to be translated into Western languages (1, 87). Later in the volume he compares rice cultivation in China and in South Carolina and finds the Chinese production superior (1, 430). This he considers a proof that the Chinese have carried the art of agriculture to a high degree of perfection. Somewhat contrary to his previous statement, however, he adds that he had inquired whether any books on the subject could be made available for translation, but that he was given negative replies.

Van Braam reports with pleasure and astonishment seeing a fleet of wheelbarrows with sails, similar to the fleet of 300 described in Franklin's Chinese letter. Van Braam gives the only detailed description of these barrows in a Western language along with the illustration of their design and appearance that I have already mentioned. Following are his comments:

> Mais qu'on juge de ma surprise lorsque j'ai vu aujourd'hui une flotte de brouettes, toutes de la même grandeur. Je dis, avec raison, une flotte, car elles étaient à la voile, ayant un petit mat exactement mis dans un étambrai ou une gaine, pratiquée sur l'avant de la brouette. Ce petit mat à une voile faite de natte, ou plus communement de toile, ayant cinq ou six pieds de hauteur & trois ou

quatre pieds de large, avec des ris, des vergues & des bras comme ceux des bateaux chinois. Les bras aboutissent aux brancards de la brouette, & par leur moyen le brouettier oriente la machine.

Il était bien facile de reconnaître à tout cet appareil qu'il n'etait pas une chose momentanée, mais bien une combinaison de plus dans la voiture, afin qu'avec un vent favorable, le brouettier puisse être extrêmement soulagé; car autrement ce moyen plus ou moins couteux & plus ou moins embarassant à transporter, n'aurait été que bisarre (1, 115).

(You can imagine how surprised I was today when I saw a fleet of wheelbarrows, all of the same size. I say, with reason, a fleet, for they were moving with sails, having a small mast placed exactly in the mast pole or scabbard, set in the forepart of the wheelbarrow. This little mast has a sail made of straw matting or more commonly of canvas, of about five or six feet high and three or four feet wide with reefs, yards and braces like those on Chinese boats. The braces end at the shafts of the wheelbarrow, and the operator uses them to steer the device. It was obvious that all this apparatus was not temporary, but rather a contrivance added to the vehicle so that with a favorable wind the barrow man could be greatly assisted; for otherwise such a means of transport, more or less expensive and more or less cumbersome, would simply have been odd.)

Van Braam refers to these conveyances as wheelbarrows, not as either carriages or wagons as they had formerly been described in Western literature. Previous pictorial representations, moreover, had shown them with four wheels. Van Braam's description and his accompanying illustration made it clear that these previous illustrations are misleading. The artist who accompanied Lord Macartney in 1797 also published a sketch of the sailed vehicle with merely a single wheel, thereby confirming the account of Van Braam. Van Braam brought one of these wheelbarrows back with him to Philadelphia, where it was placed in Peale's famous museum, but it has unfortunately been lost (II, 45).

The journey overland from Canton to Pekin was extremely tiring, and Van Braam complained that the circumference of his body had diminished by at least five inches from fatigue, poor food, and other hardships (1, 87). Apparently he was endowed with a more than substantial waistline, for de Guignes frequently witnessed ecstacies of the mandarins over his corpulence. De Guignes affirmed that " 'l'embonpoint' in China is absolutely necessary to obtain consideration, and that a man ambitious of honors or fortune must be fat and corpulent enough to fill 'a large armchair' " (Waln 1822). Van Braam grumbled that the food was wretched on the road and just as bad at Pekin (1, 141). He also complained that the "inferior mandarins" entrusted with handling baggage had grossly over-

Chinese sailing carts, from A. E. Van Braam Houckgeest's Voyage de
l'ambassade . . . *(1797–1798).*
Reproduced with permission of The Library Company of Philadelphia.

charged (1, 157). But he mused philosophically that no place in the universe is impregnable to corruption. The Chinese would have replied, moreover, that the losses the visitors complained of did not come out of their own pockets since all of their expenses were being taken care of by the emperor. The party had brought with them a number of cases of wine. More than half of the bottles were broken en route, but this was the fault of the extreme cold and of the coolies. After discovering this catastrophe, Van Braam resolved to make no further complaints (1, 159). Soon after the arrival of the party in the capital, its members received from the emperor a sturgeon twelve feet long. The emperor was eager to see his visitors as soon as they arrived without waiting for them to retrieve their state clothes that had been sent separately. If their health was good, he was not concerned with their sartorial appearance (1, 180).

Despite the emperor's sturgeon, which Van Braam apparently was happy to receive, further culinary attentions from the court failed to arouse his appetite. He particularly characterizes as disgusting the food provided during an excursion on which he and his entourage accompanied the emperor. They were served on a dirty plate a mixture of bones with almost no meat "that seemed rather to be fit for a dog's treat than for a man's meal" (1, 195). In Holland, he affirmed, the lowest beggar would receive a cleaner dish, and yet this was the reception accorded an ambassador by an emperor. Van Braam speculated that perhaps the despised delicacies were bones left over from the emperor's own plate and that it was a mark of favor to receive them. But this reflection gave him little consolation, for no attention to cleanliness had been manifested anywhere in the service.

Van Braam was not impressed by the palace grounds, but instead continually astonished by the lack of elegance (1, 145). He commented on the contrast between the imposing exterior and humble interior. The buildings were poorly maintained, the passageways narrow, and the rooms simple with little decoration. He and his party were well received, however, and made to understand that they were regarded in a more favorable light than the English who had preceded them. Because of this auspicious reception, Van Braam entertained hopes of being shown things never before seen by foreigners and thereby gratify his great desire of enlightening the West about China (1,153). As it turned out, however, he did not have enough time even to visit the Great Wall. The exceptionally good treatment accorded to the party at court was probably more than conventional politeness. Lord Macartney had steadfastly refused to kowtow on the grounds that the gesture symbolized the tributary status of the nation of the person performing it. He did not realize that the ceremonial gifts from George III that he had presented at court were considered by the Chinese as the equivalent of such an acknowledgment. Van Braam was tipped off that Macartney's obstinancy was one of the five reasons why his mission had failed. Van Braam and his superior, therefore, decided to conform scrupulously to the Chinese custom and performed the kowtow at least eighty times during their visit (Loehr 1954: 191). Van Braam indicates that one of the causes for Macartney's ejection from China arose from one of his gifts to the emperor, a planetary [or ossory] that had been purchased in England but executed in 1750 in Herford, Germany. It was presented as having been manufactured in England expressly for the emperor, but when being reconstructed by Portuguese missionaries from the disassembled state in which it had been packaged they noticed inscriptions in German and so informed the emperor. He was indignant and ordered Macartney to leave immediately. As a result, Macartney and Staunton on their farewell courtesy call deliberately dressed in casual attire (2, vi).

The emperor ordinarily held audiences between 3 and 6 in the morning, a custom Van Braam found extremely painful, especially in winter when the cold was severe and penetrating (1, 197). He expressed surprise that during his audiences the emperor was protected only by eunuchs without any military presence, for he had heard from an English officer that the Chinese army comprised nearly two million men (1, 197). He later retracted his implication that the Chinese military presence was inadequate, however, admitting that the emperor had a palace guard exactly like those in Europe (1, 241).

Van Braam was not awed by K'ien Long, and by and large he considered Chinese society as primitive. He was astounded by Chinese ignorance of the rest of the world despite the presence among them for over a century of Catholic missionaries. He concluded that the Chinese had no desire to acquire knowledge of other nations, and since they granted very little respect to the missionaries, it would have been poor strategy for the latter to commend anything European. Also policy made the priests praise their individual Chinese protectors, and this adulation fed the latter's vanity. Even the masterpieces of craftsmanship such as clocks and other instruments brought from Europe made little impression, for these works were superfluities, and the Chinese were accustomed to judge only by necessities. Van Braam affirmed philosophically that the Chinese, like other primitive peoples, were happy in their own fashion. Why should they seek to learn about matters that they would then regret not having for themselves and which being deprived of would seem a great evil? In the vein of Diderot discoursing on the natives of Tahiti, Van Braam asked the question: have the peoples of the South Sea become more or less happy because of their relationships with Europeans during the past thirty or forty years? It is only too true, he mused, that we have given them the knowledge of and taste for things that their countries cannot produce (1, 183). Van Braam is unique among eighteenth century authors, European as well as American, in thus treating the Chinese as a primitive race and placing them on a level with the natives of Tahiti.

One of the reasons Van Braam adduced to account for Chinese backwardness is the veneration of the ideas and commandments of their ancestors, particularly in pretending not to be more instructed than their fathers (1, 244). From ancient precepts such as this, of which the sense is moral rather than literal, comes the fear of advancement in all the sciences and the worship of venerable customs. Despite this apparent denigration of Chinese science, Van Braam elsewhere, like Franklin, praised the Chinese method of heating houses in winter by means of exterior fires with pipes leading into the walls of houses, almost like a modern furnace. This, he admitted, is an invention reflecting Chinese industry (1, 255).

During one seance with the emperor, the Dutch party was introduced into a small area furnished as a tiny but rather pretty theater, seated on floor mats, served fruits and sweets on small tables, and presented with various souvenirs. The emperor, K'ien Long, observed that he was then eighty-five years of age and that Van Braam was the only native of Holland ever to have approached this close to him (1, 168). Because of this close contact, Van Braam was able to give a detailed description of the emperor's physical features, unique in Western writing.

> His personal appearance exhibits all of the marks of old age, particularly his eyes. They are watery, and so weak that it is with difficulty he raises his eye-lids which hang down in folds, especially that of the left eye. He is in consequence obliged, whenever he wishes to look at anything that is not very close to him, to raise his head and even to throw it a little back. His cheeks are shrivelled and pendant. His beard, which is short, is very gray. . . . His dress consists of clothes lined with fur, which appeared to me to be that of the sea-otter; and round his cap, which is sometimes ornamented with a large pearl, was a border of the same kind. In this season, as well as in all others, the Emperor's dress is very plain, although he is served and honored like a god. (1, 240–41)

During all the conversation, eating and gift giving in the theater, an acrobatic performance also took place, very much like those offered by Chinese circuses today. Van Braam was greatly struck by a man who lay on his back with his feet vertically in the air holding a ladder of six large steps. Using his feet in this position he made the ladder turn around in circles while a boy of six to eight years climbed to the top and performed various movements. Next an enormous earthern vase of more than 125 pounds weight was placed on the man's feet and similarly caused to rotate. After the boy was introduced into the vase, he climbed in and out, making bows to the emperor and other guests.

Van Braam was amazed by the small size of the theater in the Royal Palace, no larger than fifteen square feet and separated from a staircase leading to another apartment by about five feet. From this description of the rooms of the first ministers of state he asks his readers to judge for themselves of the minuscule size of rooms in ordinary dwellings, for the "grand sallons" [sic] were used only for feasts or public assemblies (1, 172). Van Braam is somewhat ambivalent in regard to the relative opulence of the imperial palace. Elsewhere in his narrative he comes to the conclusion that he has seen less than one twentieth of its beauties to which, in his words, "not a one of the dwellings of the Princes of Europe is comparable" (1, 269). At Hong-tcheou-fou (Hangchow), Van Braam visited another theater that he described as superb. Once again the entertainment consisted of acrobatics.

Van Braam was also brought into contact with dramatic performances of a more conventional type, those put on for the public rather than for the privileged few and foreign guests. These were the *ouayangs* or public dramas, presented throughout the year in all sections of the city. He found these plays "in general very boring and accompanied by blaring music and much noise because these things appeal most to the spectators" (2, 344). He was also introduced to private performances for European visitors held in the homes of rich merchants. These theatrical companies, he wrote, present beautiful dramas accompanied by sweet music, "having much in common with the sentimental genre" (2, 345). He still remembered from his residence twenty years previously one of these dramas named *Chon-fou-Kan*, or *Fidelity Rewarded*, which he asked to have produced for him. His request was granted, but with difficulty, for few actors of the time remembered this antiquated play. It was, nevertheless, superbly acted with such skill that even though Van Braam did not understand the language he followed the entire meaning of the play, and his sentiments were touched to a high degree. For this reason he believed that if the drama could be translated by an elegant European pen for the Western stage, it would please all sensitive spirits. Hoping that some celebrated author might undertake this task, he summarized the action.

A mandarin, Thaye, summoned to the court, regretfully leaves behind an old servant Atay and a maidservant Aouana. After he has been absent for several years, his two wives overcome with boredom decide that while they are still young and beautiful they will seek a richer life elsewhere. Aouana attempts to dissuade them by taking Thaye's child, Siou-ye, in her arms, but the wives still leave. Atay and Aouana rear the child, paying particular attention to his mental development. One day in his thirteenth year when he falls asleep over his studies, the servant Aouana sings about his plight, deprived of riches as he is and facing an uncertain future, and strikes him lightly with a leather strap to waken him. Siou-ye rebukes her for daring to chastise him, for she is not his real mother, and she breaks into tears over his ingratitude. The child is touched and they are reconciled. Somewhat later the mandarin returns home in a river boat, noticing on the bank two women who appear familiar to him laboring in a menial condition. When he arrives at home, Atay acquaints him with the infidelity of his wives, identified as the two women he had seen reduced to servitude, and also informs him of the loving care that had been accorded to his son by Aouana. As the mandarin promises to make her his wife, Siou-ye appears clad in graduation clothing and renders homage to his father and future stepmother. At the end the emperor orders an arch to be erected to commemorate the noble conduct of Atay.

Although Van Braam admired this play for its sensibility, or, as we would say today, sentimentalism, he charged elsewhere in his book that Chinese culture is devoid of these qualities. He admitted the obvious fact that the Chinese respond to normal sex impulses, but affirmed that their instincts in this regard are purely animal and that the notion of kissing was nonexistent throughout the entire empire. Marriages were arranged and had nothing but procreation and domestic comfort as their aim. The diplomat's unconcealed sentimentality led him to commiserate with the unhappy Chinese for their lack of sentiment or romance. "How they are to be pitied for living without being subjected to the ineffable power of love, this love that nature has created in order to console man by itself alone for all the evils by which he might be overwhelmed and to elevate him so to speak above himself" (2, 131). Van Braam then suggested that because of the recent translation of a very interesting and well-written Chinese novel concerning the pure love of a couple in the upper classes, his readers might doubt his testimony and assume "that a sentiment that nature seems to have placed in all hearts is not foreign to those in China" (2, 134). Van Braam was referring to the anonymous novel *Hau Kiou Choaan*, or *The Fortunate Union*, the novel Jefferson had recommended to his brother-in-law and which had been translated into English by Thomas Percy and published in 1761 as *The Pleasing History*. Justifying his remarks on Chinese social behavior, Van Braam interpreted the novel as a moral romance deliberately designed to celebrate virginal chastity, a virtue venerated in China by monuments throughout the country. In a significant paragraph of literary criticism, he compared *Hau Kiou Choaan* with the novels of Samuel Richardson. "C'est le portrait d'une héroïne toute platonique, qu'à mon avis il ne faudrait pas envier à la Chine, ou l'on a, au surplus, comme en Europe, pour les romans, des modèles inimitable[s], & des Grandisson pour creer des Clarisse que nous admirons d'autant plus, que nous sentons que nous sommes plus éloignés de leur perfection pour laquelle l'auteur n'a presque rien laissé à désirer" (2, 132). Moreau de Saint-Méry's translation of Van Braam's Dutch seems ambiguous, if not inept at this point. This is my best try at an English version: "It is the portrait of a completely Platonic heroine, for whom in my opinion we should not envy the Chinese, who possess among their novels, as do the Europeans, inimitable models and Grandisons for the production of Clarissas, that we admire all the more as we regard ourselves further removed from their perfection concerning which their author has left almost nothing to be desired." Van Braam seems to be comparing the heroines of *Clarissa* and of *Hau Kiou Choaan* as models of virtue, but so perfect in their idealism that readers of the novels would be unable to aspire to imitate them.

Despite his approval of the treatment of women in *Hau Kiou Choaan*, Van Braam considers that the secluding of females in Chinese society is a further sign of the backwardness of the nation (1, 183). The custom contributes to national isolation and detracts from agreeable society, for convivial pleasure and gaiety cannot be had without a feminine presence. Van Braam reports that in a sense all Chinese women are objects of commerce. The daughters of the poor are sold as concubines and those of the wealthy must be provided with a substantial dowry. A husband has the right of selling his wife if she does not measure up to various legal requirements. Women of the upper classes are kept in continual confinement; those of the middle class are less secluded but have no liberty; and those of the lowest class perform all kinds of menial labor along with the men. Van Braam's opinions on regional distinctions are contrary to those of other Westerners. In general, he finds that the most civilized Chinese are those of Canton because of contact with Europeans; even though admitting that in theory those of Pekin the capital should be more urbane, he affirms that they have unfortunately acquired elements of rudeness from the Tartars.

Van Braam was anxious to correct a great deal of misinformation that had been printed in Europe, particularly in connection with the practice of footbinding. He remarks that the Chinese of both sexes have small feet, except those of the lower classes, who go about with their extremities bare. It is not difficult, he adds, to maintain the smallness of the girls' feet by applying at the age of six months a band designed to bend the four smallest toes so that the foot eventually assumes a pointed form and is seldom more than three and a half or four inches long. Van Braam gives these and many more details because he imagines that he was the first foreigner ever to examine the foot of a Chinese woman. A young person of eighteen years had allowed him this privilege, and he was pleased to report that neither her leg nor her feet had anything deformed or repulsive (2, 51). Anderson had exercised the same privilege in the previous year with a young lady of twenty, whose foot measured no more than five inches and a half (Morse 1796: 2: 527). Van Braam was unique in observing that Chinese women also bind their breasts in order deliberately to make them smaller (2, ix). Unlike some other Americans, Van Braam found Chinese women attractive. He reports being in a barge and witnessing several very beautiful ladies passing in another barge and as a result experiencing the tortures of Tantalus and Ixion (1, 320).

Despite Van Braam's originality and the quite adequate translation by Moreau, his work did not find a good press, probably, as I have already said, because it was overshadowed by books about the rival Macartney mission. The most extensive notice that I have found anywhere before the twentieth century concerning Van Braam or his embassy is contained in Amasa Delano's *Narrative* which also gives Delano's personal opinion of the Macartney expedition. His information concerning the latter came to him in consequence of associating with the officers of an English snow that had previously been attached to the squadron escorting Macartney. Delano reports that when the emperor learned that the commission was on its way, he dispatched orders to all his sea ports to provide its members with any materials they might be in need of and to furnish them with pilots when required. In spite of this hospitality, Delano did not believe that Macartney obtained a single privilege for his nation that it did not enjoy before (1819: 536).

> My fellow officers informed me, that while the negotiation was going on, the ships were constantly crowded with all kinds of refreshments, and that when they were first boarded by the Chinese they received every attention from them that could be shown; and that the presents received by the different officers belonging to the embassy, were of immense value. That the natives of this part of China were of different complexions and manners from those in and near Canton; their colour being nearly white; and in their manners were much more free and candid; and that they were of a larger stature, and more athletic than the southern Chinese—that they were much more sociable, and not so particular respecting their women being seen by the men. And were even fond of receiving the officers into their houses, when on shore, provided it could be done without the knowledge of the mandarins.

Delano obtained his knowledge of the Van Braam embassy from two Dutch supercargos, a "young Van Braam" and another named Blatterman, who had joined the embassy at Canton and accompanied it to Pekin.

Their statement was, that they left Canton in beautiful covered boats, and proceeded on through the canals. Some of the party would go on shore, and walk near the water whenever they chose, along by the side of the canal, while the others remained in the boats. When they came to a place where the canal did not carry them in the most direct course, or to where it was frozen, they left their boats and proceeded on horseback. It was in the winter season when they made the journey, and the country of course did not appear to so much advantage as it would have been in the summer. The mandarins, who accompanied them, indulged them in everything they asked that was reasonable, and shewed them every curiosity worthy their attention, and that they seemed very desirous to please their guests. . . .

When the embassy arrived at Pekin great parade was made, and they were received with all the attention and politeness that could be shewn them. It was said in Canton, that there was more attention paid to the Dutch, than there was to the English in their embassy, which was thought to be in consequence of the Dutch not asking any favours of them. (537)

Delano's informants repeated essentially the same details about the northern Chinese that he had heard from his fellow officers who had been with Macartney; they also agreed that Staunton had given excellent descriptions of the country and the canals. These Dutch friends indicated "that while their embassy was at Pekin, parties were frequently formed to skate on the ice, in which the emperor always joined, and seemed to be much amused by the diversion." Some of the Chinese who participated in these parties were archers who performed "very extraordinary feats, both on their skates and with bows and arrows." The Dutch supercargoes declared that these exploits on skates "exceeded any thing of the kind that they had ever seen in Holland," even though it is well known that the Dutch themselves are great proficients in skating. "They were likewise entertained with Chinese musick and dancing. Their musick however is the most disagreeable to the ear of an American or European of any thing that can be conceived of."

Although Van Braam's account of the Dutch mission was overshadowed by that of Sir George Staunton about the Macartney embassy, it would seem that American readers should have accorded the former a warm welcome, printed as it was for the first time in Philadelphia and bearing a dedication to George Washington. Notwithstanding these advantages, it was apparently given no more regard in America than in Europe. Indeed I have not been able to find a single review of the 1797 Philadelphia edition. And even more strange, the reviewer of the London edition in the *Philadelphia Magazine* for April, 1799 (1, 189–93), was not even aware that an earlier edition in his own city had already appeared. His review begins on a hostile note, apparently because he considered Van Braam as native of Holland rather than as a citizen of the United States.

> Some of our Readers will have their curiosity particularly gratified in perusing the following article, extracted from *Van Braam's Embassy to China*. It was once intended by the author that this work should have made its first appearance in Philadelphia; when much was boastingly asserted of the superior respect that was shown to the representatives of the high and mighty states of Holland, at the court of Peking: how justly will appear, in some measure, from this specimen.

The extracts that follow concerning primarily Van Braam's entry into Pekin in 1795 and his reception there, including the emperor's sending him partially gnawed bones from his table. The only original material in the piece consists of a long footnote on Chinese coolies and the labor that they perform.

A more friendly notice of the Paris edition appeared in the New York *Monthly Magazine* in May of the same year, 1799, (1, 148–50) but the manner in which the work is announced indicates that this reviewer also was not aware of a previous Philadelphia edition: "Citizen M. L. E. Moreau de Saint Méry has lately published, at Paris, an extract from Van Braam's Journal . . . , one volume quarto, being the first. The second, accompanied with maps and engravings, is announced as about to appear." The reviewer also quotes Van Braam's modest disclaimer that he was unable "to make known the usages, public and private manners, the legislation, arts, industry, productions, the temperature, commerce, religion, and government" because he was not allowed any kind of intercourse with the inhabitants. We shall see in chapter 12 that a young man of Philadelphia twenty years later attempted to cover all of these matters and some others with relatively little more opportunity of contact with the ordinary Chinese citizen. Instead of merely giving extracts, the notice in the *Monthly Magazine* paraphrases key passages, those for the most part that confirm notions about China already circulating. Readers are told, for example, that "the horse, the most beautiful and useful animal in Europe, is despised there." Perhaps under the influence of Pierre Poivre, this reviewer also affirms that "in no country does agriculture flourish so much as in China. This art is there beheld with almost religious veneration. On this subject there are treatises, brought to perfection by the application and experience of several ages: these treatises, suited to the soil of each canton, are deposited in the hands of the mandarin who acts as first magistrate; and he takes care that the neighbouring farmers shall be made acquainted with, and turn to advantage, the lessons which these treatises contain." The reviewer indicates that Van Braam speaks of Chinese monuments (or pagodas), but does not explain the use of these towers and hazards his own theory that they are parallel to obelisks in Egypt. In connection with religion, the reviewer affirms that foreigners in China are watched and confined because of a Spanish Jesuit who had told a former emperor that the Spanish gained control of South America because they had first converted the people to the Catholic faith, "after which their subjugation followed as a matter of course." Chinese religion is represented as on the whole superstitious: "The people to whom Confucius preached his simple and sublime morality, the people who erected temples to that philosopher, ought to be rational in their worship: but they are vilified and degraded by the most absurd idolatry; their pagodas are filled with idols of the most monstrous and whimsical figures." The Chinese are, nevertheless, tolerant, for Van Braam speaks of a Christian to whom they have erected temples and whom they style a saint.

It is doubtful that Van Braam was ever reviewed in London or Paris or anywhere else outside of the United States although his book is mentioned in various British accounts of the Macartney and Amherst embassies, and disparaging comments on his narrative appeared toward the middle of the nineteenth century in the *Biographie Universelle* in the article "Titsingh," the ambassador who led the Dutch mission to China. According to this article, Van Braam's book "contains very few interesting facts and even less that is new." Its lack of sparkle is given as the reason why volume two was not reprinted in Paris. The real reason, of course, is that the Paris edition was translated from one of the 500 copies of the first volume confiscated by a French privateer, and the unauthorized printer did not have the second volume at his disposal.

In contrast to the neglect of Van Braam in the American press, the accounts of Staunton and Anderson were well received, particularly the latter. The earliest notice of Anderson in America appeared in the *American Monthly Review*, for August, 1795 (2, 348–60), but it is not clear whether it is based on the American edition or that of London. The reviewer indicates that Anderson does not seem to be conversant with books, art, or science and that his situation as Macartney's valet kept him from intimate knowledge of the political aspects of the journey, but his descriptions are good and he writes a satisfactory, plain style.

The Rural Review or Vermont Repository for December, 1795 (1, 609–13), published "Particulars of the late British Embassy to China," not a review but a historical summary or narrative of what had taken place. No book is mentioned as the source of this article, which affirms that the English had two objects in undertaking the mission, to gain knowledge of the interior of the country and to establish new commercial relations between China and the English East India Company. After they arrived, however, they were considered as spies rather than emissaries. The article concludes: "It has seemed to be the policy of the Chinese court, to keep all nations on an equal footing in commercial concerns, during good behaviour. The view of the British embassy being to obtain exclusive privileges for the East India Company trading to China, interfering with this policy, rendered the whole design abortive." This article was duplicated in *The Time Piece*, 16 May 1797 (1, 109–14). Issues of *The Rural Review* in the following year published short extracts from Anderson: on customs and manners and the city of Pekin (2, 230–37); on modes of fishing (2, 300–302); and on the Great Wall (2, 336–8). The latter material was repeated in the Newark *Rural Magazine* for December, 1798 (No. 43) and in the *Weekly Magazine* for February, 1798 (85–87). Extracts from Anderson on the wall appeared also in *The Key*, 1, (24 March 1798) 83–84, and in the *National Magazine*, 2 (No. 8, 1800), 394–95. These and other extracts from Anderson, moreover, covered thirty pages of closely-packed small type in the 1796 edition of Jedidiah Morse's *Universal Geography, or, a View of the Present State of All the Empires, Kingdoms, States and Republics in the Known World*. In keeping with his practice of naming his sources, Morse indicates that he is taking this material "in Mr. Anderson's own words" from the New York edition of his *Narrative*. He also states that because of Anderson's "judgment in selecting, and his talent at describing, we are led to conclude that this little work contains more true and useful information, respecting the present state of this wonderful country, than all other publications beside" (Morse 1796: 502).

An article titled "Customs and Manners of the Chinese" in the *Massachusetts Magazine* for March, 1796 (8, 135–39), begins by denouncing abbé Grosier's description of the marriage ceremony, calling Grosier ignorant of the country. Grosier is also termed wrong about slavery, for there are no slaves in China. Finally, the article shows particular interest in the free dramatic performances in the streets during the month of March.

A long and glowing review of Staunton's *Account*, featuring an extract on the city of Pekin and remarks from English reviewers, appeared in the *Philadelphia Magazine* for March 1799 (1, 159–64). Extracts from Staunton also appeared in several numbers of the *Weekly Magazine* in 1798, including a narrative of the entrance of his ship "The Jackal" into a Chinese port (1, 185–86); a description of Chinese soldiers (2, 25–26); an account of Pekin (2, 209); a survey of religion in China (2, 241–42); and a report on the duties incumbent on consanguinity among the Chinese.

A very unflattering reference to Staunton, however, crept into *The Time Piece*, 24 November 1797 (2, No. 31). A news column with no heading devoted to statistics on the revenues of China and its military forces adds the following paragraph.

Sir George Staunton, secretary to the late British embassy to China, has published, it is said, a pompous account of the diplomatic proceedings while on that expedition. London papers mention the writer having received five thousand pounds sterling for the copy right. It is not yet said whether this narrative differs materially from that of Eneas Anderson, who was in the service of the affair. The whole expedition lord Macartney at head, appears to have been received with indifference, treated with coldness and neglect, if not insult; and absolutely dismissed out of the Chinese dominions rather as vagabonds, or intruders, than the legal representatives of a great monarch.

An open attack upon the British mission—indeed a virulent one—appeared in verse form in *The Rural Casket*, 21 August 1798 (1, 190–91). Titled "Ode on Lord Macartney's Embassy to China" and written by W. Shepherd, the poem describes the Chinese empire, personified as the genius Old Cathay, erupting in anger and horror at the approach of the English with their guilty record of rapine, slave-trading, and bloodshed.

Swift shot the curlew 'thwart the rising blast,
  As eve's dun shades enwrapt the bellowy main
Hoarse broke the waves against the sandy waste,
  And dim and cheerless swept the drizzling rain:
    When, bend'ing o'er the briny spray,
    Stood the genius, old Cathay;
    With angry glare, her eye-balls roll,
    Horror shakes her inmost soul,
  As thus along the strand swells her portentous wail:

    Athirst for pray [*sic*], what ruffian band
    Dares approach this happy land;
    Glimmering thru' the gloom of eve,
    What canvas flutters o'er the wave,
    Plunging thru' the swelling tide,
    What prows the whit'ning brine divide?
—'Tis Albion's bloody cross that flouts the air,
  'Tis Albion's sons that skirt the peaceful shore;
Her cross-oppression's badge—the sign of war,
  Her sons that range the world, and peace is seen no
                            more.

Insatiate spoilers! that with treacherous smiles,
  In wreaths of olive hide the murderous sword:
Ill fare the tribes, unconscious of your wiles,
  Whose honest candour trusts your plighted word
    Hence! ye harbingers of woe—
    Too well your deeds of blood I know:

For 'mid the thickened gloom of night,
Oft as I speed my watchful sight,
A monitory voice I hear—
Keen Sorrow's thrilling cry awakes my list'ning ear.

A cry resounds from Ganges flood,
There Oppression's giant brood
Wide the scythe of ruin sweep,
And desolated districts weep;
Terror waves the scourge on high,
Patient Mis'ry heaves the sigh.
Lo! meagre Famine drains the vital springs,
And points from far, when yawns the darksome grave:
Her gifts in vain profusive Plenty flings,
-Stern Avarice guards the store, nor owns the wish to
save.

From Niger's banks resound the shriek of woe,
There inly pining mourns the hapless slave;
Fraud proudly braves the light with shameless brow,
And floating charnels plow the restless wave.
Behold in desolate array,
The captives wind their silent way;
Amid the ranks, does Pity find,
A pair, by fond affection join'd;
Fell Rapine, reckless of their pain,
Blasts Mercy's final hope—denies a common chain.

Hear, O my sons the warning cry,
And while you breathe the pitying sigh,
Deep on Memory's tablet trace
These triumphs of Britannia's race,
From age to age, from sire to son
Let the eternal record run:
And when, with hollow hearts, and honey'd tongues,
These slaves of gold advance their blood stain'd hand,
Shrink from the touch—Remember India's wrongs—
Remember Afric's woes—and save your distin'd [*sic*]
land.

This denigrating view of the Macartney mission, rather than the official flattering one of the British press, was again expressed in Philadelphia by Robert Waln, Jr. twenty years later—a development that I shall treat in Chapter Thirteen. But even though Staunton was given mixed reviews in America, he attracted considerably more attention than Van Braam, who was greatly eclipsed by his British competitors. The neglect of the latter's literary achievement has continued to the present day.

The Premises of Proclus

T he French comparatist Etiemble has richly documented the process in eighteenth century Europe by which the favorable attitude toward Chinese religion and philosophy deriving from Jesuits and deists gave way to suspicion and distrust generated in large measure by travelers and merchants. We have seen that in America the reports of the latter group similarly tended to dim the prestige of China as a nation of philosophers. The European transition from excessive admiration of China to prudent wariness had taken place gradually, having originally emerged at the beginning of the century in the observations of Defoe and Montesquieu and somewhat later in those of Rousseau. Conscious American reaction against Chinamania seems to have begun with Timothy Dwight, who in a satirical poem *The Triumph of Infidelity*, 1788, ridiculed what he considered the exaggerated respect accorded in Europe to Chinese culture in large measure because of the influence of Voltaire. In reference to the emperor who had built the Great Wall to defend his country from the Tartars and then burned all its ancient records, Dwight caustically inquired in a footnote in which of these two actions he had done most good for his countrymen "if the books, he burnt, were like those written by them afterwards" (1969(1): 344–45). In the verse passage to which this note is affixed Dwight similarly ridiculed the philosophy, religion, and boasted antiquity of China.

> There, mid a realm of cheat, a world of lies,
> Where alter'd nature wears one great disguise,

> Where shrunk, mishapen bodies mock the eye,
>   And shrivell'd souls the power of thought deny,
> Mid idiot Mandarins, and baby Kings,
> And dwarf Philosophers, in leading-strings,
> Mid senseless votaries of less senseless Fo,
> Wretches who nothing even seem'd to know,
> Bonzes, with souls more naked than their skin,
> All brute without, and more than brute within,
> From Europe's rougher sons the goddess [of infidelity] shrunk,
> Tripp'd in her iron shoes, and sail'd her junk,
> Nice, pretty, wondrous stories there she told,
> Of empires, forty thousand ages old,
> Of Tohi, born with rainbows round his nose,
> Lao's long day—Ginseng alchymic dose.

In another footnote, Dwight maintained that the medicinal virtues ascribed by the Chinese to ginseng are as illusory as is placing the date of the origins of the Chinese empire as far back as 40,000 years.

Dwight's disparagement of China was immediately attacked by the famous lexicographer Noah Webster in a review of *The Triumph of Infidelity* in the *American Magazine* for July 1788. Webster berated the poetic author, whose identity he may not have known, for unjustifiably denigrating the Chinese merely because they are not Christian. "Is it possible," he asked, "that a man who attempts to vindicate christianity can seriously call the *Mandarins, Kings* and *Philosophers* of China *Idiots, babies,* and *dunces,* and the Bonzes, *brutes* and something below brutes?"

> The chief men of a nation too, celebrated thro' the world for the most perfect system of ethics and civil government ever carried into execution—and for improvements in philosophy and the arts that vie with those of ancient Greece and Rome? And all for what? Why merely because they are not *christian* . . . because they lived two thousand years *before Christ* without any knowledge of him, and because they expelled from their empire the christian missionaries, whose vices were so glaring as to give the lie to their doctrines, and whose avarice and ambition threw whole provinces into confusion. Such language will never pass with men of christian candor and meekness, either for sense, satire, or reasoning; much less for an honest zeal for religon.

In his later *Travels in New England and New York,* published in 1805, Dwight several times compares the physical extent of the American continent with that of China. Although the Chinese have very corrupt morals, he affirms, they also have as a nation "mild and gentle manners." He then queries, "May not such manners grow as effectively out of freedom, intelligence, and Christianity, as out of idolatry, ignorance, and slavery" (1969(2)4: 371)?

Dwight compares the American colonists with the immediate descendants of Noah, when the world was "of one language and one speech" and recognizes that modern China also possesses a single language in an extensive territory (1969(2)4: 368–9). He predicts, however, that "in less than two centuries the population of the American States will in all probability exceed that of China, and the extent of territory occupied by it will be quadrupled" (1969(2)4: 368). Here he was following the preface to the first volume of the *Transactions* of the American Philosophical Society, which predicted in 1771 that "could we be so fortunate as to introduce the industry of the Chinese, their arts of living and improvements in husbandry . . . America might become in time as populous as China," a prospect that American public opinion at the turn of the present century no longer views with equanimity. In regard to language, Dwight, like several of his contemporary Western observers, remarks that English is wonderfully superior to Chinese. "It is written with alphabetical letters. It already includes nearly all the learning and science, and generally all the useful information found in the world. In words which denote different ideas, it is more copious than any other" (ibid.).

Dwight's attack on China was relatively mild and motivated more by opposition to Voltaire and the deists than by personal antipathy toward Chinese culture. An unrelieved vitriolic portrayal of the Middle Kingdom appeared, however, in 1811 in a lengthy essay entitled "On the Genius of the Chinese" in four numbers of a Philadelphia Magazine, the *Port-Folio*, (vol. 5: April, 342–56, May, 418–36, June, 493–506, vol. 6, August, 112–23). Outdoing the worst of Defoe, Rousseau, and the European travelers in undisguised animosity, the essay was written by a citizen of Baltimore, using the pseudonym Proclus. So far I have been unsuccessful in my attempts to identify him further. This author had never visited China; indeed at least three-fourths of his material is derived from merely three sources: the compilation of Du Halde and the travels of two members of the Macartney embassy, Sir George Staunton and John Barrow. He completely ignores the work of his fellow American Van Braam, the existence of which he was probably not aware. For special topics Proclus draws in addition upon abbé Barthelemy, Blackstone, Burlamaqui, Campbell (Phil Rhetoric), De Pauw, Hume, Sir William Jones, Adam Smith, and Philip Strahlenburgh. The last name on this list, Strahlenburgh, is notable because no American besides Proclus seems to have mentioned this Swedish geographer or his *An Historical-geographical Description of the North and Eastern parts of Europe and Asia* (London: 1736). Proclus also introduces

Hume, Gibbon, and Voltaire in order to denounce their anti-Christian views which he associates with their favorable opinions on China. Completely lacking firsthand knowledge of his subject, Proclus builds his essay on conclusions and theories derived entirely from literary sources. He freely contradicts Du Halde when the latter is favorable to China, and uniformly accepts the disparaging testimony of Staunton and Barrow.

He affirms that he had originally adopted the usual favorable notions concerning the antiquity and civilization of the Chinese, but had come to diametrically opposite conclusions as a result of further reading (5: 420). Although rejecting Athanasius Kircher's theory that the Chinese are racial descendants of the Egyptians, Proclus, nevertheless, specifically argues that the Egyptians along with the Assyrians are older than the Chinese. He discards the related notion of Joseph de Guignes, father of Vam Braam's interpreter, that China was an Egyptian colony on the grounds of racial differences in countenance and figure, but gives no evidence of greater Egyptian antiquity. His arguments are limited to denying any great age to China without specific comparisons to other cultures. One of his main arguments is linguistic, that Chinese writing was originally hieroglyphic, in other words, that ideograms are pictorial, and that no major change in them has taken place for more than two thousand years. He then adds to this assumption the charge that the failure to alter the written system of communication is a proof of national inflexibility and tyrannical government rather than of great age. From these enormous steps in illogic, he comes to the conclusion "that the growth of genius and learning, will ever be in proportion to the degree of civil liberty and freedom of discussion allowed to the people, and the means they might have, for the facile acquirement of the language" (5: 349). After establishing to his own satisfaction the inferiority of Chinese linguistics, Proclus accepts the opinion that the Chinese are racial descendants of the Tartars, but rejects the Noachide conjecture that he ascribes to Barrow that the Tartars are the direct progeny of Noah.

Proclus's final method of denying Chinese antiquity is to challenge Chinese records and traditions. He argues that universal history shows that knowledge develops slowly and gradually among all peoples; whereas the history of China indicates a sudden access to wisdom and knowledge in the reign of the first emperor Fo-hi followed by centuries of obscurity and ignorance. As late as the seventeenth century, he charges, the Chinese were deprived of even elemental knowledge of geography and astronomy and possessed no monuments or remnants of antiquity by which to substantiate their claims of great age.

Since the Great Wall would seem to offer concrete evidence of a venerable monument, Proclus in his next essay denies its antiquity, dating it as no earlier than 200 B.C., and describing it as a "huge memorial of folly, and loss of labor" (5: 419). He next alleges that "the extreme superstition and credulity" of Chinese philosophers and literati completely rule out "the possibility of their having any *science* or *knowledge* peculiar to them-selves." Their philosophy, he affirms, comprises "a few trite maxims," no doubt a reference to Confucius. Somewhat puzzling, however, is his cate-gorizing the ranks of the literati as being somehow degenerate because of the "admission of *foreigners* to the first literary posts, to the exclusion and injury of *natives*, equally endowed with the requisite qualifications" (5: 420). This is probably a reference to the preferential treatment accorded to Ricci and later Catholic missionaries. Reverting to his doubts concern-ing the antiquity of the Chinese nation, he repeats his charge that no monuments or other proofs of great age can be produced and alleges that the Catholic missionaries had accepted the tradition of antiquity for politi-cal reasons, for to deny it would have subjected them to banishment or popular indignation (5: 423). After left-handed compliments to Du Halde concerning "the force of his genius, and the logical nature of his deduc-tions," Proclus attacks his affirmation that the Chinese recorded an eclipse of the sun in the year 2155 B.C., citing the astronomer Cassini as authority that an eclipse could not have occurred at that time. In the same spirit he denies the authenticity of coins and books that Du Halde had accepted as ancient. Then on the basis of these denials, he affirms that the Chinese as a people are "debased by tyranny, immersed in superstition, and sunk in vice" (5: 429). He then proceeds to excoriate Voltaire and Gibbon for their complimentary treatment of China, remarking that the most captious and skeptical minds on some subjects may be the most passive and credulous on others. He introduces the two renowned infidels primarily because their opinion that China had an enormous population two thousand years B.C. necessarily conflicts with the Biblical theory of a universal flood shortly before. In concluding this essay, Proclus quotes Sir William Jones to the effect that "they have no ancient monuments from which their origin can be traced" and that "their sciences are wholly exotic; and their mechanical arts have nothing in them characteristic of a particular family" (5: 436).

In his next essay, dealing with science and the arts, Proclus returns to linguistic arguments, ascribing much of the alleged backwardness of the Chinese to the nature of their language based, as it is, on a prodigious number of characters and to their method of rote learning. He disagrees with the opinion of Staunton that the absence of grammar makes learning the language easier, arguing that "the labour of storing the memory with all their characters, and a huge volume of the works of Confucius" far overbalances the supposed impediments of grammar (5: 495). The minute attention to sounds and figures, moreover, prevents the Chinese from understanding the workings of the mind. Not only is the Chinese language "utterly unsuitable as an instrument of philosophy," according to Proclus, but the "mental imbecility, abasement, and indolence" of the people have kept them from acquiring the rudiments of logic, mathematics, astronomy, and geography (5: 498).

Spanish writers more than those of any other Western countries have concerned themselves with the development of medicine in China, and Proclus is unusual among writers in English in following their example of stressing the healing art. He derives nearly all his information, however, from Staunton. Ever since the thirteenth century voyages to Asia of Guillaume de Rubruquis, the Chinese have been given credit for discovering the use of the pulse in medical treatment (Etiemble 1988: 102). But Proclus characteristically minimizes the value of this procedure. He also takes pleasure in citing from Staunton the account of the treatment of a patient by opening passages for the escape of an adverse vapor or spirit (presumably the use of acupuncture), a treatment that gave no relief until a Western physician using Western methods discovered that the patient was suffering from rheumatism and a fully-formed hernia (5: 502). The invention of gun powder and printing was also generally attributed to the Chinese throughout the eighteenth century. Proclus says absolutely nothing about printing and only grudgingly admits the Chinese priority in gunpowder. He has considerably more to say about their ignorance of the use of muskets and the inferiority of their cannons to Western ones. He also passes over with a single sentence the Chinese invention of silk manufacture, which, he adds, they have not improved in any way. Immediately after acknowledging the celebrity and excellence of Chinese porcelain, he indicates that the manufacture of glass was not known in China until introduced in the seventeenth century and that the Chinese had no knowledge of clocks until they received models of them from Europe. Despite this series of grudging admissions, Proclus concludes that the Chinese depend for their art upon mechanical dexterity and that a nation that has little but the play of animal ingenuity to its credit cannot be considered "one jot above barbarity" (5: 405).

In his final essay, on Chinese political relationships, Proclus adopts Hume's opinion that the nature of a people is reflected in its government (6: 113). Characteristically Proclus charges that the Chinese political system at the time was the only one in existence that could be characterized as purely arbitrary. For him this meant cowardly weakness of the people and tyrannical oppression by the rulers. Proclus was not opposed to a monarchical system like that of England; he was denouncing what was known in the period as "absolute" in contrast to "pure" monarchy. Popular belief both in and out of China held that its system of government was that of patriarchy, but Proclus insisted that it was tyranny. The much admired appearances of the emperor on ceremonial occasions such as spring planting, Proclus converts to spectacles of pomp and power to impress imbecile minds with awe and adoration (6: 118). He argues, moreover, that the Chinese system of taxation is oppressive and wasteful, devoted to imperial magnificence and splendor rather than to provision for times of famine. In his opinion, periodic famines did not result from overpopulation but rather from inadequate governmental regulation. Although he had never seen China, he maintains in opposition to one of his authorities, Sir George Staunton, who had visited the country, that the tax burden in China was greater than that in any European nation. I shall not summarize his argument, but rather quote his conclusion, which not only encapsulates his economic arguments but betrays his prejudiced attitude toward China throughout his treatise as a whole. The nation of China exhibits, he contends,

> the prevalence of customs, absurd and trivial, giving the brightest sanction, though repugnant to reason, to the most important and serious actions of life; the utmost degree of tyranny, in its basest form, exercised in oppression, under the deceptive mask of paternal affection and authority; the property of the subject extorted without reason and dissipated upon objects neither necessary to the welfare, nor tending to the benefit of the state; a system composed of ingredients, pernicious, cruel, and base, and operating to produce a temperament, rather not wretched than happy, not diseased than wholesome. (6: 133)

Crude, prejudiced, and uninformed, the essay of Proclus is a diatribe rather than a serious portrayal. It cannot be considered as representative of American attitudes, but unfortunately neither can it be dismissed as an aberration, for there was no generally accepted Western attitude by which it can be judged. One explanation for the anti-Chinese prejudice of Proclus may be found in the editorial policies of the periodical in which his essays appeared. The reactionary ideology of the *Port Folio* was clear, visible, and well-recognized. The editor, Joseph Dennie, was a staunch conservative, a defender of classical taste, the church, and inherited wealth. As an outspoken adherent of the Federalist party, he bitterly opposed Jeffersonian democracy and the ideals of the French Revolution. His editorial policies, therefore, consistently rejected the theological and political notions generally associated with the French philosophes. It can hardly be argued that throughout the Enlightenment only deists and writers with liberal political views were friendly toward China, but it is historically true that concepts associated with the Middle Kingdom such as Confucian morality, patriarchal government, and religious toleration conformed to the views of most deists and were not entirely compatible with religious orthodoxy. It is not merely coincidental that the three American authors to deliver panegyrics on China, Franklin, Paine, and Jefferson, were all deists.

A more moderate view of China appeared in the *Port Folio* in February, 1819, in an article with the modest title "Careful observations by one having had a long residence among the people in China" (8 [series 3] 91–111). Like that of Proclus, the identity of this author has remained unknown. An editorial introduction indicates that he is "a gentleman of this city, now abroad," but I am not aware of any Philadelphian who in 1819 could claim a "long residence" in China. Robert Waln, Jr., who is treated in the next chapter, did not go to Canton until the same year, 1819, and his residence there was measured by months rather than years. A remote possibility is that the Philadelphia gentleman is the author of a work titled "A journal of a residence in China by a young American during the years 1817, '18 and '19" listed under "Recent Publications" in the *American Magazine* for 1824 (1: 380). Unfortunately I have been unable to discover any other trace of this publication. The introduction to the *Port Folio* article further affirms that the author "does not bewilder himself and his readers in dissertations on absurd ceremonies and ridiculous rites, nor does he appear to think it worth the trouble even to name the wretched drama of this country." The reference to drama may have been intended as a slight upon Van Braam's enthusiastic description of the sentimental play that was acted for his benefit and treated in the previous chapter.

The author stresses the uniformity of the Chinese: they all perform the same rites and ceremonies and follow the same customs, habits, and manners except those arising from the possession of wealth or an exalted station. Nearly everyone can read except members of the lowest class, but the average ability is greatly limited. Most people are familiar with only a few of the thousands of characters of which the language consists. The education of the poor is so circumscribed as to convey little instruction, "merely exercising the memory to retain a few characters, only sufficient for the commonest purposes of life, or to read those numberless absurd, as well as obscene tales and fables, with which the literature of China abounds" (8: 92). This is the only comment on literature in the article, and it is somewhat surprising in its reference to obscenity. Other observers to the contrary praise the high morality of Chinese letters. It may be that this writer had encountered the great social novel of the seventeenth century *Ching Ping Mei*, but even this classic should be termed erotic rather than pornographic. The writer adds in a footnote that the obscene works to which he refers may be obtained by paying the police a trifling sum (ibid.). He affirms that there is not a single public hospital or humane institution of any description anywhere in the empire and calls this condition a "great national disgrace to China." He asserts, moreover, that crowds of homeless beggars live and die in the streets and vividly describes the sordid sight of indigent souls starving in the open air.

Crime is widespread. A strict penal code prohibits people from walking the streets at night, and those who have permission to travel must carry a lantern. Since most homes have only one story, they are easily entered by thieves. Pawnbrokers shops established by the government contribute to the prevalence of robbery and housebreaking. This writer affirms that there is not a single institution in China, regardless of intent, that has not become useless or pernicious through corruption. He asks rhetorically, "who is there that does not feel a glow of pleasure when he reads of the humane intentions of the Chinese emperors in opening the public granaries established to relieve the poor when there is a famine?" He wishes that he could speak in favor of this praiseworthy custom, but instead reminds his readers that "it is well known, that such calamities are frequently augmented by the cruelty and avarice of those who are appointed to alleviate them. The emperor is often obliged to take off the heads of the mandarins who superintend the granaries, in order to suppress the popular tumults which are executed by the extortions of these faithless servants" (8: 98).

The only possibility of reform that this author envisions is the total subversion of the Tartar dynasty and placing the descendants of the ancient emperors on the throne with the aid of a European army or through the revolt of the people themselves. He does not expect the latter to take place, however, since the people are too debased, abject, and corrupt to maintain a unity of sentiments and action. They are even known to sell their chiefs when difficulties arise. "Notwithstanding his flaming manifestoes, it is the emperor's money, and not his arms, that keeps him on the throne" (8: 98). It would, therefore, be "an act of real humanity, if the powers of Europe were to combine against an usurpation and tyranny of the very worst sort; a ferocious despotism which has brought misery and wretchedness on a once happy people, perverted their native dispositions, ruined their morals, and made them slaves to vice as well as injustice" (8: 101). The Philadelphia author maintains that previous writers are incorrect in assuming that a populous country such as China could easily resist an invasion. In his opinion, the people are not only divided and disaffected, but "entirely ignorant of the arts of war, and as pusilanimous as unskillful." They would fall before a well-disciplined European army like the largest flock of sheep before a peasant with a well-directed club (8:

101). These are precisely the sentiments of Daniel Defoe, who in *The Farther Adventures of Robinson Crusoe*, had affirmed a century earlier that "a million of their Foot could not stand before one embattled Body of our Infantry" (1905: 548).

The Philadelphia author grants that most of the Chinese are naturally quick and intelligent (8: 92), and he feels that their industry, ingenuity, and economy "are worthy of the protecting arm of a wise and good government, which would know how to punish their faults and reward their virtues" (8: 101). He maintains, however, that they cannot on their own become a great independent nation because they lack the "energy of soul and physical conformation" to bring it about. "They are constitutionally, a feeble race of men, and where policy, habits and customs, all conspire against the growth of noble sentiments and physical strength, we must expect to see much submission; but when it is joined to some native good and valuable qualities, we cannot help deploring their misfortunes and grieving to see mildness trodden under foot, instead of being cherished and encouraged" (8: 101).

The concluding paragraph of the article embodies a similarly moderate tone, combining severe judgments on the shortcomings of Chinese society with a tolerant attitude toward the moral nature of the people.

> If I have attributed to their government, or the nation, a character they do not deserve, my ears and eyes deceived me, for I could not discover, with all my care, the slightest indications of that proud preeminence which they assume over Europeans, and which the Jesuits and others are so prone to concede to them. On the contrary, they exhibit a most deplorable contrast to every thing that is great, wise, noble and honourable; and their government, which has been so highly extolled, is the impure source from whence the black stream of vice flows to infect the whole nation. . . . I believe the Chinese generally, to be naturally deficient of courage; but in other respects, they are an excellent, mild, well-disposed people, who, under a good government, might be made most valuable subjects, and probably, by the force of education, good soldiers. At present they are literally a flock of sheep, in comparison with Europeans, and their armies of millions would be as easily routed and slaughtered.

Not only does the author evince a wholesome impartiality, notably lacking in Proclus, but his opinions, based as they are on personal observations, have a certain ring of authority perhaps founded on the residence in Canton that he claims.

CHAPTER

12

The American Marco Polo: The Magnum Opus of Robert Waln, Jr.

O ne of the most curious and rare books in the entire history of the relations between America and China appeared in Philadelphia in 1823. Written by a young native of that city, Robert Waln, Jr., who had passed several months in Canton as supercargo of his father's ship the *Caledonia* in 1819–20, the book is massive in size and comprehensive in coverage. It comprises 475 quarto pages of 650 words each or a total of about 308,000 words, an undertaking that for the time and place can be compared only to Cotton Mather's *Magnalia Christi Americana: or, the Ecclesiastical History of New-England* that has roughly twice the number of words. In scope, however, Waln's work is vastly more comprehensive than Mather's, limited as the latter is to the progress of religion in the colonies of New England. Waln published only half of his thoughts on the Middle Kingdom in book form. If the other half, now in manuscript in the Library Company of Philadelphia, were taken into account, the total numnber of words would approximate that of Mather's colossal work. Waln's perspective covers the entire history of the Chinese nation and much of its culture.

Mather, of course, adorned his history with a theme—that of divine providence establishing America as a privileged land for a chosen people; Waln's work has no central theme and is presented entirely as information. Mather when his work was published was fifty-five years of age; Waln at his publication date was merely twenty-nine. The half title of his book reads simply *History of China*, but the title page lists an all-encompassing range of topics: *China: Comprehending a view of the origin, antiquity, history, religion, morals, government, laws, population, literature, drama, festivals, games, women, beggars, manners, customs, &c. of that empire, With Remarks on the European Embassies to China, and the Policy of Sending a Mission from the United States to the Court of Pekin. To which is added a Commercial Appendix, containing a synopsis of the trade of Portugal, Holland, England, France, Denmark, Ostend, Sweden, Prussia, Trieste, and Spain, in China and India: and a Full Description of the American Trade to Canton, Its Rise, Progress, and Present State: with Mercantile Information, Useful to the Chinese Trader and General Merchant.*

Considerable information concerning the sources and process of composition of Waln's *China* may be gleaned from an extensive collection of his manuscripts in the Library Company of Philadelphia upon which the following account is based. While carrying on his duties as a supercargo in Canton in the years 1819–1820, Waln had already entertained the notion of writing about China and toward that end had begun research in the library of the British Factory in Canton, which at the time he thought contained among its 3,700 volumes "all the published accounts of China." He soon realized that the Canton collection was inadequate, however, and compiled a bibliography of thirty-three titles to be procured on his return to Philadelphia. Sometime after 1822, he made up a companion list of nineteen "authors on China," only two of which were carried over from the preceding one. On the homeward voyage of the *Caledonia* early in 1820, he conceived the general plan of his work, writing out two separate title pages almost identical to the one eventually published and composing essays on most of the topics mentioned in the title. Some of the individual essays he published separately in the local newspaper, the *National Gazette*, before soliciting subscriptions for his *China* in book form. He issued the call for subscribers in the *National Gazette* on 30 October 1821 and on three days of each week for the subsequent two months. The book was to be issued in parts at $1.50 for each one, consisting of about 125 quarto pages, payable on delivery and "printed at discretion," that is, according to the printer's time schedule. The final number, it was promised, would be issued within six months from the commencement of publication. Waln's printer, J. Maxwell, however, was dilatory, for the first part comprising 133 pages did not appear until April 1823, when the *National Gazette* welcomed it editorially on the first day of the month.

> This is one of the most considerable literary enterprises in which an American has ever embarked, whether we consider the bulk which it must have, or the historical and philosophical research and erudition which the proper execution of it implies. . . . What he has published furnishes abundant evidence that he has explored, with the utmost

assiduity, all the writers, ancient and modern, within the reach of an American, who refer to his subject. . . . He has combined with the most interesting and instructive details concerning the geography and history of a nation whose annals and situation are eminently curious, much judicious enquiry and criticism, which reduce the statements of other writers to their true value and circumscribe general results within the bounds of probability and real testimony. This production is a creditable specimen of a kind of investigation and toil, new in this country, at least in the walks of profane, constradistinguished from sacred literature [perhaps a reference to Mather's *Magnalia Christi*]. We contemplate this elaborate digest of recondite facts and speculations touching a vast Asiatic empire, and this great body of reference to the text of historians, travellers, classics of all ages, and of various languages, with equal surprise and pleasure. There are few among us, who have the leisure and ability to follow the example of Mr. Waln; but it may be enjoyed as a foretaste of what will at some period be accomplished by other Americans in a similar way, in relation perhaps to the countries of our own continent, as well as those of the old world.

Although presented in somewhat grandiloquent language, this justly-deserved tribute to Waln has an importance of its own as the first recognition that history writing represents a significant genre in American literature and as a prediction of the achievements of historians such as Parkman and Bancroft who later in the century would attain international recognition.

The second part of Waln's book also appeared in 1823, but the third part, according to an ink inscription on a four-part set in the Library Company of Philadelphia, did not appear until April 1824 and the fourth part not until June of the same year. This was considerably beyond the time limit of six months set forth in Waln's proposal. These four parts, moreover, covered merely the first four topics of the title, that is, the origin, antiquity, history, and religion of the Chinese people. Further parts were never printed in book form, although most of the later topics set forth in Waln's title were treated as essays in the *National Gazette* between June 1821 and August 1823. In the single printed volume of *China*, comprising the first four parts, there is no summarizing paragraph or even final sentence indicating that any kind of a conclusion had been reached. Probably Waln or his printer Maxwell was discouraged from publishing a second volume because of a lack of public response. Since his work was "printed and published for the author," it presumably had no commercial potentialities. Also Waln died in 1825, two years after the appearance of the initial parts of his book.

Even though Waln wrote one of the most comprehensive books of history and cultural anthropology in early American letters, all that Simpson's *Lives of Eminent Philadelphians* says about his intellectual background is that he received a "liberal education." Apparently, therefore, he did not study at the University of Pennsylvania or any other institution of higher learning. He published four other books before his *China*. Two of these satirized Philadelphia society by means of the device of placing a foreign traveler in the Quaker city, *The Hermit in America on a Visit to Philadelphia*, 1819, and *The Hermit in Philadelphia*, 1821. Waln's traveling recluse is an octogenarian native of Guiana, whose features and color are identical with those of the citizens of Philadelphia. His two other books are also satires, but in verse, *American Bards*, 1820, and *Sisyphi Opus: or, Touches at the Times*, 1820. He wrote several of the entries in *Biographies of the Signers of the Declaration of Independence*, 1823–24, a *Life of the Marquis de Lafayette*, 1825, and an account in a medical journal of an asylum for the insane established by the Quakers near Philadelphia.

A preliminary manuscript version of *China* now in the Library Company of Philadelphia was composed at sea on the *Caledonia* in 1820. The printed version, however, based as it is on nearly all the major books on China available at the time, required months of research later at the Athenaeum Library and the Library Company. Since his father was a director of the latter institution, Waln had permission to withdraw books for use at home. It is, nevertheless, astounding that such a comprehensive book on a subject as esoteric as Chinese history and culture could have been written and published in America in the first quarter of the nineteenth century. It is equally astounding that it could have been almost completely neglected until the present day. Even now it is fascinating reading.

Although Waln had spent a brief period in Canton as a supercargo, he makes clear in his preface that he is not using his own experiences as his major source. Indeed he admits relying primarily upon the relations of Catholic missionaries and the narratives of modern travelers, despite the characteristic drawbacks of each one.

> The descriptions of the Fathers, in their original and undefined state contain all the important points relative to the country and people which they describe [but they are] so confused by the credulity and superstitions of the narrators, and intermixed with such gross exaggerations and improbable statements, that, without the advantages of modern experience, by which they are characterized and explained, it would be almost impracticable to obtain from them a proper, or even probable, insight into the character and condition of the Chinese nation.

Waln adopts an equally cautious attitude toward the reports of travelers. The route of ambassadors through China, he affirms, is in general unvaried and offers little opportunity for personal observation. Anticipating accusations leveled at organized tourism in some modern societies, he charges that foreign visitors are "restricted in their excursions, prohibited from entering cities, and even in many instances confined to their houses." The best writers on the subject, he maintains, "are precisely those who weighed, at a distance, the merits and demerits of the people, and formed their deductions in a cool and dispassionate manner, unswayed by temporary excitement, beyond the reach of personal bias, and secure from the influence of local misrepresentation." Despite this rational caveat against subjectivity, it is somewhat surprising to read Waln's further remark that "there is not a modern traveller in China, whose narrative will convey such just and well settled information in relation to the Chinese, as the learned Dissertations of Renaudot, and the Recherches Philosophiques of De Pauw." Today neither Théophraste Renaudot nor Corneille De Pauw is considered an expert on Chinese affairs. Renaudot edited *Anciens relations des Indes, et de la Chine*, an extremely informative manuscript concerning two Mohammedan visitors to China during the Middle Ages, and De Pauw in his *Recherches philosophiques sur les Egyptiens et les Chinoises*, 1774, accepted Kircher's notion that China had been peopled by the ancient Egyptians. Neither of these writers had ever left Europe. In the body of his work, however, Waln cites practically all of the contemporary authorities on China, whether missionaries, travelers, or philosophers, and he does not in any way accord Renaudot or De Pauw preferred treatment. Indeed in one passage he ridicules De Pauw for writing "from his easy chair at Berlin" instead of going in person to discover that Chinese tombs, contrary to his assertion, are not always shaded by trees (1823: 164).

In an ironical reference in his preface to Voltaire and the Encyclopedists, Waln affirms that "we may, like the enthusiasts of France, magnify the profound knowledge of this wonderful people, in civil polity, in morality, in literature, and in all the useful arts and sciences; or, by critical analogies and careful comparisons, establish . . . the corruption of their political system, their neglect of moral duties, their deficiency in real science, their ignorance in every branch of literature," and their generally depraved principles. This summarizing statement leaves little doubt about Waln's personal aversion toward China, although he attempts to give the impression of objectivity by affirming that he has not been influenced by the "*Chinomania* of the Romish writers, or the immoderate incredulity of more modern travelers." In his preliminary version and other materials in manuscript, Waln reveals a strong antipathy to practically all aspects of Chinese life and culture, but in his printed volume he moderates his criticism and even occasionally introduces words of praise.

Even though among his authorities he relies more on travelers who had recently set foot on Chinese soil than on any other group, he disparages the importance of personal experience even at the risk of detracting from his own credibility. Admitting that he has never penetrated "beyond the verge of the Southern frontier" during a short residence in Canton, he describes his method of composition as combining "such personal knowledge of the habits, character, appearance, and peculiarities, of the natives, as might enable him, with more confidence, to form his opinions from a general review of those writers who possessed greater practical advantage than himself." Today his work would be considered primarily as a study in the history of ideas, and as such it contains a considerable amount of valuable material not to be found in even the most authoritative modern texts.

Between his preface and his first chapter, Waln inserts 133 pages of "Preliminary Observations" comprising a geographical view of China and a survey of how Western knowledge of the country had grown progressively. I could not hope to summarize this part or any others of Waln's book without turning the present chapter into a bare digest. Instead I shall merely draw attention to some of his comments that seem to be pertinent to contemporary interests.

Waln observes that the name China is completely unknown to the inhabitants of this area, who refer to it in their language as the Middle Kingdom, for which, however, he does not supply the Mandarin word, *Chung Kuo*. He indicates that the English word for the country, like the Italian *Cina* and the German *Schina*, derives from a conquering family named Tsin. The Latin *Sina*, Waln maintains, originally had no reference to China, but instead to Siam or other westward lands (11). He also argues that the Arabs used the word *Sin* or *Sines* in reference to Cochin China [78]. Pekin, he informs us, was known to Marco Polo as *Cambalu*, the capital of *Khatai*, that is, Cathay in English. Cambalu is based on the Mongol name Khan, a northern province (26). The name appears in *Paradise Lost*, and some modern critics have suggested that Milton did not realize that Paquin and Cambalu in the following lines both represent the city of Pekin:

> . . . from the destined walls
> Of Cambalu, seat of Cathaian Can,
> And Samarkand by Oxus, Temir's throne
> To Paquin, of Sinaean Kings. [lines 387–90]
> (Etiemble 1989: 124)

Waln cites the extreme variation in the population figures for Pekin given by different writers, extending from one million in some accounts to twenty million in others [35] and points to similar extremes in the computation of the size of the city. One estimate indicates the entire length of the walls from east to west as equivalent to a journey of twenty-three days and another considers the circumference as only fourteen and a half miles (28). Waln may have been familiar with the meticulous calculations of William Maitland in *The History of London* (1739), indicating the length of London and its suburbs "where shortest" as "Six Miles, Three Quarters, Ten hundred and Ninety-one Yards" and the breadth of London as three miles, 170 yards and a half. Through his own statistical computation of the number of people in each square mile of the land area of China, Waln rejects the claims of Jesuits and others for "the exuberant population of China" (32). He attributes the absence of offal, or filth and nastiness, in the city streets, not to cleanliness, but to the scarcity of conventional manure for agriculture (32).

His colorful description of these streets provides an excellent example of his crisp and variegated literary style.

The numerous body of barbers, in particular, have no fixed shops, but perambulate the streets, with all the necessary apparatus for shaving the head, and cleansing the ears; they carry a stool, and a small vessel of water, and whoever wishes to undergo either of these operations, sits down in the street, whilst the operator performs his office. To these may be added, itinerant showmen, whose puppets in Canton are too filthy for description [dirt-encrusted or pornographic?]; itinerant booksellers, with their tales and song books for the lower orders; itinerant florists, with large panniers of blooming flowers; pedlars, with their moveable shops of bamboo lattice-work; traveling tinkers, with all their implements of trade, and a portable forge; itinerant jacks of all trades, called in China, *Fia-con-culk-tziang*, with their forges, anvils, coal, furnaces, and tools; china-menders, with their diamond-pointed piercers and fine brass wire; toymen, with their painted pasteboard animals, houses, and boats, their punchinellos and scaramouches; jugglers and merry-andrews, and mountebanks, floating and refloating ribbons in the air, of one hundred feet in length, rolling china vases along their arms as if by spontaneous impulse, or exhibiting their astonishing feats of balancing; story-tellers, beguiling their hearers of a few *tchen* by the most gross fabrications; auctioneers, standing upon platforms, and bawling to the crowds around them; quack doctors, distributing their medicines, and describing their admirable effect with rhetorical flourishes; comedians, musicians, fortune-tellers, pork-butchers, ballad-singers, blacksmiths, braziers, coblers; troops of dromedaries laden with coals from Tartary; wheel-barrows and hand-carts stuffed with vegetables; Mahommedans with their red caps; Tartar ladies on horseback, sitting astride like men; carmen, porters, chairmen, horses, mules, asses, camels, carts, chairs, wagons, and the processions of men in office, attended by their numberous retinues, bearing umbrellas and flags, painted lanterns, and a variety of strange insignia of their rank and station; the buying and selling, and bartering of merchandize, arrayed before the doors; the loud bawling of the venders; the wrangling of others; the squalling of music, and the twanging of the barber's tweezers; the cries of the porters;—altogether constitute a scene of bustle and confusion in the principal streets, to which the secluded cross streets afford a miserable contrast. (37)

Who could doubt that Waln had been an eyewitness to these wonders? At this point in his narrative he could well be described as the American Marco Polo.

After treating the great destruction and loss of life brought about by an earthquake early in the eighteenth century, Waln turns to the restriction of dwellings in Chinese cities to a single story. He denies that this limitation represents a precaution against potential harm from natural disasters, but views it instead as a result of sumptuary laws applying to all classes from the meanest to the most elevated person. In this connection, he cites an anecdote "of a mandarin who had transgressed this law, as well as the law of custom, by raising a house to more than the usual height of one story, and who was compelled to pull the building down" (34). The importance of this citation does not lie in the anecdote itself, but in its provenance, "the notes to 'the Pleasing History,' translated from the Chinese." This work, "The Pleasing History," is the novel turned into English by Thomas Percy that Jefferson possessed in his personal library and had recommended to his brother-in-law. For some reason Waln does not cite Percy in his footnotes even though his textual reference quoted above to one of the notes in the latter's edition would seem to indicate that Waln had a firsthand knowledge of the novel itself rather than merely a casual acquaintance with its title. If so, this knowledge must have been acquired after the writing of his unpublished essay "Poetry, General Literature," that is now bound in the fifteenth volume of his manuscripts bearing the date 1820. In this essay he charges that Chinese novels consist of "a tissue of uninteresting details and dry matters of fact, selected from the most vulgar occurrences of life, and abounding in the adventures of strumpets, the prospicious [*sic*] devices of vice and the triumphs of lechery." He also affirms that in China "there are no Pamelas, no Clarissa Harlowes, no Sophia Westerns; . . . the female character is even too degraded to be thought worthy of virtuous record in the pages of a novel." The novel *Hau Kiou Choaan* translated by Percy under the title *A Pleasing History*, however, belongs to a genre of Chinese fiction known as the scholar-beauty romance in which feminine virtue is highly extolled. The female protagonist of *A Pleasing History* actually has many striking resemblances to Clarissa Harlow (Cheung 1989), and, as I have noted in chapter 10, Everard Van Braam highly approved of these resemblances.

Waln continues his discussion of Chinese houses with the remark of a Chinese emperor to a Western missionary "that the ground must be certainly very scarce in Europe, since the inhabitants were forced to build one house on the top of another" (34). This is a variant of the surprised reaction of Emperor Wanli, reported by Ricci, to the report of his eunuchs that the rulers of Europe "sometimes lived on the upper floors of their high buildings." Waln does not cite Ricci as his authority, but instead Guthrie's "System of Geography."

In addition to his preoccupation with the origin of words and civilizations, Waln enjoyed myths, fables, and tales of monsters. He cites from the *Atlas Chinensis* of Montanus, for example, a four-eyed fish with six feet that produced pearls; a fish with the head of a bird, yielding precious stones; sea-crabs that turn to stone when emerging from water; gold fish that leap up and down at the commands of their owners; a yellow creature that is a bird in summer and a fish in winter; birds with beautiful plumage growing out of a flower and living only as long as the flower continues to bloom; tortoises that fly and others that leap about in the manner of grasshoppers; and human beings with two nails on the little toe (24). He also lists a number of miraculous streams from various writers, including one that is always as red as blood; one that shines at night because of its vast quantity of precious stones; one that becomes blue during harvest; one with water too light to float timber; one that is sweet-scented; one that transforms iron into copper; and one that overflows every year on the eighth month (48). On the same page Waln cites a fountain that issues in two branches, one hot, one cold; one that is ice cold at the surface and boiling hot at the bottom; and one that responds to a stone thrown into it by producing thunder and rain. Among fabulous lakes he lists one that petrifies everything falling into it; one that turns copper into iron; one that becomes red as blood when a stone is cast into it and changes leaves into living swallows; one that turns leaves into black birds; and one "that possesses the estimable quality of becoming clear when the city has a good and pious governor, and muddy and thick when it has a bad one" (49). In a note to this passage, Waln offers natural explanations for some of the marvels reported by early European travelers: a mountain of adamant that drew to itself the darts and arrows of a body of Tartars, a nation of monsters with men's heads and dogs' faces, a race of savages with the entire body except the face and hands covered with hair, a land of naked men and women with the faces of dogs, men without heads, and men with mouths in their breasts. He lacked the ingenuity to explain, however, shoals of sirens in Brazil, monopeds in South America, negroes in Africa with feet like the tail of a lobster, one-legged men in Tartary who join together in couples to run with great swiftness, enormous serpents whose only employment is to ravish young girls, a tree with leaves that acquire feet and run away as soon as they fall to the ground, and men and women eighteen inches in height with ears large enough for one to be used as a mattress and the other for a cover (49).

Waln suggests that the annual spring ceremony in which the emperor wields a plough as a stimulus to agriculture is a propaganda event since it is held in an outdoor enclosure or theater. Following Marco Polo, who reported that 25,000 public women reside in the suburbs of Pekin, divided into cadres like an army under the direction of a captain general, Waln remarks on the large number of prostitutes available in Chinese cities. The custom of providing one of these courtesans nightly to foreign embassadors, he speculates, may not have descended to modern times or "perhaps the notice of it, from motives of delicacy, has been suppressed by the gentlemen of the late embassies" (31). Similarly, many of the pleasure boats in a lake to the south of Nanking, he slyly reports, "are rowed by a single female, . . . supposed to follow more than one profession" (56). This rather clever innuendo, however, is a direct quotation plagiarized from Sir George Staunton (1799: 2: 174). His early manuscript version is more caustic and specific. Here he affirms that "these miserable beings who live by prostitution are licensed by the government. On the Pearl River in Canton, their residence is almost exclusively on the water, or in cabins built upon piles below low water mark. . . . They ride in boats of a peculiar construction richly ornamented with bright colours."

Waln's observations of the seamy side of Canton night life are corroborated in an excellent English compilation in concise, straightforward prose summarizing nearly all aspects of Chinese culture under the title *The Chinese Traveller* (London: 1775). This work affirms that English sailors on the river at Canton bargain with fathers and mothers on sampans for kisses from their daughters, but adds that the trade is illicit and subject to fines or corporal punishment. Other vessels called Lob Lob boats, however, have a special understanding with the mandarins and "are well stocked with a number of beautiful young women of different ages, to whom every body, Chinese or European, may have access at any time" (1: 48). A Chinese autobiography written about a decade prior to Waln's visit to Canton also supports his description of the river traffic. The author, Fu Shen, describes his visit to brothel boats as "making the rounds on the river" (1979: 240). He reports that these vessels, known as "flower boats," were anchored in "two parallel rows with a clear space in the centre for small boats to pass up and down. . . . Between the boats, there were wooden piles sunk into the bottom of the river, with movable rattan rings on top allowing the boats to rise and fall with the tide" (1979: 251). Some customers used to go from one girl to another, a practice called in sing-song slang "jumping the trough," and others enjoyed two girls at the same time (1979: 271). Waln was a disapproving critic; Shen, an unabashed satisfied customer. But their facts agree perfectly. More than a curious coincidence, this corroboratory evidence from Chinese literature attests to the authenticity of Waln's recollections.

The final sentence of the geographical review in *China* prefigures the generally denigrating attitude of the body of the book: "If the spirit of scientific researches were once admitted into the great wilderness of China, (for such it relatively is,) the wonderful fertility of nature would assume a still more luxuriant character, and vast and varied sources of knowledge be opened for the general benefit of mankind, which are now pent up or adulterated by the jealousy and ignorance of a half-civilized nation" (58). Again Waln's manuscript version is more extreme

> I may be wrong in not according to this nation, the title of a civilized people, which is granted to them by many writers. They are certainly neither savages, or anthropophagi, but a removal from a state of nature does not alone amount to civilization; there is no progressive improvement in any of the most requisite qualities of civilized man, and if barbarity of disposition, corruption of heart, and propension to fraud & deceit, can confer this dignity upon the Chinese nation, it is eminently entitled to it. There are many virtues among savages which do not exist here, & many vices in the country unknown to the children of nature.

Waln begins his treatment of the progressive increase of knowledge about China in the West with the incursion of Alexander the Great into India and concludes with the relations of the Catholic missionaries at the beginning of the eighteenth century. During the course of this summary, which still has much to offer, he maintains that the navigation of the ancients never extended to the coast of China, that the Sinae were a distinct people from the Chinese, and that silk production may have originated in India (92). Waln accuses the Chinese of falsifying their annals, ascribing to the Chinese scribes the same motives that allegedly led the Jesuits to insert in the same annals records of eclipses and other astronomical data derived from other sources. They did so, he charges, to gratify the vanity of Chinese monarchs (69). Waln's ironic portrayal of the Enlightenment vision of the Middle Kingdom succeeds in disparaging both China and the philosophes:

The French academicians extolled to the skies the profound knowledge of this wonderful people in civil polity, in morality, in literature, and all the useful arts and sciences: and the laborious encyclopedists considered them as not only superior to the rest of Asiatic nations, but at least equal to the most enlightened Europeans. The incredulous philosopher of Ferney condescended, in this instance, to swim with the stream, and to prostitute his talents in the propagation of what, in his heart, he could not possibly believe to be true. (124)

In his own times, Waln concludes, information about China has been limited by the banishment of the missionaries and the vigilant system by which official visitors are kept under surveillance. No additional knowledge would be forthcoming, he predicts, until events would force the restrictive policy of the government to be changed (133).

In his chapter on racial origins, Waln first of all refutes the notion that the Chinese were descendants of Noah, a belief, he charges, founded on the fancied similarities of the builder of the ark to Fo-hi, the legendary first emperor of China. While disposing of the Noah legend and its proponents, he summarizes various theories concerning the universal deluge of the Old Testament. Despite his earlier praise of De Pauw, he dismisses the latter's notion of the descent of the Chinese from the Tartars and also rejects the competing theory of ancient Egyptian origins together with the related hypothesis of a resemblance between Egyptian hieroglyphics and Chinese ideograms. He accepts instead the opinion of Sir William Jones that the Chinese descended from the Hindus. As one of many examples of obvious fabrications and absurd suppositions, he ridicules the debate on whether American Indians were Jews (162). Strangely enough, Waln does not introduce the notion of a possible racial connection between the Chinese and the American Indians, and he does not seem to be aware of it. In the next year, however, he referred to the theory in one of his *National Gazette* essays and took a strong stand against it.

In addition to De Pauw, his main authorities are Adams, Anquetil, Morrison, Sonnerat, Barrow, De Guignes the elder, Montanus, Kircher, Renaudot, Martin Martinius, Du Halde, Winterbotham, Sir William Jones, and Murray's account of Asia, together with at least twice this number of other authorities on subsidiary points. He mentions Van Braam two or three times, but without page references.

Among topics of particular interest, Waln summarizes the alleged similarities between the Chinese Lao-tse and the Greek Pythagoreans (151–52) and rejects biographical parallels between Confucius, Pythagoras, and Herodotus, who were roughly contemporaneous (172). In regard to the Lo-chu, a famous geometric figure introduced in a chapter of the Shu ching of the Confucian *Wu ching*, Waln cites Barrow's ridicule of its alleged sublimity "by comparing it to the common school-boy's trick of the magic square, or placing the nine digits so that they shall make the sum of fifteen every way" (151). Waln concludes "that the whole Chinese nation descended from the *Chinas* of *Menu*, and mixing with the Tartars, by whom the plains of Ho-nan and the more southern provinces were thinly inhabited, formed by degrees the race of men whom we now see in possession of the noblest empire in Asia" (189). Although thus characterizing the Chinese as "the noblest empire in Asia," he was far from accepting Franklin's verdict that they were "the most ancient, and from long Experience the wisest of Nations."

Waln's main source for his subsequent chapter on Chinese history was apparently abbé Grosier's history of China supplemented by nearly all the authorities cited previously in his book. He repeats as one of his chief points that Chinese annals are completely unreliable. As supporting evidence he provides a table of the varying dates attributed to twenty-two dynasties by four Western authorities, Du Halde, Fourmont, de Guignes and Morrison. He, therefore, feels free to restrict his own remarks "to peculiar occurrences and glaring discrepancies, which may afford at the same time a general outline of the history of the people, and the tables with which it is intermingled, and of which it is composed" (229). He similarly points out glaring errors in the recording of eclipses in the *Ch'un-ch'iu* of Confucius. Only one sixth of the occurrences recorded, he charges, are free from suspicion (233). He derides the *Shu-ching* as "a mass of unintelligible fables" (249) and seems to consider the *Wu ching* as more important than the *Ssu shu*. The following passage illustrates his opinion that scant literary merits may be discerned in the *Shih-ching* (the book of poetry or second book in the *Wu ching*):

> Its poetry, say the missionaries, is so beautiful and so melodious, its language so charming, so sublime, and so marked by antiquity, its descriptions so artless and minute, that nothing more is requisite to confirm its authenticity. Father Ko, after honestly confessing that capacity did not permit him to pronounce any opinion of its merit, when compared with Pindar and Horace, affirms without hesitation, that in sublimity of expression and magnificence of ideas, when speaking of the deity, of providence, and of virtue, it is only surpassed by the psalms of David. To prove this he should have cited the ode recording an eclipse of the sun, beginning thus: *"Tenth moon's conjunction, first-day sin-mao, sun had eclipse. All portend bad. Whether sun covered or moon covered, people in general fear bad,"* &c. &c. All this we are assured by the French missionaries is *"très superbe;"* they, moreover, aver that the Chinese poets study nature, and may therefore be compared with Boileau and Horace. Another, with great naïveté, asserts

that none of those passages of Homer, wherein the sound is meant to be "an echo of the sense," are surpassed by *tang-tang*, as an imitation of the sound of the gong. (261–62)

Some of the language in this paragraph, including the poetic quotation, the ridicule of the missionaries' "très superbe," and the comparison to Boileau and Horace is taken without acknowledgment from a review in the *Quarterly Review* (4 [1810] 361–372) by John Barrow of an English translation of some of the poems of K'ien Long.

In his discussion Waln does not take into consideration the difficulties in translating from one language to another or the difference between Chinese, which is composed chiefly of verbs and nouns, that are neither conjugated nor declined, and English, that has both conjugations and declinations as well as adjectival and adverbial designations and prepositions to clarify the meaning. He does recognize these limitations of translation in an unpublished essay in his manuscript volumes (No. 15), but even here displays an unfortunate insensitivity to Chinese esthetic effects.

Waln further ridicules Confucius as a historian because of the "striking similarities" in his account of the lives of the last emperors of two subsequent dynasties. "In both cases they were completely ruled by their respective wives, and both those wives were the most barbarous and wicked wretches of the age. Their peculiar dispositions were remarkably similar; each amused herself with lakes of wine, trees garnished with meats, posture-making drunkenness and debauchery" (244). Waln concludes from the falsities and contradictions of the Chinese annals that "no satisfactory evidence can be adduced in their support, either from astronomical data, from their own records, or from the suggestions of probability itself. Instead of a clear and distinct chronological and historical series, we find a tissue of prodigies, superstitions, and impossibilities" (258). In other passages, he describes the Chinese legendary beginnings of the human race in terms reminiscent of the Western Golden Age. In an account of a reign during which the sun allegedly stood still for ten days, he draws a parallel with Joshua of the Old Testament, typically rejecting the Chinese belief in the event, but accepting that of the Christian scriptures (218).

Probably following Du Halde (1736: 1: 329), Waln describes "two odd sects" that grew up during the Chow dynasty that have some resemblance to competing ethical systems in the West; one affirming that fundamental human relations are based upon benevolence and the other, that they are based upon selfishness. One of the Chinese sects held that "all men were to be loved alike, strangers as well as kindred: the other maintained, that every man ought to take care of himself and his own affairs, without concerning himself about any body else" (278). Waln gives an emperor ruling in A.D. 64 credit or blame for introducing the worship of Fo. Having dreamed of a man of gigantic size, this monarch remembered a saying of Confucius that the Holy One was in the West and, therefore, sent missionaries to India to seek for the true religion. They brought back Fo, idolatry, and the doctrine of transmigration (289).

Throughout his historical summary, Waln continually contrasts his own dim view of Chinese culture with the contrary perspective of Enlightenment thinkers. This dichotomy is particularly evident in the concluding paragraph of his chapter.

> The freedom and felicity of China, so highly extolled by the enthusiasts of Europe, no longer afford food for the reveries of a Vossius or a Voltaire. The mask in which the exaggerations of biassed travellers had concealed the real features of the government has fallen; and it is now firmly established, that the general conduct of that government is unjust, corrupt, partial, and tyrannical; that one chain of servile dependance fetters every rank, from the highest to the lowest: and that not one particle, of what is deemed political freedom, is enjoyed within the precincts of the Chinese empire. (332)

In treating religion, Waln affirms that "an innate belief in the necessity of adoring a Supreme Being does not generally exist" in China; and he ascribes the multiplicity of temples, sacrificial rites, and prayers to superstition and to the fear of temporal misfortunes rather than to a spirit of worship (333). Here he cites his own observations of the temple of Ho-nan in Canton during a "temporary residence" in that city. "Not a single individual, with the exception of the priests, was at any time engaged in acts of devotion; nor, during various visits to the same temple, did I observe any Chinese, not attached to the establishment, within its walls, excepting a party of females, whose pursuit appeared to be pleasure rather than devotion" (333). In another part of the chapter, Waln describes the custom of keeping sacred pigs in a stye in the precincts of the temple, where they "wallow in the filth and stench of years" (390). Waln's colorful style is again worthy of quotation.

> Food is constantly kept before them, and they are suffered to die of old age: whenever this event occurs, the deceased hog is buried with certain ceremonies prescribed by custom. The result of this fattening system is almost incredible: the miserable animals become so loaded with fat that their bellies rest upon the ground, and their features are almost lost; the eyes are completely sunk into the flesh, and a latitudinal crevice alone, extending from ear to ear, marks the precise point beneath which they are concealed.

Waln comments also on the human visitors to the temple.

> Upon entering this theatre of idolatry, we fortunately surprised a party
> of ladies, returning from the performance of their devotions; or, more
> probably, from consulting the sacred oracles, or rubbing the bellies of
> the gods. Our guide was extremely anxious to prevent a meeting, and
> was ably seconded in his exertions, by an old duenna, who, appar-
> ently, had some command over the others: good management, how-
> ever, and a portion of obstinacy, on our part, entirely defeated their
> joint efforts, and the young ladies, by their smiling faces and knowing
> whisperings, seemed to triumph in our success. The whole party,
> with the exception of the old woman, were ornamented with small
> feet, and dressed in a neat and becoming manner. Their features, of
> course, were not handsome, but if their charms had exceeded those of
> "the most beautiful Ophelia," the horrible deformity of their feet,
> and their hobbling gait, could have excited no other feelings than
> those of commiseration and disgust. (391)

Waln's reaction to bound feet is exactly the opposite of Van Braam's, who,
as we have seen, found nothing distasteful in the practice. In his manuscript volume Waln has considerably more to say about Chinese women,
almost none of it favorable. He admits that he has had no contact with
those of the upper or middle classes, except by accident when glimpsing
their faces as they ascended or descended from their palanquins. In his
opinion, not one was beautiful by American standards, with their "small,
half-shut eyes, almost forming in shape the sides of an inverted pyramid,
with corresponding eye-brows, and the pupils drawn towards the center,
joined to their 'cream faces,' 'sicklied o'er with the pale hue of death.' "
The whiteness of the skin, never exposed to the sun, he maintains, has a
"most disgusting effect" despite the use of red and white paint to conceal
the pallor (Vol. 15).

While denying that the Chinese share the innate attachment to a
supreme being noticed in other nations, Waln affirms that "most of the
forms of mythology which figure in the pages of history now exist in
China, except that their indecent parts, and their direct tendency to injure
human life, have been cut off" (334). This apparent reference to the
absence of human sacrifice in China would seem to be praise, rather than
otherwise. He finds in China the equivalent of the Western Diana, Escula-
pius, Mars, Mercury, Pluto, Jupiter, Neptune, and Ceres. After referring
to his doubts concerning the antiquity of the *Shu ching* of Confucius, Waln
observes that it contains "unceasing references to the power and attributes
of Chang-te, *Sovereign Lord*, Hwang tien, *Supreme Heaven*, and Tien,
Heaven" (336). He then provides a fairly accurate, though brief, summary
of the rites controversy in the Catholic Church. "Tien signifies both the

spirit in heaven, and the material heaven: hence, while one order of missionaries admitted the worship of Tien, as the Supreme Being, another forbade it, as idolatrous; thus sowing the seeds of destructive dissentions, which rendered necessary the mediation of the Pope, and degraded the general Christian faith in the eyes of the Chinese."

In his further consideration of Confucius, Waln again concentrates on the *Wu ching* rather than the *Ssu shu* that Franklin and most Europeans considered as the key to the Confucian philosophy. The translation Waln uses is that of the elder de Guignes in volume 23 of the *Mémoires de l'Académie d'Inscriptions*. In regard to Lao Tse, he rejects the hypothesis of previous writers that the Chinese philosopher was the same person as Abaris, a Scythian teacher, who travelled in Greece during the eighth century B.C.

> The idea that Abaris, the Hyperborean, was the same with Lao-tse, is one of those palpable improbabilities, which, without even the recommendation of ingenuity, are so often foisted into the philosophical discussions of learned men, with little other design than that of displaying new ideas, and starting new game, to afford amusement to, and be finally hunted down by, brother sportsmen in the chase of philosophy. Whether M. de Guignes believed that Abaris actually possessed the golden arrow presented to him by Apollo, with which he could travel without taking nourishment, and that he could foretell earthquakes, calm the winds, and drive away pestilence, does not appear; but they are nevertheless equally certain with the alleged appearance of a Chinese philosopher in Greece, seven hundred and sixty-nine years before our era. It may also be remarked, that the Travels of Abaris have occasioned much learned discussion, and that the opinion of Mr. Toland, making him a Scotsman, instead of a Chinese, is quite as well founded as any other. . . . The affable character of Abaris, who, as it is said, sought and cultivated friendship, was totally opposite to that of the solitary and selfish cynics of the Taou-keaou; of whom none are more remarkable than Kwang-shing-tse, who bearded old Hwan-te, and Shan-foo-tse, who passed his life perched in a tree, like a bird in its nest. (351)

Waln does not, however, consistently denigrate the Chinese in relation to the West. After an account of gross superstitions among Chinese seamen, for example, he describes equally absurd instances among those of England, America, and other Western nations (401). "What example of Chinese superstition," he asks, "is more gross than that of the insurance company of Cadiz, which once took the Virgin Mary into formal co-partnership, covenanting to set aside her portion of the profits for the enrichment of her shrine in that city?" (403). Affirming that "superstition is indeed an universal principle," Waln refers to legends concerning the voluntary transformation of men into beasts of prey as a notable illustration. He cites the wizard-tigers of Mexico, the were-wolves of Armorica, the vampires of Slavic countries, the witch-procuresses of Italy, the elegant and yielding fairies clad in white of France, the masculine elves of England, and the gnomes of Germany (404). He also admits that religious persecutions in China have never come near the horror of those recorded in the history of Christianity and presents a sizable listing of infamous cruelties systematically practised in Christian controversies. The persecutions during the Reformation alone, he maintains, "far exceed, in their sanguinary nature, the collected cruelties which have been exercised by all the various sects which have existed in China, and all the governmental persecutions which have occurred."

After separate sections on the existence of Jews and Mohammedans in China in ancient times, Waln turns to accounts of Christians in the same period. He accepts from a variety of sources the report of a Nestorian monument dating from A.D. 782 that was dug up in Si-gan-foo, the metropolis of Shen-see. He denies that it is a forgery of the Jesuits and rejects the treatment of it by Voltaire in his *Essay on General History*. Voltaire, he dismisses as "a poet, who recounts facts, or denies them, without deigning to produce his authorities" and who, therefore, "must not expect to meet with the credit that is due to an historian" (431). Waln also accepts the tradition that the legendary Prester John was an authentic Nestorian and considers as reasonable the view that he was the same person as the Dalai Lama (435).

As I have already indicated, the final paragraph of this chapter and of the fourth and last to be published part of Waln's book has no indication of being a formal conclusion. This paragraph consists for the most part of his own notes on the installation in Canton in 1819 of the first chaplain of the English East India Company, significant to him and to the readers of this book because of the presence of many Americans at the ceremony.

> It is a remarkable fact that this symbol of homage to the Deity has never been officially instituted before the present year. It is inexcusable that a body of Christians should have been so long permanently established amid the allurements of an idolatrous people, without a religious monitor to guard against the seductions which estrange the mind from the fountain of all good, in a country where the day of rest is not held sacred, and the affairs of the world trespass upon the holiness of the Sabbath.—The pulpit is erected in the library of the factory, and together with the temporary pews, is of plain china-wood without ornament or beauty. It is, however, remarkable for being the first that has been raised within the empire of China, for the admission

of a Protestant minister. The pews will not contain more than fifty persons, and not more than one hundred could be accommodated in the whole apartment. The congregation, to-day, consisted of about sixty persons, among whom were many Americans; the chief of the factory having given a general invitation through the medium of the American consul. (475)

Although copies of Waln's *China* are extremely rare today, absent from even some of the major East Coast libraries of the United States, the work was presumably well-known in contemporary Philadelphia. After the advertisements for subscriptions appeared in the *National Gazette* in October 1821, the same periodical published in succeeding months several essays by Waln described as emanating "From the Port Folio of a Canton Supra-Cargo." Those associated with China will be discussed in the next chapter. They cover many of the topics listed in the complete title of Waln's book that were not represented in the parts printed in 1823, but which he had obviously planned to include in subsequent parts. In an editorial comment, the *Gazette* on 27 April 1822 affirmed that one of these essays "gave great pleasure" and another was "not less curious and interesting." From parts of this author's "large work on China, which we have seen," the *Gazette* continued, "we augur full success for the whole, as far at least as abundant, valuable, and well-digested information, presented in a sound, good style, may be sufficient to obtain success."

The true significance of Waln's monumental work—for such it is despite some plagiarized passages, two of which I have pointed out—lies not so much in the narrative it comprises and its anticipation of the great historical literature of the later part of the century, but in the evidence it provides of the accumulated knowledge concerning China available in the United States before 1825. Waln refers to almost every major European work on any aspect of Chinese culture. Since he had never been out of the United States except on his single voyage to Canton, he must have obtained these books in Philadelphia bookstores or libraries, particularly in the Athenaeum and in the Library Company. Many of the titles he used, moreover, had been available in America since the middle and late eighteenth century. Waln's magnum opus, in other words, provides convincing corroborating evidence of the view that Enlightenment America had at its disposition a great deal of information about the history and culture of the greatest empire of the East.

13

The Relevant Writings
of Robert Waln, Jr.

Waln's essays in the *National Gazette* reveal a considerable variety in style and subject matter, ranging from transmission of factual information from European authors to original essays on relations between China and America. I shall treat those which I consider to be of greatest contemporary interest. In one of them on Chinese history he translates and edits from *De Bello Tartarico* of Martin Martinius the biography of "Chang-hien-Chung, or the Nero of China" (13 May 1822). The essay affirms that the history of this tyrant affords "a series of the most atrocious and exquisite cruelties that ever degraded the character of man, and which place their perpetrator on a level with the wild beasts of the forest," but Waln admits that the "alleged atrocities of this monster evidently owe some portion of their enormity to the imagination of Martinius."

Three numbers of the *Gazette* were needed for Waln's related essay on cannibalism or anthropophagy, a topic that has reemerged in popularity in our own times (5, 10, 13 September 1823). In its editorial columns, the *Gazette* remarked that "so much curious research and interesting fact, connected with the history of human nature—one of the most important of subjects—may not be found elsewhere in a narrower compass or more agreeable form" (10 September 1823). The question of cannibalism in China had been a troubling one for the Sinophile Voltaire, for if the practice could be attributed to the Chinese on a large scale, it would tend to reduce the effect of panegyrics on Chinese morality and humanitarianism. Voltaire exculpated the Middle Kingdom by the simple expedient of

THE DRAGON AND THE EAGLE

accusing other nations of greater cruelties, particularly the Spanish for massacring millions of American Indians and opening butcher shops for the sale of human flesh (Etiemble 1989: 218).

Waln was more interested in the topic of cannibalism itself than in the extent to which it was practiced in China. He cites the British traveler Dalrymple, who claimed to have read all travels and voyages ever published, to the effect that he could find no instance whatsoever "in which the eating of human flesh from choice was related," a conclusion that has recently been repeated by some modern anthropologists. Waln, nevertheless, loads his essay with innumerable examples of cannibalism in both ancient and modern times both in Europe and America, particularly among the Indians of the two American continents. After all of his horror stories, however, he concludes that in his own times the practice occurred only in New Zealand and Sumatra. In regard to the earlier existence of cannibalism in China, he quotes Renaudot's two Mohammedan travelers in the ninth century, Marco Polo, Martin Martinius, and several modern authorities. He concludes that the practice never existed in China to the degree which has been represented and that when it did take place it was the result of "the spirit of hatred and revenge, or, more generally from famine."

In a similar article, he refuted what he labelled the distortions of Catholic missionaries about Chinese infanticide (15, 16, 17 January 1821). He argued that if the practice ever existed it was only in times of famine and that it was just as prevalent in Western countries during similar periods of privation. Pointing to government-supported foundling hospitals such as one he had himself seen in Canton, he hurled a counter charge at the missionaries that they were deliberately portraying Chinese culture as primitive or barbarian in order to elicit financial contributions for their own institutions. Although he and Delano agreed that it is unjust to accuse the Chinese as a whole people with infanticide, his somewhat rosy picture of Canton does not square with Delano's portrayal of drowned Eurasian and Amerasian babies floating down the Pearl River nor with the parallel testimonies of Samuel Shaw and of the Swedish naturalist Peter Osbeck. He seems to have overlooked his own insinuation that prostitutes had been supplied to members of recent embassies from the West as well as his observation in one of his manuscript volumes that nearly all Chinese boatwomen had babies in their care.

One of the most original of Waln's essays concerns "Secret Associations in China" (6 August 1823), a topic which as far as I know has not been treated in print by any other Western writer and which seems to be based on knowledge gleaned by Waln from a prize essay, presumably written by an Englishman in Canton in 1820. These secret fraternities, he reports, have ostensibly religious or ethical principles as their foundation, but in practice they engage in various kinds of petty crime. Their names are quaint and ludicrous such as "The Great Ascending Society," "The Society of Glory and Splendour," "The Red Beards," "The Short Swords," and "The White Water Lily." In the initiation ceremony, the person being inducted performs the kowtow to the leader, who ordinarily professes skill in curing diseases. A certain phrase is given as the watchword, a stick of incense is burned to solemnize the occasion, and the initiated one acknowledges the leader as his master. Waln ridicules the author of the prize essay for anathematizing the Roman Catholic religion for its potential to "roll on and spread by degrees, until it enters China"; whereas, as Waln points out, it was common knowledge that the Catholic faith had entered the country two centuries previously. According to Waln, the secret societies are strictly forbidden by the government, but they flourish despite strict punishments mandated against their members.

Waln introduces a good deal of his own personality in an open letter to the *Gazette*, 19 February 1821, indicating mistakes relative to China in recent numbers of the *Edinburgh Review*, particularly in regard to trade with America. The British writers had said that American commercial relations with China had begun in 1792, instead of 1784, and had given the impression that the British trade in tea was more substantial than the American. Waln explains that regardless of actual consumption the American trade was more important since the British drink black tea principally, which is the least expensive, whereas the Americans consume green tea, which is from two to four times more valuable. He accuses the *Quarterly Review* of making even more erroneous statements amounting to an attack on the honor of the United States by equating American commercial integrity with that of the Chinese, charges he dismisses with the comment that "they bear upon their face the imprint of their character."

In the following year Waln contributed a related essay on "Novel Varieties and Consumption of the Tea Plant" stretching over two numbers of the *Gazette* (18, 19 April 1822) and containing considerably more facts about tea than I have given in chapter 7. Waln affirms that the two Mohammedan travelers of the ninth century drank the beverage during their sojourn in China as did the ambassadors of Mirza Schah Rokh in the fifteenth. Dutch ambassadors in the seventeenth century, however, seldom mention tea, even though it was introduced into London in 1666. According to Chinese legend, the origin of tea was miraculous, deriving from the eyelids of a saint. A holy man of the sixth century who had taken a vow to go without sleep for several years was unable to keep himself from slumbering. As penance, he tore his eyebrows from his head, and they were turned into tea leaves. Anthropologists would no doubt consider this tea myth parallel with Franklin's legend concerning the origin of corn and tobacco. Reporting the affirmation of the French Jesuit Michel Benoît in 1772 that tea improves its flavor by traveling and that a chest carried from China to France and back again increases enormously in value, Waln in order "to prevent erroneous impressions," adds that "there is much less gospel in these words of the worthy Father than his profession would lead us to imagine."

Another of Waln's references leads to a literary digression. After citing an "Ode to Tea" by the Emperor K'ien Long that was then widely known in Europe, Waln caustically remarks that the poem could be seen "flourishing upon one half the tea pots of the Empire." To illustrate the emperor's epicurean imagination, Waln quotes a culinary simile from a translation of one of his choral songs, "The blast of our artillery choaked up the embrazures of their fortresses as *the breath of a fish is stopped when thrown into a cauldron of boiling water.*" But in extenuation of the emperor he cites Homer's comparison "of one of his heroes tossing to and fro in his bed and burning with resentment, *to a piece of flesh broiled on the coals*" as well as Solomon's resembling "the nose of his beloved to the tower of Lebanon, which looketh towards Damascus." In connection with the varied and dissimilar ways in which tea is served in different parts of the world, Waln expresses the principle that taste preferences depend primarily upon local resources.

> The Kamschatdate would prefer his putrid fish, the Esquimaux his train-oil, the Tarter his horse-flesh before all the dainties of an American bill of fare. The choicest vintages of Madeira, could not seduce the Chinese from his warm rice wine; nor the fairest products of Virginia and Kentucky, win the Malay from his betel and areka. We turn with disgust from the horse tripe, mare's milk, and fried locusts of the modern Scythian, and regale ourselves upon living shell fish, water snakes, and fricasseed frogs. Worms, ants, and spiders, have been converted into food, by the wretched inhabitants of New Holland, of Van Diemen's Land, of the Andaman Islands, and even of our lately acquired Florida; and we feel the nauseating influence of a bare recital of the fact;—yet we cull out and feast upon the living tenants of a Gloucester cheese. (18, 19 April 1822)

Drawing upon his own experience, Waln affirms that during his four months residence in Canton, he "never saw a solitary example either among the higher or lower classes, of a Chinese taking a draught of pure water," even though foreigners indulged in it freely.

In an essay on the related subject of "Edible Bird's Nests; or, *Hirunda Nidis Eduibus* (29 April 1822), Waln affirms that these delicacies rank first among the delights of Chinese epicures and constitute "an important dish at all entertainments given by the richer classes." Apart from their delicious taste, the Chinese believe that when converted into soup birds' nests give "firmness to the flesh, strength to the nerves, and general health and spirits to the body and mind." Waln admits that neither he nor anyone else is quite certain of the composition of this esteemed broth, but he assumes that the nests are formed "from a viscous substance gathered upon the surface of the ocean." After summarizing the opinions of two dozen European authorities from the seventeenth century to his own times on the manner in which these nests are produced, Waln suggests that they come from a floating substance on the sea, "which undergoes a certain process in the stomach of the bird, previous to its application, in thin filaments, to the construction of the nests." He has not seen any description of "the manner in which that fermented substance is ejected, although it is a point upon which its claims to delicacy might considerably depend." Despite the pretentions of the Chinese concerning the delicious taste and salubrious effects of bird nests and their extremely high market prices, Waln himself proclaims "the vaunted bird's nest soups of China, to be nothing better than a weak concoction of common glue."

In treating birds' nests, Waln preserves a certain degree of objectivity, but in a related essay on "Chinese Delicacies" (16 May 1822), he betrays considerable prejudice against Chinese customs. Declaring that the food of the common people is extremely simple, he affirms that "the higher orders indulge in every delicacy that can pamper their appetites, or excite their passions."

> It is worthy of remark, that precisely those parts of the animal structure which are rejected by almost every other nation, civilized or savage, are converted by the prejudices or singularity of Chinese taste, into articles of great value, and general consumption. The tendons, and hoofs of deer, the paws of bears, the maws of fish, and the fins of sharks, are luxuries peculiarly devoted to the tables of the rich. The poor indulge in not less singular, but more disgusting dainties, common to most people in a savage state, where self-preservation is the first law of nature, and no refinement opposes, nor resources avert, the indulgence of a depraved appetite. But among a people such as the Chinese, whose claims to civilization are more than coeval with the creation of the world, and one of whose emperors was contemporary with Adam, it really appears surprising that any portion of the community should be found, with dispositions and tastes so closely assimilated to the acknowledged barbarities of more modern times.

Waln affirms that it is attachment, not necessity, that causes the Chinese "to eat such disgusting food," much of which is extremely expensive. The common people eat "rats, bats, cats, mice, dogs, frogs, toads, snakes, horse-flesh, badgers, lizards, locusts, owls, storks, and worms;" whereas the wealthy feast upon the choicest cuts of horse meat, birds' nests, dried ducks, bears paws, sea slugs, and shark fins. Waln suggests that he is exposing the "excessive and luxurious eating" habits of the Chinese to combat the prevailing good opinion of Chinese morality and behavior.

> The uniform regularity of Chinese habits, their strict adherence to those temperate rules which cement the moral structure of society, their rigid abstinence from the vices and excesses which strike at its foundation; in fine, their general observance of temperance and sobriety, have been so highly extolled, not only by the primitive missionaries and their successors, but by the enthusiasts of France, that it appeared a perilous attempt to endeavour to unveil the real character which pompous professions and studied duplicity had so long successfully concealed. But Voltaire and all his host were defeated, and the united testimony of all modern writers have, in a greater or less degree, served to remove the delusion.

Despite the overtones in the preceding passage suggesting that the reports of Chinese sobriety are exaggerated, Waln is forced to admit that the Chinese as a nation are not addicted to intoxication. He, nevertheless, cites a few travelers, chiefly ancient ones, who have recorded instances of drunkenness.

Among all of Waln's essays, the ones that reveal most of his personal experience in China are concerned with the arts, one on "Painters of Canton" (4 August 1823) and one on drama (28 June 1821). Perhaps unconscious of prejudice, he remarks in his essay on painters that those employed by foreigners at Canton "possess a more extensive knowledge of their profession" than Chinese painters in general. His summary of Chinese pictorial art reveals both preconceived ideas and keen personal observation.

> Chinese painters offend against every rule of perspective, which, with the effects produced by the proper disposition of light and shade, they affect to consider unnatural. Always taking a horizontal view of their subject, they place themselves alternately in front of the objects, whatever may be their position or extent; thus, in their paintings, houses are placed one on top of another, and the method which they have imagined to express objects at a distance, is to represent clouds intersecting trees, buildings and men. They absurdly contend that it is proper to represent the objects in the back, of the same size as those in the fore ground, because they are so in nature. They have another singular idea, that the Emperor should not be painted like other men, and if he be the most remote object in the painting, it is

necessary that his head should be the largest in the company. Having no idea of demi-tints, or softening shades, or indeed of any shades at all, and no variety of colouring being commonly used, a Chinese landscape appears at first to be a mass of black marks, representing nothing; and a closer examination only discovers the bare outline of an unsuccessful and rude attempt to imitate nature.

Waln admits that the Cantonese painters are able to work according to Western rules, producing landscapes and views of boats, women, trades, and punishments, commonplace subjects that are encountered in museums today. They are particularly skilled, he affirms, in delineating birds, reptiles, insects, fish, and flowers with such exactness that "not one plumula of a feather, nor a single scale of a fish escapes them." Waln mentions Topaqua as the most accomplished of portrait painters, "both as to resemblance, execution and colouring." Specialists in this genre, according to Waln, have plenty of customers because of their reasonable prices, but their failures are also numerous.

> The artist commonly regales himself with a pipe during the sittings, and his visitor may read, write, or smoke, at his option. Another reason why likenesses are badly executed, and the colouring bad, is the quantity of *blanc* used in all their colors. But their manner of proceeding may offer a still more weighty cause; they first cover the oval of the figure, with a flesh-coloured tint, and begin with the first part of the face that happens to come uppermost in their ideas; sometimes with the eye, at others with the mouth, passing thus from one point to another without any fixed rule. In full length portraits they seldom succeed, from their ignorance in delineating the proportions of the human figure.

Waln reports the artifice of some of the Cantonese painters who had been engaged to paint portraits of foreign clients, but had been left with their work not paid for when the sitters returned to their native lands. The revenge of the painters consisted in exhibiting the portrait with a rope around the neck of the delinquent and suspended from a gallows. Waln compares this practice to that of Lucas Giardino of Naples, who placed upon rejected portraits the inscription "I am here through want of money." Apparently a fair amount of eroticism or pornography appeared in the ateliers of the painters Waln visited, for he remarks disapprovingly that the state of Chinese morality could be determined by the "lascivious and indecent paintings hanging in the galleries of the most respectable artists." He would not accept the excuse that these provocative subjects emanated from the presence of other Westerners. Chinese moral fiber must have been weak indeed, he says, for the transitory residence of a few foreigners to be strong enough to permit the exhibition of "the most disgusting delineations."

He applies the same reasoning to the "gross representations of the Chinese actors," during dramatic entertainments presented for foreigners by the Hong merchants. Western observers of Chinese theatrical performances disagreed on the subject of their alleged obscenity. De Guignes and Barrow in company with Waln reported offensive scenes; whereas Van Braam, Staunton, and Davis had nothing to say about lubriciousness. Indeed the comments of the latter observers uniformly stress the high moral tone of dramatic exhibitions. Waln's statement conforms, however, to the opinion of the writer in the *Port-Folio* in 1819, who condemned the obscenity of tales and fables available to Chinese readers.

Like Shaw and other observers, Waln affirms that Chinese artists are excellent copyists, but lacking in imagination. In his words, "when left to his own resources, a Chinese painter has no mind to convey the idea of distance, solidity, expression, and magnitude of objects, by fore-shortening, perspective, and a due proportion of light and shade; yet in a picture, he will copy them all with scrupulous accuracy." Among the copied subjects in the shops of Canton, Waln had noticed Miss O'Neil and William Penn; Miss Mary Ann Clarke and Adam & Eve; the Prince Regent and Jupiter; the Princess Charlotte and Peasant's Little Maid; American Naval Victories and Lord Viscount Nelson; the prayer of Innocence and Bonaparte; the Nabob of Oude and John Elwes, Esq.; Roderick Dhu and Houqua; Lady Hamilton and Hebe; Jupiter and Danae; Washington, Jefferson, and Madison; scenes from the *Lady of the Lake*, and representations of Bible stories.

Another essay in the *National Gazette* that I assume to be Waln's concerns Chinese drama. It appeared two years after Proclus maintained in the *Port-Folio* that in his opinion it is "not worth the trouble even to name the wretched drama of this country." The *Gazette* essay is introduced by the following heading: "If you consider the subsequent extract from a Note Book, kept in China, worthy a place in your columns, it is at your disposal" (28 June 1821). My only reason for not unequivocally claiming it for Waln is that the appended signature consists of the letter E. This I take, however, to be a typographical error for W. The essay has many similarities to a section in one of Waln's manuscript volumes titled "Drama—Sing Songs—Pantomimes—Puppet Shows." Close parallels between the two accounts may be seen in regard to the antiquity of Chinese drama and the presumed resistance to change in Chinese culture. In the present chapter, I shall confine my remarks to the printed essay, however, and consider it as by an unknown pen even though I am satisfied in my own mind that Waln is the author.

Throughout his discussion the essayist demonstrates a love-hate relationship toward the Middle Kingdom. He alternately damns with faint praise and savagely condemns elements by which he is obviously fascinated. "Notwithstanding the Chinese boast of the great antiquity of their plays," he remarks in his opening sally, "the rudeness of their dramatic performances may be inferred from the total want of theatres and scenery; and from the vagrant life of their performers." If the author intends to deny an extensive past to Chinese drama, the two parts of this sentence are in a sense contradictory: the itinerant nature of the acting profession could in itself indicate great age, for primitive conditions bespeak antiquity rather than the reverse. The author also observes in a pejorative vein that "in the barbarous jargon spoken by Chinese to foreigners, the term *sing-song* is applied to public entertainments whether they consist of music alone or are accompanied by acting." E is not, moreover, referring to young girls exercising their vocal talents, as the term *sing-song* is usually taken to mean in our times, but rather to male performers engaged in any aspect of the dramatic art. His objective description of a street performance conforms to that of other Western travelers of the time.

> The stage usually consists of a scaffold erected in the middle of a street, elevated just high enough to allow persons to walk under without stooping. It extends from one side to the other, though it need not be very large to do so, and has a temporary roof above it. To heighten the effect of their representation, the vicinity of the stage is often decked out in a most singular style. Transparencies, variegated lamps, figures of giants, dragons, and other monstrosities are liberally distributed in all quarters. These with the profuse display of shining tinsel, and childish gew-gaws of a thousand descriptions, afford a singularly fantastical spectacle.

After commenting that these decorations are usually designed to honor native gods, either to solicit their protection or forfend their baleful machinations, the essayist is reminded "of the ancient Greek and Roman usage of consecrating public games and exhibitions to religious purposes."

The essayist displays considerable interest in the economic aspects of the street performances. He indicates that the expenses are defrayed by the inhabitants of the street on which they take place and that the shops and stores suffer in addition a loss of business since the lower classes crowd the street for a considerable distance and wedge themselves so firmly together that the establishments are closed while the entertainment lasts. The pay of a first-rate company like that previously described, he calculates as amounting to 300 American dollars for three days. The company consisting of from 60 to 100 persons performs, he says, from early morning to sunset, and the approbation of the sponsors seems to be commensurate with the "actual muscular exertion of the actors," sweat being equated with talent. Through the kindness of a Chinese acquaintance, the narrator and a friend were able to witness the dramatic action from the window of a house overlooking the stage. Although utterly ignorant of the Chinese language, he "found ample food for curiosity and spent much time in witnessing their most eccentric actions." Not surprisingly he admitted that he was unable to derive from the action any conception of Chinese psychology, but, nevertheless, maintained that some prominent national traits could be discerned and some amusing comparisons drawn.

> The strongest touches of character, and the greatest actions of life are usually selected as subjects for the stage, which like a mirror, may be generally consulted to discover the leading and characteristic feature of nations. In the Chinese drama, caprice and fashion seem equally unknown. Every thing bows to their veneration for antiquity, and the veil of time appears absolutely necessary to render events interesting. The stage may be considered a striking monument of their political code. Every thing is a copy of "olden time," and the dresses, arms and manners, are reckoned exact counterfeits of the remote ages when the real characters acted their parts on earth.

E seems quite unaware of the contradiction between this insistence on the Chinese obsession for antiquity and his previous effort to deny the Chinese a long dramatic tradition. He continues in the same strain. "The origin of many of their plays like that of their pagodas is unknown, and hence it may be inferred, that the drama has had a long and inglorious reign in China." E terms the reign of drama inglorious because in his opinion it had subsisted upon tradition alone rather than upon popular acclaim. "Such a thing as an audience summoned to decide upon the merits of a new play has perhaps not been known for centuries. Thus by adopting with scrupulous punctuality the laws and opinions of their avatars, they have shackled improvement which is no longer able to keep pace with time." Here E attributes to Chinese culture the characteristic of unchanging continuity, a quality which Paine and others also ascribe to Chinese history in general. E compliments the actors' costumes as "rich and splendid, shining with gold and of a fashion well adapted to the end of adding new attraction and dignity to the human form," but he adds that this luxurious effect is completely unsupported by any corresponding scenery, "not the least attention being bestowed upon this department."

Turning next to the content of Chinese plays, the narrator affirms that their most laudable characteristic consists in their morality. "Government is said to be very strict in its attention to this particular, and although there is no female audience, most of the spectators belonging to the lower classes of men, every thing like obscenity is carefully avoided. Nothing is to be seen that might bring a blush upon the cheek of modesty." This may seem contrary to Waln's objections in his essay on Canton artists to the "gross representations of the Chinese actors." This is only an apparent contradiction, however, for E's essay specifically describes one of the identical scenes that Waln repudiates—the portraying of a character "with his bowels ripped out." Several European writers on China had reported that female roles were taken by men as in Elizabethan England. The Philadelphia essayist explains that actresses in China are banned by the laws of the empire, but affirms that the want of them is scarcely felt because the men who "counterfeit the fair sex . . . succeed so admirably well, that . . . not one in a thousand could discover the imposition unless previously acquainted with it. The effeminate features, soft modulation of voice, disposition of the hair, general carriage, *little feet*—in fact all the striking peculiarities which serve as distinguishing marks are imitated with the most surprising success." As proof of this assertion, the essayist cites the example of one of his personal friends who "actually lost his heart, and became quite enamoured with one of the fair ones who was performing a part on the stage. He could not or would not be convinced by the round assertions of the Chinese about us, that the fair object of his admiration belonged to his own sex." Waln in his manuscript volume cites a case in actual history of a sailor who in Tahiti had fallen in love with a dancing girl who was in reality a boy.

Turning to the unfolding of the action, the essayist explains that the various parts of the drama are introduced by signs placed on the stage, describing what is to take place in the following scene. He considers as striking defects in the typical plot the disregarding of normal connections of time, place, and natural events. A play may incorporate incidents of a long life, a century, or even an entire dynasty, he remarks, and yet the hero may have the same appearance at the age of eighty as at twenty. The essayist comments that "Chinese women are allowed the privilege of figuring in romance, if not in real life," by which he means that they are portrayed as invincible warriors. Even in Chinese fiction of the twentieth century, the woman warrior remains a stereotype. The scenarios E describes strongly resemble those of a modern Kung Fu movie.

> Nothing is more common than to see a heroine of common mold put a dozen men to flight, dispatch as many more with their own weapons, she having been unarmed at first. . . . Whenever . . . a woman was brought forward with her arms pinioned, and other disadvantageous circumstances, you might expect to see her—turn upon and vanquish

all before her. . . . The life of the stage seems to depend upon the most extravagant contests in which attempts are made to display incredible feats of valor and savage ferocity. Occasionally some most horrid scenes are represented, which, for the credit of the people, I suppose, are indebted for their popularity to their improbability. I have seen a character with his bowels ripped out in a conflict, staggering about the stage with them trailing after him—bleeding hands and trunks thrown before the spectators, and many other sights not less revolting, received with the strongest applause.

The narrator characterizes as ludicrous and inconsistent the combination of realism and acrobatics, when in the midst of a fierce encounter, the combatants "clear round upon their heels to strike a blow or drop a lance and turn a somerset in picking it up."

The essayist is impressed slightly more favorably by the use of make-up to depict personal traits. Bad characters in particular, E says, "may be always known by their face, before their deeds inform on them; for the countenance is so disfigured by paint, as to produce the utmost distortion, and expressions of demoniacal wickedness. . . . According to the stage rules, a Richard, a Shylock, and a Iago would be converted into the most horrible monsters." The essayist assumes from this circumstance that the Chinese place more faith in physiognomy than Westerners do, but presumes that they are frequently deceived if they attempt in real life to discern character from appearance. He reports the Chinese expression that a person who has forfeited his good name has "lost face" and compares it to the English adage "pretty is as pretty does." He concludes with remarks on the musical accompaniment, which he affirms "always corresponds in vehemence to the violence of the actions, and during a combat makes a most terrible and discordant din." As he had equated the Chinese standard of histrionic skill with sweat, he equates that of musical excellence with volume. Like the visitor to a modern disco, he found the music "extremely annoying at first, and was almost deafened by it." He explains that when pantomime is in process, "the orchestra which is mounted upon the stage in full view, keeps up an incessant noise"; when dialogue takes over, "the speaking is recitative, each pause being filled up by a clattering, mingled with the loud crashes of metallic plates or cymbals, and the squeaking of wind instruments somewhat resembling the harmonious noise made by a dozen ill tuned hautboys."

The essayist explains that the spectators in the evening are treated to acrobatics and tumbling as a kind of afterpiece. Since these exhibitions are the most intelligible parts of Chinese theatrics to foreigners, they are the most popular among them, and for this reason while Chinese drama is almost unknown in the West, "the wonderful feats of their tumblers and jugglers are talked of all over the world."

Two of the most important of Waln's essays published in the *Gazette* with his initial W concern contemporary political issues and personalities and even today carry a high degree of authority. Under the title "Embassy from the United States to China" (5,7 February 1821), Waln explores the merits of a proposal to establish diplomatic relations between the United States and China. He points out that among all the Western nations at that time engaged in the China trade, the United States was the only one that had never sent a mission to the Middle Kingdom—even though England and the United States held almost a commercial monopoly and the latter's trade during 1818–19 exceeded that of the English by the enormous sum of $1.5 million. The Chinese feared the English, moreover, and had been reluctant to grant them access to their shores beyond the confines of Canton because the fate of India, "deluged in blood and groaning in slavery," plainly indicated that if the British merchants ever established a firm footing, "there would be no bounds to their avarice or ambition." The Americans, on the other hand, holding no territories in the Far East and carefully avoiding all conflicts with the Chinese during their thirty-six year period of contact, had aroused neither fear nor jealousy. The advantages of commercial relations with the British had brought in their wake massive misgivings, but those with the Americans had not been in any way alloyed by ambivalent consequences. Waln admits that if an embassy were sent from America to China, no return courtesy would be extended, but he argues that such a response should not be expected, for the European nations had firmly established the tradition of unilaterally affirming a friendly disposition.

There were, however, urgent reasons for seeking a formal expression of bilateral understanding between China and the United States. Without some kind of a supporting treaty, the Chinese "barely endured" the connection with American merchants, who were as a result subject to vexatious exactions from the local authorities together with private defalcations. Every other state engaged in the trade had sought a written understanding, but all had failed in their quest because of a reason not applicable to the United States: that the European missions pretended to be from government to government, but were actually from trading company to government. "But a mission from the President of the United States would appear under very different features; emanating directly from a powerful government, it would be received, and treated with respect; demanding redress for no grievances, imploring no important favours, and no associated body of merchants, from whom it might be supposed to arise, existing, it would be considered in no other light than an amicable overture to a more frequent and friendly intercourse." A further reason for timely action, according to Waln, was that if the British should ever gain the power of influencing the Chinese, American trade would be either annihilated or reduced to an injurious status, and American citizens would be forced to depend upon other nations for the exotic luxuries which "time and habit have transformed into real necessities." No doubt Waln imagined himself as playing a major role in an American embassy should it ever be sent.

Waln suggests as the main reason for fearing that Britain might gain control of China, the strong possibility of a revolution occurring there. History shows that the empire had repeatedly been dismembered, re-united, and once again dismembered. Should a revolution take place, Waln speculates, foreign aid would be needed to put it down and the Chinese government would call upon Europeans to provide this aid. Waln provides a historical sketch of Chinese dependence upon outside help since 1643, when the court called on the Manchu Tartars, who thereupon seized control of the empire themselves. The Portuguese obtained their foothold in Macao because their assistance had been necessary to control piracy; in 1662 the emperor formed an alliance with the Dutch at Batavia to put down a rebellion led by General Coxinga; in 1788 the emperor of Cochin China—an empire exactly parallel with China itself—made an alliance with the king of France in order to quell a rebellion, and the French would have taken control of the entire country if the revolution in their own country had not intervened.

According to Waln, there were only two main objections to sending an embassy from the United States: fear of its being improperly received and the necessity of performing the kowtow. Waln affirms that in China the latter ceremony is not considered degrading or disgraceful, but a mark of honor comparable to smoking the pipe of peace with American Indians, or "kissing the king's hand at St. James's, or the pope's toe at the Vatican." He argues that the bad odor surrounding the ceremony was due to the exaggerations of the English, who needed an excuse to account for the Chinese rejection of the mission of Lord Amherst. British accounts condemned it as "a vile mark of obsequiousness" in order to eulogize in contrast the alleged "manly firmness of the ambassador." But their reaction was "nothing but an ebullition of anger, excited by the contemptuous dismissal of the British embassy." Waln counsels his countrymen that in avoiding the "fastidiousness" of the English that they not "adopt the submissive humility" of the Dutch, who, according to Waln's interpretation of Van Braam's relation, had not only saluted pieces of silk considered as symbols of the emperor, but also prostrated themselves before government officials and even before the gate of the viceroy's palace. Waln maintains that it would be possible for the Americans to avoid the ceremony on all occasions except in the imperial presence. He also advises that an American embassy not seek to match the Chinese in splendor, but to shun "all useless, expensive, and vain ostentation." In keeping with his Quaker heritage he maintains that an embassy should be conducted "in the full spirit of republican simplicity," particularly since the Chinese observed the maxim of Confucius, "Give much,—receive little," the reason for their rejecting the splendid presents of the last British embassy.

Advantages to the United States in establishing formal relations with China, according to Waln, consist in collecting facts and information that previous travelers may have overlooked or concealed; becoming officially acquainted with the views and dispositions of the Chinese; providing the Chinese with a parallel understanding of the character of Americans; and placing American traders at Canton "on that footing to which their birthright has elevated them."

In a separate essay in the *National Gazette*, (26, 27 February 1821) Waln gave his own history of "European Embassies to China," reflecting the attitude in the following passage of a French missionary, Joseph de Grammont, in regard to the embassy of Lord Macartney.

> These gentlemen, like all strangers who know China only from books, were ignorant of the manner of proceeding, of the customs and etiquette of this court; and to add to their misfortunes they brought with them a Chinese interpreter still less informed than themselves: the consequence of all which was, that, in the first place, they came without any presents for the minister of state, or for the sons of the Emperor, Secondly, they refused to go through the usual ceremony of saluting the emperor, without offering any satisfactory reasons for such refusal. Thirdly, they presented themselves in clothes that were too plain and too common. Fourthly, they did not use the precaution to fee the several persons appointed to the superintendence of their affairs. Fifthly, their demands were not made in the tone and style of the country. Another reason of their bad success, and, in my mind, the principal one, was owing to the intrigues of a certain missionary, [the Portuguese Bernardo Almeyda] who imagining that this embassy might be injurious to the interests of his own country, did not fail to excite unfavourable impressions against the English nation.

Waln also quotes Barrow to the effect that Lord Macartney's "immediate object was just about as reasonable as if the Emperor of China had sent to demand from us a cessation of the Isle of Wight." Waln takes no notice that de Grammont's opinion is directly opposite to his own on the subjects of appropriate attire and the offering of presents. He begins his essay with the mission of Thomas Pereira in 1517, but I shall limit my coverage to his remarks on Van Braam and Lord Amherst. The latter's expedition took place in 1815 ostensibly to register a protest against alleged wrongs committed by the Chinese on Chinese territory against British subjects.

By this time, Waln had presumably read Van Braam's memoir and used it as the basis for his recounting "the constant series of self degradations," which accompanied the progress of Titsingh and Van Braam in China. According to Waln, their bad treatment arose from their "total lack of self-respect,—that of the English, from their total want of courtesy." Considered as traders, not ambassadors, the Dutch were forced to perform the kowtow nearly fifty times on their way to the capital and about thirty more during their residence there.

> Before they left Canton they were displayed in a religious procession, and performed the prostration in a public temple; they were insulted by the Vice-Roy, to whom they desired personally to pay their respects, who informed them that persons *in their situation* were not permitted to enter his palace; and that an officer would receive them at its *gate*! They accordingly visited "*the gate*." They suffered the ministers of state to trick them out of the most valuable presents intended for the Emperor;—they were accommodated during their journey in the worst manner;—together with miserable vehicles, and worse horses, they were even obliged to remain in the open air, "with the thermometer below freezing point"—they were denied the common necessaries of life, and remained sometimes without eating "four and twenty hours together"; [in a note Waln quotes Van Braam's statement that he was "a bulky man" and that he lost on his trip 3 inches of bodily circumference] they were lodged in a stable at Pekin; they were laughed at by the Emperor, owing to the bulk of M. Van Braam, and the difficulties he met with in making what he denominates "*le salut d'honneur*"; . . . on every trumpery present of a plate of meagre venison, or insipid sweetmeats, the two embassadors were duly called upon to bow the knee to the absent Baal.

Waln's interpretation, it is just to observe, is contradicted in Delano's account of the statements of the two Dutch supercargoes who accompanied Van Braam to Pekin. According to their testimony, "when the embassy arrived at Pekin great parade was made, and they were received with all the attention and politeness that could be shown them" (1817: 537).

According to Waln, Lord Amherst's mission came about because the East India Company asked the British government to obtain the right for them to have direct communication with the court at Pekin rather than through local authorities at Canton. But the time was not propitious because the British had recently taken high-handed action against an American vessel in Chinese waters and subsequently against local Chinese authority in Canton. The embassy might have succeeded had it been confined to commercial arrangements, Waln suggests, but it was extended to embrace other concerns such as allowing the British to trade in other parts of the empire as well as Canton, to trade directly with any Chinese merchants, not merely with members of the hong, and to send a minister to Pekin as a channel for submitting grievances directly to the throne. Waln explains that the first point would never have been granted, for the protection of the country required even greater restriction rather than extension of foreign contact, which could only "expose their weakness and incapacity." The second point could also never have been admitted since the hong was composed of the most wealthy and powerful group of merchants and carried great influence at court. Finally, a British resident minister would have been regarded as a spy and never tolerated.

In addition to these disadvantages, the conduct of the ambassador showed no "appearance of cordiality or friendly regard," and the presence of the Sinologist Sir George Thomas Staunton in the mission was a decided liability, despite his knowledge of the language and the culture of the country, for he had been declared by the emperor himself a "dangerous person" and committed on that account to the "surveillance of the local authorities." When the mission arrived in Pekin by an overland route, they were told that they must return to Canton by water, but they, nevertheless, sent their boats away, making the return by land necessary. They engaged in a long and ridiculous negotiation over the kowtow, that Waln makes seem even more ridiculous than it probably was, and the dispute was known about all over Europe before Amherst's return. AEneas Anderson and others suggest that Lord Macartney had even performed the ceremony on the previous mission, and all the mandarins as well as the emperor himself concur that he did. Waln reasons that since Macartney had already set a precedent and since it had been hinted to Amherst in London that he might perform the ceremony in secret and deny it in public, his adamant refusal to do so made the success of the mission partially dependent "upon the private feelings and prejudices of its directors."

As though issuing a warning to a potential future mission from the United States, Waln observes, "Embassies conducted upon the same haughty, unbending, and unconciliating footing, may always anticipate similar treatment: it should be remembered that the Chinese are a peculiar nation, and in our intercourse with them we have no other customs but their own to guide our proceedings. We are at the best but intruders on their soil; no social bonds of affection or hospitality exist between them and other nations, and it is the love of gain alone that prevents us from leaving their uninteresting dominions." Waln's caustic attitude toward the British experience in China may also have been in part founded upon the American climate of ultra-national feeling widespread in the 1820s. He, therefore, chuckles over the discomfiture of the British envoys when an order of the emperor to the viceroy of Canton was carried out to invite them to dinner, to give them a lecture of paternal advice, to refuse any more presents, and to rid himself of their annoying presence. "To these ridiculous scenes, may be added the grave and formal discussion respecting a band of fiddlers which the Emperor had prohibited from attending the embassy to Pekin;—and the paltry accommodations afforded his lordship on his arrival at Canton, in the *Joss-house*, or Temple of Worship at *Honan*, opposite that city, where a single room—only in part sheltered from the weather—served, for nearly three weeks, as the residence of the Embassador Extraordinary from his Royal Highness the Prince Regent, *as well as his whole suite!*" Waln abruptly concludes his essay with the comment, "Thus ended this famous mission, without the attainment of a single object, connected with the honour, or profit of the company, or the nation."

Prior to Waln, complete coverage of the Amherst mission had been available in American newspapers. In Boston, for example, *The Athenaeum, or, Spirit of the English Magazines* prefaced a lengthy review of Clarke Abel's *Narrative of a Journey in the Interior of China* (15 Nov. 1812) with the observation that "The *Literary Gazette* has already performed the *Ko tou* to the various interesting works which have emanated from the Chinese Embassy, and in more than nine of our Numbers will be found the bowing of our heads over these pages. We do not regret that we are again called upon to repeat the ceremony, since nothing relative to China can be otherwise than curious and amusing." Not unexpectedly the American reviewers found little in these accounts to reflect credit upon the undertakers of the mission, which they summarized as disastrous, costly, and disgraceful.

The most important of Waln's essays in the *National Gazette* concerns further diplomatic relations between China and the Western nations, including the United States, and even today these essays carry a high degree of historical authority. These essays concern events that I have discussed in chapter 8, the execution of a British soldier during the so-called "Canton war" and that of a sailor on an American vessel in a later episode. Waln gives an extended treatment of both of these incidents from the perspective of international justice in the longest of his essays, "Homicide in China," that extends over five issues of the *Gazette* (6, 8, 11, 12, and 13 June 1822). His essay had been inspired by a further incident, some

British sailors robbing a potato field and several Chinese being killed in the aftermath. By affirming the right of the Chinese to enforce their own laws and vindicating their past actions in this regard, Waln presents a point of view quite contrary to that of Samuel Shaw and American opinion in general.

Since the execution of Terranova, the sailor belonging to the American ship the *Emily*, had been condemned by some observers as legalized murder and defended by others as a legitimate dispensation of Chinese law, Waln begins his essay with an examination of the Chinese criminal code, revealing an apparently incredibly detailed and sophisticated knowledge of the subject. He does not disclose the source of his legal expertise, but it is readily apparent in his manuscript volumes in the Library Company. One of these contains a combination paraphrase and abstract of a famous English summary of the Chinese legal system, Sir George Thomas Staunton's *Ta Tsing Leu Lee: being the fundamental laws . . . of China . . . translated from the Chinese* (London: T. Cadell & W. Davies, 1810). In his *Gazette* essay on the treatment of homicide in China, Waln includes all of the relevant aspects in the legal code without disclosing the source of his information. I shall limit myself to his personal observations. He corrects the erroneous impression held by foreigners that all Chinese convicted of homicide are automatically sentenced to death by indicating that cases of "pure accident" are accompanied with slighter penalties. He does not dispute, however, that the Chinese tenaciously adhere to the precept that "whoso sheddeth man's blood, by man shall his blood be shed." As in his other writings, Waln's general attitude toward the Chinese is ambivalent; he criticizes harshly at times, but almost immediately adds some words of retraction or extenuation. He declares that one of the most odious features of the Chinese legal system is the iniquitous distinction between husband and wife, parent and child, and master and slave, the subordinate of each pair being subject to extremely harsh penalties and the dominant one to relatively mild ones. He gives an "example of savage barbarity committed by the benevolent 'Father of the People,' a title then vested in Kien-lung, the late Emperor of China" that will demonstrate "the solicitude of the Chinese government, to encourage those feelings of filial dependence, by which it is mainly supported." Two children for beating and disgracing their mother were by the express orders of the emperor flayed alive, the head of their family and the elders of the village were strangled, and various neighbors and officials of the village were given strokes of the bamboo and transported to other parts of the realm. Waln particularly impugns the motive of K'ien Long, the "Son of Heaven" in decreeing these harsh punishments, that is, "to render the empire filial." At the same time, Waln admits that the "treatment of slaves in China is incomparably more humane than in America, or the West Indies" and that the institution is mitigated by "being almost entirely domestic, and seldom praedial." He admits that a large number of crimes are punished by death, but explains that this severity is designed for the protection of the lives of all subjects.

Waln devotes the second part of his essay to a summary of the historical relations between Chinese authorities and foreign traders when sovereignty was at issue, including cases of homicide of foreigners committed by Chinese and those of Chinese committed by foreigners. He concludes that the Chinese have invariably punished their own subjects guilty of crimes against foreigners, but that foreigners, particularly the English, have asserted a right to try their nationals accused of offenses against the Chinese, and he unequivocally asserts that this is an assumed right completely contrary to international law. In his discussion, an attitude intrudes that can only be described as racism; Waln does not himself declare that Western people are superior to Chinese, but he suggests that Westerners in general have this belief. This is the first direct expression of this attitude that I have encountered in any American publication, and because of the attention now being given to aspects of racism in East-West scholarship, I shall give Waln's own words:

> The estimation in which the Chinese are generally held by foreigners, is of such a nature as to require the most energetic and coersive [*sic*] laws, so as to prevent a wanton waste of life, and protect them from the most gross oppression. A Chinese, physically weak, and timorous in disposition, is looked upon with contempt, and treated with indignity by the smallest sailor in the foreign fleet. These feelings, indeed, are fully reciprocated by the weaker party, but self-interest, or a sense of their own weakness, in general, prevent their expression: it is only under circumstances of perfect safety, that they give vent to the sovereign disdain with which they regard men, who forsake their native country, and live in thraldom, for the purpose of gain. This constant and increasing state of irritation, and reciprocal contempt, have given rise to the most disgraceful scenes, in which foreigners, as proportionally the most powerful party, have generally been the victors, as well as the aggressors.

Waln provides another historical summary to support his opinion that the English from the advent of their first fleet in China in 1637 "have caused more troubles, created more difficulties, committed more crimes, and conspired more strenuously against the peace and dignity of the Chinese nation, than all other European powers collectively." Waln's portrayal of the *Lady Hughes* affair, as I have said in chapter 8, is quite different from that of Samuel Shaw. In answer to an English writer who had hoped "for the honour of his country that such a cowardly concession will never again be made to the Chinese," Waln affirms that "it might also be hoped for the honour of human nature, that the sacrifice of innocence should never again have shielded the guilty." Drawing his account of the affair from the French Sinologue de Guignes, who was residing at the time of its occurrence in Canton, Waln argues that the guilty person was a British officer, not the sailor who was executed, and that international law required that the officer should have been surrendered to the Chinese authorities. According to Waln, the officer of the *Lady Hughes* gave an order to the Phillipino sailor to fire a salute to a group of visitors then leaving the ship. The sailor warned some Chinese in a boat alongside to drop behind and fired the first two of three shots on the opposite side, but hesitated over the third. When the officer inquired why he was delaying and heard the sailor's explanation, *"the officer compelled him by threats to fire immediately."* As a consequence one of the Chinese was killed and another severely burned and died soon after. In retaliation the Chinese placed the supercargo of the ship in prison and affirmed that he would be released only in exchange for the sailor who had fired the shot. The representatives of the other nations at first made a show of force, but later decided to remain peaceable. The Chinese ordered all trading to be stopped, and in the face of this economic sanction, the sailor was surrendered, and "Captain Williams, the accountable perpetrator of the deed, sailed from Whampoa, leaving his substitute to suffer death." The commanding officer should have been the one surrendered, Waln maintains, "because he was actually apprized of the result before he forced the fatal gun to be fired."

Before treating the case of Terranova, Waln compares the conduct of American sailors in China with those from Great Britain. Among a number of authorities, he cites the report of a committee of the House of Lords to the effect that "every witness without exception, who was examined upon the subject, testified to their uniform good conduct, and relative superiority over those of the [East India] Company, and they all concurred that no dispute whatever had ever taken place between the Chinese and Americans." Waln suggests two reasons for the superior behavior of the American sailors: they were better paid and less addicted to drunkenness. In regard to Terranova, who was accused of killing a Chinese woman by throwing a jar at her, Waln insists that whether he threw the jar deliberately or whether he did so without any design to kill, "it was a capital crime; and the American government has no right whatever to take offence at the prescribed penalties, but if the defence set up by the American residents can be fairly supported, and it can be proved that the jar was safely delivered into the hands of the woman by the accused,—that she fell overboard at the distance of 30 feet and upwards from the *Emily* while in the act of sculling her boat, . . . it is not only the right, but the duty of our government to resent the non-admission of that evidence." He goes on, however, to suggest that Americans who would lie in Terranova's favor in a Chinese court would not do so in an American one where they would be under oath. Also he points out that a Chinese woman expressly testified that she had seen the victim fall overboard as a consequence of the throwing of the jar. When the Americans refused to surrender Terranova, Waln maintains, "the Chinese exercised their undoubted right by seizing him on board the *Emily*."

Waln's various publications on China gave him a local reputation at least as an expert on the Middle Kingdom, and he was consequently asked by Richard Peters of the American Philosophical Society to express an opinion concerning a book from China that had been discovered in the unlikely hands of some local Indians, and which the officials of the society thought might be of some antiquity. Accordingly Waln examined the book and wrote a formal letter, 2 July 1824, now among the society's manuscripts, analyzing the physical features of the book and attempting to account for its presence among the Indians. The officers of the society wondered whether it might be an almanac or at least have some kind of astronomical significance, but Waln was reasonably sure that it had nothing to do with the heavenly bodies. The leaves of the book had been detached when turned over to him. After rearranging them in the order in which he believed they had originally been placed, he came to the conclusion that the work was "one of the school or toy books" printed in large numbers every year.

The first page contained a map or plan, which he assumed was that of a walled city, and the next two, a map of the Chinese empire. The fourth page contained the symbol of a hand, which Waln conjectured was used to illustrate the tones of various syllables, referring to a parallel symbol in "Morrison's Chinese Grammar." The next three pages contained diagrams of the abacus, for which Waln gave the Chinese name "Swan-pan," adding arithmetic to geography and grammar to his taxonomy. The next section, comprising nearly forty pages, he took to be a series of lessons designed for the instruction of youth. Later pages he conjectured concerned ancient empires. These were followed by twenty or so pages with drawings of common objects of interest to children, including houses, fruits, flowers, animals, birds, household and agricultural implements, and furniture. A separate group of objects, Waln assumed, concerned the creation of the universe, among them the famous metaphysical symbol of the *Lo-choo*. Some of the objects Waln could not identify, he explained, because many implements exist in China the use of which is not known in the West. A final section appeared to be pictures designed merely for amusement. One of the most intriguing of these Waln described as "Love à la Chinoise," without any further explanation. Another reminded him of "an offence of the same nature as that which caused Actaeon to be transformed into a stag," hardly a fit subject for a children's book. Another illustration might have been appropriate for Franklin's Chinese letter, a "Lady riding in a kind of wheelbarrow, as is now the custom."

Waln's most ingenious comments consist of his explanation of how the book came into the possession of the Indians. Of three possibilities, he firmly rejected the first, that the book was of great antiquity and had made its way to the West in the possession of ancient sailors from Asia. "The idea that any Chinese vessel ever sailed across the North Pacific Ocean," he affirmed, "can no more be admitted than that the original Indians have paddled their canoes to China. The state of Chinese navigation, the construction of their vessels, the ignorance of their mariners, all forbid the notion." To support his conviction, he quoted estimates, that he admitted were only approximate, that ten thousand sailors, fishermen, and others living on the water around the port of Canton were annually destroyed by tempests. Although the extreme limit of a Chinese voyage at the time was Batavia, he added, a Chinese navigator going anywhere to sea takes solemn leave of his family and makes the same financial arrangements as if he were going to certain death. No Chinese junk ever survives a strong gale, Waln asserted, and the Chinese sailor's only hope of safety is in not encountering one. Waln was willing, therefore, to contemplate only two other explanations as reasonable.

The first was that given the large numbers of such books in circulation and their extreme cheapness, a common sailor might have acquired the book and used it as an object of trade with the Indians, imposing "his useless book upon these simple beings, as a powerful cabalistical work of sorcery or magic, which fraud its strange & uncouth characters served to support." This hypothetical sailor, moreover, may have claimed that the book "came from a country situated far to the west," or in the words of the Indians, "towards the setting sun." Waln explained that he could not have said "towards the east" because the Indians could not have conceived of another country situated beyond Europe. Waln was certain that the book came from the Atlantic rather than the Pacific coast.

The second realistic possibility and the one that Waln accepted as the most likely explanation is linked to the theory of the Chinese mariner that he had already rejected. Waln's final opinion, in short, was that some philosophical theorist or "scientific traveler" who had imbibed the notion that American Indians descended from the Chinese had gone among the

Indians, taking with him the Chinese book to assist his researches. Waln, however, had no faith in the theory of a Chinese-Indian racial connection. "Even those who are so extravagant," he wrote, "as to trace Chinese features, language &c. among the aborigines, confine their hypothesis to South America; but—I speak with deference—nothing appears to me to be more certain than that Chinese Indians, are as little known in any portion of this continent as the descendents of Madoc," a reference to a similar theory based on linguistic resemblances that North American Indians had descended from the Welsh. Franklin had published an article in his *General Magazine*, February 1741, using the alleged interpenetration of the Welsh among the Indians as evidence that Britain's claim to America had existed before that of Spain.

As a further example of an untenable hypothesis, Waln referred to the notion that the Chinese had descended from the Egyptians that he had previously considered at length in *China*. In his letter, he ridiculed the advocates of the Egypt hypothesis by narrating some of their excesses. They had uncovered, for example, a bust of Isis near Turin on which were inscribed on the forehead, cheeks and breasts thirty characters that a professor of Chinese at Rome declared to be of Chinese origin, thereby making a connection between ancient Egypt and ancient Rome. Further investigation, however, revealed that the bust had been manufactured in Piedmont, and the characters were a mere whimsy of the artist of no significance whatsoever. On a more sober note, Waln affirmed that many similar efforts to penetrate the veil of time had served merely to dim the little light on the past that already existed. Appealing to the "Word of God" as his beacon, Waln affirmed that we may "overthrow the fabrications of sceptics, who would create an Ararat in Scythia, & place the patriarch of the flood upon the plains of China." But he asked rhetorically, "where are we to establish boundaries to the reputed conquests of Sisostris, [*sic*] or fix limits to the adoration paid to Noah & his immediate posterity, who are assimilated to almost all the primary gods of the eastern world, not excepting Fo-hi, the first emperor of China, or Fo, or Buddah, the progenitors of the Hindu, Chinese, & Japanese idolatries?" Here Waln seems to place the deists among the ranks of the Noachides, those who argued that the Chinese were the descendants of Noah. So far as I know, however, all of the Noachide polemicists were Christian. In our times, Etiemble is still exposing the ridiculousness of the theories that Egypt and Chinese languages are related, that the Old Testament preceded ancient Chinese texts, and that the Chinese race descended from Noah (1989: 231–32).

Waln gave other examples of serious scholars offering incredible examples of linguistic resemblances or the provenance of strange objects in order to support pet theories. Hugir developed an analogy between the Roman numerals I, II, III and similar Chinese horizontal lines, and Webb derived the Greek word for *woman* from the Chinese *nu-jin*. A copper coin found in an Irish bog with an Oriental inscription was said to have been imported by the Phoenicians until it was discovered that the coin had been stamped in China during the reign of a modern emperor. An authentic Egyptian relic, *la vivix à anse*, was proclaimed by Bishop Clayton of Clogher to be an instrument for planting cabbages; by Kircher, the image of the creator; and by the famous Steward, a compass. Eventually everyone realized that it was a phallus, a conclusion that does not appear in Etiemble's exposé of the various interpretations (1989: 231–32). Waln had presumably never heard of Lafitau or read his comments on the possibility of direct contact between Chinese and native Americans. If he had, he would no doubt have included him in his list of unrealistic theorizers.

The notion of an ethnic link between the Chinese and American Indians had been presented to the English reading public in America several times before Waln wrote his letter. The *United States Magazine* in June 1794 (169–74) published extracts from Bryan Edwards's *History of the West Indies*, which in its second chapter treats ancient writers, chiefly Greek, who suggest an oriental origin for some natives of America, particularly the Caribs. The poet Freneau in a note to an essay series *Tomo Chichi* in his periodical *The Time Piece* (1, 93) refers to America and Asia having at one time being joined as one continent. A uniquely American version of the Chinese-Indian relationship, moreover, was presented in the *Port Folio* in June 1816 (N.S. 1, 457–63) by John P. Campbell. In an essay "Of the Aborigines of the Western Country," he argues that the Israelites were the common source of the Tartars of Asia and the original inhabitants of the Western boundaries of the United States before the Indians. His argument is based solely on the discovery of remnants of drawings, artistic designs, pottery, and metal work in various Indian emplacements; since the allegedly barbarian Indians were not themselves capable of producing these artifacts, according to Campbell's reasoning, they must have been the work of some more advanced race, presumably one linked to the Chinese, but now lost. This is a crude type of racial prejudice, but it is directed not against the Chinese but against Native Americans. Waln's moderately prejudiced attitude toward Chinese culture is by contrast a model of objectivity.

CHAPTER
14

An American Travel Liar

Alllll of the American literary works that I have so far discussed, with the possible exception of Franklin's treatment of Indian mythology and his Chinese letter, must be ranked under the heading of functional rather than belletristic writing; that is, they belong to the genres of history, religion, and travel rather than to the literature of imagination in which the giving of pleasure and the creating of esthetic effect take precedence over the transferring of information. In eighteenth-century America, however, China had its place in works of imagination as well as in those of utility, and even some genuine literary works from China itself were known on the American continent.

One of the most intriguing imaginary works profiting from the vogue for China belongs to the same genre as Franklin's Chinese letter, that of the fictitious voyage. Since this particular work has been catalogued by the Library of Congress as a genuine travel book, I would seem to be presumptuous in labeling it, like Franklin's, a literary hoax, but there is no question that its section dealing with China at least is pure fabrication. I am, accordingly, suspicious of everything else. This book, *The Adventures of James Sharan: compiled from the Journal, written during his Voyages and Travels in the Four Quarters of the Globe*, was published by subscription by its author, Sharan himself, in Baltimore in 1808, while he was presumably living in Charleston, South Carolina. In the preface, Sharan affirms that his work is a transcript from his journal apart from a few stylistic improvements and that he has sent it the press at the solicitation of a great number of respectable people in the neighborhood where he resides. He says in the body of the work that he was born in 1762 near Liverpool, England, and was impressed into the British navy at the age of ten. The narrative then breaks off until the year 1775, when he participates in an engagement repelling a band of pirates during which twenty-five of his shipmates are killed and in a subsequent engagement off the coast of America during which he is disabled by a heavy block of wood falling upon him. The captain of his ship places him in a hospital in New York in August 1775, discharges him honorably from the service, and makes him a present of five guineas. Sharan recovers, makes his way to Pennsylvania, learns the trade of a wheelwright, and travels to Charleston, where he remains until the end of the American Revolution. Interjected in the narrative is a section describing England, its topography, religion, government, navy, and revenues; another section on the city of London with encyclopedic statistics; and a third comprising a brief history of the final stages of the Revolutionary War. The rest of the book similarly incorporates sketches of Scotland, Niagara Falls, Capetown, Canton, The Great Wall, Batavia, St. Helena, Copenhagen, and Naples.

After Sharan amasses a capital of $1,000 by miscellaneous trading in Philadelphia, he buys a load of furs and embarks with them for Holland on the *Hope*, with Captain Bennett, 2 September 1784. He lands, however, at Edinburgh on 17 October and disposes of his furs without difficulty. On 2 December he returns to Philadelphia on the same vessel, arriving 16 January 1785. Here he makes the acquaintance of a Captain Barry, presumably not the naval hero of the Revolution, and sails for Ireland on Barry's ship *Howland* on 7 June 1785. Here takes place the first of a series of miraculous escapes in Sharan's apparently charmed career. In the midst of a calm, he and several sailors take to the water and swim around the ship, but he alone drifts out of sight and is left by himself in the midst of the ocean. His absence is eventually noticed, and the captain turns the ship around and after several hours picks him up. On 27 July he enters the Liffey River at Dublin. At this point Sharan tells several Irish jokes, including the following: "A doctor advertised the infallible cure of deafness and blindness. The *deaf*, he says may *hear* of him at a house in Liffey-street, where the *blind* may *see* him from ten in the morning until three in the afternoon" (1808: 88).

On 1 May 1786 Sharan embarks at Dublin with a load of Irish linen and arrives back in Philadelphia on 18 June. In only three weeks, he takes ship again, but does not arrive at his destination, Bordeaux, until 7 October. Here he has no extraordinary adventures, but relates the story of a convent which countenances illicit sex among its members. It is customary for two nuns to be allowed to leave the convent each year for the purpose of begging, one of them old and ugly and the other young and attractive. Often the younger of the pair has had affairs in her past. The duo for the current year visit the abode of a wealthy nobleman, leaving at his door a bundle containing an infant of two months that the nobleman had fathered upon the younger of the nuns together with a letter declaring that she belonged to an aristocratic family and had been sequestered in the convent against her will. The nobleman thereupon institutes measures to have her released and takes her as his wife. After recounting this episode, Sharan returns to his own experiences. He leaves Bordeaux on 10 December 1786 and arrives at Fort Johnson, South Carolina, on 15 February of the following year.

Up to this point, Sharan's exploits apart from his mid-Atlantic swimming are believable and buttressed by specific dates and names of vessels and their captains. As he subsequently expresses time lapses in ambiguous terms, the ring of truth almost completely vanishes. He proceeds on an overland trip to New Orleans, where he resolves "to penetrate into the United States by a course up the river Mississippi, and endeavor to find my way through the forests and Indian tribes, until I had seen that wonder, the Falls of Niagara" (1808: 101), the mecca of all travelers in America of the time. He advances by foot and boat up the Mississippi to the mouth of the Missouri and retraces his steps to the Ohio. En route he passes several months with "the Collapissas," an Indian tribe he describes as "very similar to the Creeks, Choctaws, Chickasaws, and Cherokees (103)," even though he is unable to speak their language. He follows the Ohio River eastward, and after passing through Pittsburgh reaches his goal, Niagara Falls. The author of a study on "Eighteenth Century Visitors to Niagara," after remarking on the dubious quality of Sharan's pages because of the absence of dates and precise corroborating details, affirms that the statements in his lengthy section on the "Falls of Niagara" seem "based on what earlier travelers had published, Peter Kalm in particular, rather than on Sharan's observation" (Severance 1911: 383). His subsequent itinerary seems incredibly haphazard. He enters New England, descends to New York, turns west again to Pittsburgh, and then south to Staunton, Virginia, and Natural Bridge. Here instead of fabricating his own account, he quotes Jefferson's description of this natural wonder and gives him full credit. He completes this journey in Charleston, having, he says, traveled for twenty-two months a distance of 10,000 miles principally on foot and alone.

The next part of the book concerns Africa, where Sharan's experiences, according to Frank H. Severance, resemble those of Mungo Park among the Moors (1911: 383). In Charleston he meets the captain of the

Lion, preparing to sail for the Gold Coast, and resolves to accompany him, not to engage in the slave trade, but in that of gold dust. He, accordingly, buys a variety of trinkets, clothes, and brandy for use in trading and sets sail on 16 May 1789, the last date he records until his return journey to America eighteen months later. On the outward voyage, his ship is wrecked on the coast of Africa, he does not know where, and he is the sole survivor, another miraculous escape. After several days waiting on the coast in vain for rescue, he proceeds inland, where he is attacked by a tiger that he successfully fights off, witnesses a herd of 237 elephants (a specific number, where such precision would have been difficult or impossible), and after several more days, is surrounded by a band of natives. They communicate in sign language and take him to their village, where he is kindly received. But when he is turned over to one of the tribe as a menial servant and required to perform hard labor, he escapes during a raid by an enemy tribe. After twenty-five days of solitary wandering, he is discovered by a group of nearly naked black men, much darker than the members of the previous tribe, who take him to their village, a month's travel away. Here it becomes apparent that they are cannibals as he is tied up next to a fire being prepared to receive him. While inexplicably released for a brief period, he pushes some children into the fringes of the fire and in the confusion escapes. He is soon recaptured and taken back to the village, where a new fire is made ready. This time he seizes a shovel, scatters the burning embers, once more escapes, wanders in the wilderness for about a month, and eventually reaches the Atlantic coast. He gives a date, 26 August 1790, for being picked up by a nameless vessel and another, 23 January 1791, for reaching New York. He embroiders his narrative of these events with an explanation of the social customs of the African villages based on insights impossible to have been discovered under the conditions which he maintains he endured.

After precisely one month in New York, Sharan leaves for the Mediterranean, sails up the Nile, and visits the pyramids, which he obligingly describes. He also recounts a harrowing tale from Aaron Hill concerning Europeans trapped in a crypt by Egyptian guides. With almost no transition, he leaves the land of the Pharoahs on a boat bound for Canton, a most unlikely itinerary.

We come now to the reason for including Sharan as a writer on China: 28 out of the 225 pages of his book are devoted to the Middle Kingdom. I have expressed my doubts concerning his previous adventures elsewhere in the world in order to prepare the ground for my absolute disbelief of every personal connection he maintains to have had in China. He does not name the ship on which he sails or mention its nationality or captain. He lands first of all at Canton, where he concludes a purchase of "nankins," or fine cotton fabric, for resale in the West, and after this transaction proceeds to Macao. Not only would this itinerary have been geographically backwards, but no boat would have been permitted to push on to Canton without stopping at Macao for a chop and a pilot. Sharan shows his complete ignorance of the required customs formalities, the existence of the hongs, and the names of the principal merchants. At Canton Sharan makes the acquaintance of a merchant, Trolaze, and communicates to him his desire of observing and describing the Chinese empire at first hand. The name Trolaze does not even sound Chinese, and it lacks the suffix "qua," the equivalent of "mister" that is included by every legitimate traveler in naming Chinese merchants. Many of the cities that Sharan mentions later in his narrative have no more resemblance to Chinese place names than Trolaze has to personal ones. Apart from Sharan's mention of "nankins," he has nothing to say about the articles of trade, not even ginseng.

When Trolaze hears Sharan's desire of penetrating into the interior of the empire, he appropriately recoils in fright and tries to dissuade him, warning that he would be killed if discovered. Trolaze, nevertheless, contacts a group of friends, who agree to take Sharan to Nankin and Pekin, insisting, however, that he dress in Chinese fashion, color his face, and pretend to be deaf and dumb in order to escape detection. After leaving Canton on 13 March 1792, the group passes through Chu-chu and Nanshu, where Sharan is scrutinized by border guards, but allowed to proceed. They spend several days at the city of Nangan, that "appeared like a piece of tiling" (1808: 178). Here, Sharan says, he acquires most of his information about Chinese life and customs. His following comments on funerals and women have a degree of verisimilitude, but they give no evidence of being based on personal observation. "In their funerals the Chinese are precisely opposite to the Americans. A number of young men dressed perfectly in white conveying small flags of different coloured silks, precede the corpse which is placed in a square case, under a covering, painted with colours that appear to us to be the most pleasing, and agreeable" (181). The only authentic detail is that of white as the symbol of mourning. Sharan finds the women of Nangan "strong and laborious" and their feet not compressed (180).

> Marriages in China," he affirms, "are consummated at a very early age; the principal reason for this, as there is such a super-abundance of population, seems to be, that as the children, especially the males are bound to maintain their parents, it is necessary to have the help of the female, who as before remarked, contributes very largely by her labour to this object. But this circumstance has produced a very great evil—that of exposing the young children as soon as they are born,

especially the females, to perish on the high roads, or of drowning them in the adjacent rivers. (1808: 181–82)

Sharan adds that the government employs a number of men to look for these infants and that if any are found still alive they are nourished and reared or, if dead, buried. He says nothing about the custom of arranged marriages, one of the most important elements of the marital process.

Sharan then continues through a list of partly imaginary towns, Hinchu, Kegan, Norcan, Vrichau, Suchu, Nankin, Caisan, and Tayinsin, before reaching the Great Wall. He treats this architectural marvel as proof of the "ability of man to overcome apparently innumerable difficulties" (1808: 191). No American at this period had actually penetrated as far as the Great Wall, not even Van Braam. Since I cannot compare Sharan's description with that of another American, I shall quote several sentences from that of Aeneas Anderson as extracted in Morse's *Geography*.

> This wall is perhaps, the most stupendous work ever produced by man: the length of it is supposed to be upwards of twelve hundred miles, and its height in the place where I stood upon it, (for it varies in its circumstances, according to the nature of the surface) is upwards of thirty feet, and it is about twenty-four feet broad. . . .
> There are also, at proper distances, strong towers, from whence, by certain signals, an alarm could be communicated, in a very short space of time, across the whole empire; and wherever the wall attains the summit of an hill, or mountain, there is a strong fort designed to watch the excursions and movements of the enemy. . . . But the most stupendous works of man must at length moulder away; and since Tartary and China are become one nation, and, consequently, subject to the same government, the wall has lost its importance: it being no longer necessary for defence or security. (Morse 1796: 517)

Sharan's entire coverage of the Wall contains little information not found in the few sentences above from Anderson.

> It is represented by the Chinese to extend at least fifteen hundred miles in length, though when the mountains are impassable, it is not so perfect as upon more level, and more exposed ground. This wall exceeds in solidity and duration, every other building of the same kind of which we read in the records of history: it stands unrivalled for the extent of country through which it is carried, the bulk of materials used to construct it, and the labour requisite to be engaged, for in some places it passes over the tops of mountains more than a mile high; and in the principlal parts of it seems to have been built with so

much strength, art, and care, that it probably will continue to stand nearly as long as the mountains and rocks upon which it is erected, having already existed upwards of two thousand years. The thickness of the foundation which is of stone, has been measured, and amounts to twenty-five feet—and the wall cannot be less than from forty to fifty feet in height. Towers built of brick in which the guards are stationed, are raised upon the wall at a distance of not more than one hundred yards from each other, but those which are situated at the gates are much larger and stronger than the others. But since the Tartar dynasty has been permanently fixed upon the Chinese throne, the wall though still considered as the boundary between the two nations, is dwindled into a mere line of military posts. (191–192)

Although Sharan's measurements are somewhat larger than Anderson's, exaggeration being a characteristic of travel liars, his description has no concrete observations or important facts not in the work of his predecessor. I am not declaring that he drew from Anderson, but it is quite possible that he did. At any rate, I am convinced that he was not the first American to see the Great Wall.

The route taken by Sharan and his escorts completely defies geography, for Canton is in the extreme south of the country, Pekin in the northeast, and the Great Wall to the north of the latter city. Sharan gives no description of Pekin, where he and his party remain only three days, after which they return to Canton as quickly as possible. His companions do not even transact their business because they have learned that Sharan's identity is suspected.

At this point Sharan introduces the tale of an English factor with some facial resemblances to the Chinese and possessing some knowledge of the language, who is taken by a similar group to the capital. After three days, he also is discovered; he is imprisoned and the others in the party beheaded. After Sharan again reaches Canton, he decides to leave on the first boat for the West, which happens to be one bound for Copenhagen with scheduled calls at Batavia and Saint Helena. Despite his hasty retreat from Canton, Sharan acquires some Chinese goods, which he exchanges in Batavia for coffee. From Copenhagen he sails to Palermo, Naples, and Leghorn, where he remains for some time until finding a boat bound for Charleston. As usual, he does not mention the vessel or its captain. Just after Georgia is sighted on the homeward voyage, the ship strikes a reef about a half mile out and everyone on board except Sharan perishes, the second time in his charmed existence that he is the sole survivor. On his return to Charleston, he retreats to a solitary cave in the mountains, where he remains for three years, returning to society at the insistence of some hikers who come upon his retreat. He then once again takes up incessant traveling, visiting "every part of the Union" and "the settlements of uncultivated worlds."

Sharan brings his book to a close with a poem "The Retrospect and Wish" in which we find the following lines concerning China.

> I saw the restless Tartar, proud to roam,
> Move with his herds, and spread his transient home;
> Through the vast tracts of China's fix'd domain,
> The sons of dull contentment plough the plain.

Sharan's ambiguous itinerary from Canton to Pekin cannot be followed on a map, and it does not include the northern plains where Sharan has the Tartars roam. He says nothing in his putative journal, moreover, about agriculture, and the two lines about it in his poem may have been inspired instead by Poivre.

As a modern scholar has observed, Sharan's "book was written either by one of the perpetual rolling stones or by a man with a good imagination. At any rate there is no moss here for the student of the period" (Clark 1956: 149). I shall go further and brand the author as an arrant travel liar of the ilk of the French-English imposter George Psalmanzar, who wrote *An Historical and Geographical Description of Formosa*, 1704, without ever seeing that beautiful island. Sharan's *Adventures* have only a superficial resemblance to Franklin's Chinese letter since Franklin did not pose as one who had actually been to China. Franklin's work is a comparatively sophisticated hoax, and it carries at least the external marks of credibility. Sharan, however, claims to have had the experiences about which he writes, and he presents his journal as historical fact. His untruths are so palpable that I am even suspicious of the list of 600 subscribers that appears at the end of his book. There may have been an edition of around that figure, however, judging by the large number of copies still to be found in libraries today.

Although Sharan's work may not have a great deal of intrinsic literary value for the modern reader, it has the historical importance of showing that the vogue for China in America could be profitably used by an enterprising author. Those of his contemporaries who did not consult Morse or Anderson may have acquired some impressions about China from Sharan.

CHAPTER

15

Timid Exoticism:
Or China of the Imagination

T he most important of the authentic Chinese writings circulating in
Enlightenment America were the sayings of Confucius. Many
Americans were aware of the style in which Confucius expressed
his philosophy even though his concepts were reported in only a cursory
and superficial manner. In addition to the various references to the morality of the Chinese sage that appeared throughout the century, the poet
Philip Freneau published a series of short poems under the general title
"The Book of Odes" in *The Time Piece* (Vol. 2, 16 October 1797 and eleven
consecutive weeks thereafter). The "Book of Odes" could refer to nothing
else but the *Shih ching* of Confucius, for Greek or English odes have never,
in Freneau's milieu or elsewhere, been classified as books. An epigraph
which Freneau attached to the first of his poems, moreover, leaves no
doubt that he intended to remind his readers of Chinese literary traditions: "He that readeth not in the Book of Odes is like a man standing
with his face against a wall; he can neither move a step forward, nor survey
any object." Freneau attributed this quotation to *Hau Kiou Choaan*, the
seventeenth-century Chinese novel that Jefferson had recommended to
his brother-in-law. The coupling of Confucius and this work of Chinese
fiction is by no means fortuitous since a strong thread of Confucian morality permeates the novel. No evidence exists, however, that Freneau had
read either Confucius or *Hau Kiou Choaan*, and the epigraphs of the remaining eleven poems have nothing to do with China. Freneau, nevertheless, wrote, as I have indicated in chapter 7, the only American poem of

any consequence in the period concerning the Middle Kingdom, his "On the first American Ship that explored the Rout to China," not one of his most notable creations and certainly not offering much competition to the Elizabethan Michael Drayton's "Ode to the Virginia Voyage," the worthy prototype of the genre to which it belongs.

A substantially complete version of an authentic Chinese classic appeared several times in American periodicals. This is the most famous story in a collection of forty tales under the title *Chin Ku Ch'i Kuan* that appeared toward the end of the Ming Dynasty, more or less contemporaneous with the Elizabethan Period in England. This story remains one of the most beloved in the canon of Chinese literature, still required reading in Chinese schools. Titled in English "The Inconstancy of Madam Choang," it has many resemblances to the portrayal of "The Matron of Ephesus" in *The Satyricon* of Petronius. In the Chinese tale, Choang-Tzu, a disciple of Lao Tzu, encounters a widow fanning her husband's grave to dry it out since she had promised not to remarry while his grave remained moist. Choang dries it completely by magic, and the widow gives him her fan in gratitude. He recounts the episode to his wife, who harshly condemns the widow and destroys the fan. Choang dies, and soon after a handsome prince who had intended to study with him appears on the scene. The new arrival and the new widow immediately fall in love and move the corpse to an outhouse. She persuades the prince that it is useless to respect the memory of Choang, and then dons her wedding garments. At this moment the prince falls ill and the widow is told that the only way to save him from death is to serve him the brain of a living or recently deceased man in a cup of hot wine. She then opens Choang's coffin with an axe and is about to split his head open, when he rises from the dead. The prince is made to disappear, and the widow hangs herself.

This tale was translated by Du Halde in his *Description of the Empire of China* in 1735. Shortly after, Voltaire used the elements of the story as the second chapter of his oriental tale *Zadig*, but transferred the action from China to the Near East and gave his characters Persian names. Also he introduced a quack doctor who has a remedy for apoplexy and substituted the nose for the brain as the nostrum to cure Choang's disciple. This was a ribald touch since the nose in the eighteenth century was recognized as a euphemism for the male organ of generation as in Sterne's *Tristram Shandy*. Voltaire's English admirer Goldsmith included the Chinese story as Letter 18 of his *Citizen of the World*, following closely the version of Du Halde, but having Choang's disciple suffer an attack of apoplexy and require a human heart for recovery. This version was extracted in the *New York Magazine* in October 1794 (5, 595–57) under the title "Story of

Choang and Hansi," but with no indication of its source or author. It reappeared in August, 1795, (1, 396–68) under the title "Story of a Chinese Matron" in *The Rural Magazine or Vermont Repository* and in the *Philadelphia Minerva* in April 1798 (4, 38) as "The Chinese Matron—A Story," neither periodical indicating its source. Under the latter title, it was attributed to the *Citizen of the World* in *The Rural Magazine* (Newark) of 17 March 1798. In May of the same year, Voltaire's version appeared anonymously in the *Time Piece* under the title "The Nose." Brief as it is, the account of the ingenious matron, an authentic example of Chinese storytelling, was apparently extensively read in the period.

The indefatigable pioneer of comparative literature Thomas Percy, the clergyman who had edited *Hau Kiou Choaan* and who would later bring out the historically important *Reliques of Ancient English Poetry*, published in 1762 a collection of stories concerning forgetful widows, now extremely rare, under the title *The Matrons. Six Short Histories*. They include "The Ephesian Matron" by Petronius, "The Chinese Matron" from Du Halde, "The French Matron" from a letter of Sir George Etherege to the Duke of Buckingham, "The British Matron" summarized from a book by Benjamin Victor *The Widow of the Wood* (1755), "The Turkish Matron" from a manuscript translation of the original Arabic transmitted by a member of the French academy, and "The Roman Matron," an ancient English reworking of Petronius's tale taken from *The Seven Wise Maidens of Rome*. The narratives in Du Halde and in Percy are much longer and filled with many more details than any of the others. After the wife hangs herself, Choang-Tzu diverts himself "by singing her funeral dirge in a burlesque manner."

Aspects of Chinese feminine behavior are revealed in a chapter entitled "Of the Chinese Women" in an anonymous work published in Philadelphia by Samuel Sansom, Jr. *Sketches of the History, Genius, Disposition, Accomplishments, Employments, Customs and Importance of the Fair Sex, In All Parts of the World*. The title page gives no date, but the British Museum Catalogue assigns it to 1780, and Luther Evans's *American Bibliography* to both 1796 and 1800. No work under this title is known to have been published in Great Britain, and it may, therefore, have been written by an American. No references to any indigenous conditions or circumstances, however, appear anywhere in the work. The author indicates that the Chinese have perhaps the best claim to modesty of all the Asian nations, even the men considering it indecent to reveal any more of their arms and legs than is necessary. The women, even more carefully wrapped up, never disclose a bare hand even to a near relative if they can avoid it. This uncommon modesty that appears in every look and every action "adds the greatest lustre to their charms" (42). Under the influence of this engaging deportment, the men behave in a reciprocal manner. And in order that virtue not be contaminated by vice, the laws require that no prostitutes may lodge within the walls of any Chinese city. "Some however suspect whether this appearance of modesty be any thing else than the custom of the country; and allege that, notwithstanding so much seeming decency and decorum, they have their peculiar modes of intriguing, and embrace every possible opportunity of putting them in practice, and that, in these intrigues, they frequently scruple not to stab the paramour they invited to their arms, as the surest method of preventing detection and loss of character" (42). The author concludes, however, with the observation that no examples of this conduct are to be found in the most veracious of modern travelers.

Early in the next century the translation of a second Chinese work of fiction appeared in an American periodical, the *Port-Folio*, (June, July, and August 1816), but this is a much less renowned tale, in China or elsewhere, *San-Yu-Low; or the Three Dedicated Rooms*. It had been translated by John Francis Davis and published in Canton during the preceding year. Since it appeared almost immediately in the *Port Folio*, it had presumably been brought directly back to Philadelphia by some participant in the China trade. Davis was an early Sinologist who had accompanied the Amherst mission and later translated *Hau Kiou Choaan* from the original Chinese as *The Fortunate Union* (1829). *San-Yu-Low* concerns a man who spends his entire fortune building an elaborate house, but is forced by financial difficulties to sell all of it except a small apartment in which he dedicates three rooms respectively to men, the ancients, and heaven. Although he dies in straightened circumstances, his heirs benefit from his virtue and foresight.

Genuine Chinese literature is highly didactic, and the plots in fiction and drama are usually accompanied by a specific moral statement. For this reason, Western writers of the Enlightenment who wished to set forth an ethical doctrine or present an example of virtuous conduct frequently used a spurious Eastern background. The genre combining these ingredients in Western literary history known as the oriental tale accommodates both Persia and other Near Eastern countries together with China and the rest of the Far East, sometimes indiscriminately mixing the names and customs of the two geographical areas.

One of the most popular sub-genres of the oriental tale in Europe was a form of prose satire based upon the persona of a foreign visitor, spy, or agent. This presumed native of some country outside of Europe visiting the nation of the author ordinarily presents his comments in a collection of letters exposing the absurdity of customs or behavior in the host country by means of naïve expressions of surprise or misunderstanding. The originator of the genre was Giovanni Paolo Marana in a work called in English the *Turkish Spy* and in French *L'espion Turc,* but titled by its author in the original Italian *L'Esploratore turco e le di lui relazioni segrete alla Porta otto-mana scoperte in Parigi nel regno di Luiggi il Grande* (Paris, 1684). In English: *The Turkish Explorer and the Secret Relations conveyed by him to the Ottoman Empire in the Reign of Louis XIV.* The most popular example of the visiting alien genre was *Les Lettres persanes* of Montesquieu, 1721; and the title most relevant to our subject was the *Lettres chinoises,* 1741, of Jean Baptiste d'Argens. The *American Magazine* of Boston published in 1743 (62–63) the second of d'Argens' *Chinese Letters,* but with no indication that it was not genuine or not even Chinese. The contents concerning French fashions, however, should have provided some clue to its country of origin. In November 1745, the same journal published the seventeenth of d'Argens' collection, "Of Philosophical Systems: In a letter from a Chinese Traveller in Paris to his Friend at Pekin," also with no indication of its provenance. The philosophies treated were exclusively those of the West. Toward the end of the century, the *Massachusetts Magazine* published in December 1790 (2, 731–33) "From the Mandarin Chamfifi to the Mandarin Kiet-ouna, at Pekin, containing a concise history of Witchcraft," but this time the editor indicated that it was translated from a European work. This source, *L'espion Chinois, ou l'Envoye secret de la Cour de Pekin,* 1764, by Ange Goudar, was not well known even in France, and today it is considered somewhat esoteric. All three of these letters are satires on European cus-toms and beliefs and are only superficially connnected with Asia.

In addition to circulating these European portrayals of the foreign visitor, the American continent produced at least one original example of the genre, an entire book published in Philadelphia in 1810 titled *The Wandering Philanthropist or Letters from a Chinese, written during his residence in the United States.* The author was a native of Virgina, George Fowler, who described himself on the title page as the discoverer and editor of the letters. Since the persona of a Chinese correspondent was merely a device enabling Fowler to satirize various aspects of American life, there are practically no genuine elements of Chinese culture displayed anywhere in the book. To account for this lack of verisimilitude and to apologize for it, Fowler has his protagonist affirm "I have seen such a variety of human institutions; and have been so long immersed in the reflection which such objects are calculated to awaken, that you will hardly be able to recognize in my letter any traits of the Chinese character. The only worthy man is the one who can look through the world and say, my attachment, my feelings, my ideas are not confined to this district or territory, or to that" (1810: 292–93). As editor, Fowler maintains that he does not care whether his readers regard his work as a fiction or whether they think the author is an American or an Antipodean: truth is always the same no matter what the source.

The letter writer is presumably sending his epistles to a friend of his youth. Although he has visited all the natural and scenic wonders of the world, he limits his comments on the United States to men and manners. Much of his satire is political. He expresses a liberal point of view, more or less that of Jefferson and the Republicans. He affirms that the founders of the republic had been attached to the state through principle and reason, but the majority of people of his times were loyal only through national partiality. At least half were uninformed concerning the principles of government or even those of their own constitution. Although the majority may have professed moderate and rational principles in general, he charges, they were violent and prejudiced in matters touching themselves.

In further comments on *The Wandering Philanthropist*, I shall limit myself to passages concerning China. After asserting that providence seems to have destined the United States for some important purpose, the Chinese citizen indicates that "perhaps no nation on earth, not even China itself can compare with it in several respects. Its first and most prominent advantage is its remote situation from the convulsions of the European world (68)" beset, as it is, by wars, rivalries and hatreds. Fowler does not draw a comparison between China and America in regard to their isolation from Europe, but others, as I have shown in chapter 6, had already done so. The oriental philanthropist indicates that another advantage of America is its "wide extent of fertile soil." "Whilst in China, every foot of land is cultivated with care, here are vast tracts which are inhabited by nothing but savage beasts" (74). Another feature of the country is the wretched state of many of its roads. "In China, as well as in some countries of Europe," the narrator affirms, "the roads are equal to the pavements of the towns, whilst here they are almost impassable" (77). Fowler must not have read Van Braam or Staunton or realized that most long-distance travel in China took place on waterways. The Chinese visitor acquires an American friend, notable for possessing neither the austerity of an Englishman nor the egotism of a Frenchman. Considering everything American superior to anything in the rest of the world, this friend urges the philanthropist to throw aside his "Chinese oddities, as he calls them, and conform to the dress, manners and customs of his own country" (99). The friend forces him to part with his "fine tail of hair" and to have the remainder trimmed and powdered in the Western manner. He even tries to persuade him to become an American citizen and abandon his "partiality for the philosophy of Confucius, and embrace the Christian religion." The visitor assures this friend that

I had no reason to be surprised that the Christian religion should be dear to his heart, since it was the religion of his country. . . . But I stated the great difficulty of suddenly believing a religion of which I scarcely ever heard the name until I left my native country. I suggested to him whether his own belief proceeded in any other cause or agency than education: whether if he had been born in Turkey or Arabia he would not have been a follower of Mahomet; whether if he had been born of Jewish parents, he would not have been a follower of Moses; and whether if he had been born in China, he might not, like myself, have been a disciple of the wise and virtuous Confucius. "We see, said I, that all mankind neither are, nor can be of the same religion; but I conceive it of little consequence what religion we may possess; or in other words, on what part of the great globe we happen to be born, so as we seek—that light of nature which God has given us, and which is not confined to this country, or to that, but is inherent in the whole human race." (101)

This sage Chinese asks why so many other religions exist if Christianity is the only true one, and why Mohammedanism has the greatest number of votaries throughout the world.

As I have said, the major purpose of Fowler's book is to comment on American political and moral issues, not to mold opinion concerning China. From the latter perspective, the most significant feature of Fowler's portrayal of the Chinese protagonist is the casting him as a rational philosopher and a philanthropist. Although its literary merit may not be extraordinary, his book is notable for its positive image of Chinese culture.

A variant of the genre in which a Chinese observer visits the United States is the one reversing the relationship when an American finds himself in the Middle Kingdom. Examples of this are Franklin's Chinese letter that I have treated in chapter 5 and Sharan's fabricated voyage in chapter 14.

Closely related to the foreign visitor genre is that of the pseudo-letter, and here again American literature produced something indigenous, a comparison of American customs with those of China and a conclusion that they were equally strange. This letter, which has some resemblance to the second of the *Lettres chinoises* of d'Argens, is headed "From a Chinese Lady, to Mrs. xxxx, of Philadelphia." It was published in the *Columbian Magazine* for June 1790 (4, 350–52) and reprinted in the *Massachusetts Magazine* for March 1792 (4, 169–70). The Chinese lady thanks her American correspondent for a letter and three gifts she has just received. She cannot understand how the first of these gifts, stays or a corset, could fit a grown female since they could not even accommodate the waist of a child of two. For this reason she asks not to be bantered any longer about the small size of the shoes she had previously sent as her own gift to her American correspondent; small shoes on small feet, she remarks, can never, like stays, impair health nor do they offend the eye by producing any disproportions. Since the customs of her country forbid ladies from leaving their homes, they experience no inconvenience from the lack of agility in their feet, and, in addition, they breathe comfortably, remain free of colic and consumption, and do not faint in warm weather.

The next gift she refers to is a cushion, the use of which as a garment she cannot understand. Her sister had worn it on her head for three days and developed a headache. Twentieth-century readers may be equally at a loss to understand the uses of the cushion. An essay "on fashion in dress; with particular remarks on certain female ornaments" in an earlier issue of the *Columbian Magazine* (2 [June, 1790], 350–52) indicates that the cushion is a device for concealing the breasts and at the same time making them seem of substantial size. The Chinese lady refers to a third gift, the bishop, apparently a type of bustle. After she had tied it on her hips, dogs and cats squalled at her, and her parrot broke his cage in trying to get out of her way. Her father then sent it to Pekin to be preserved in a museum among articles of dress worn by the Tartars before being civilized. Turning to generalities, the letter writer remarks that her countrymen had been told that Americans follow the British in dress and manners; she assumes, therefore, that the report that they had recently become a separate and independent empire must be without foundation. She realizes that Americans laugh at Chinese religion, but questions the benefits of Western science and religion if they do not teach people to live according to reason. She also admits that some Chinese merchants of an inferior class may be guilty of fraud, but maintains that Chinese laws, unlike those of America, are just; she has been told that the Americans "defraud not only strangers, but even your own citizens by *law*." She charges her correspondent no longer to reproach the Chinese for the words demeaning to foreigners on the chop or pass given to ships in their waters: "Permit the Barbarians to pass the fort. They can do no harm." She affirms that "many of your customs belong to barbarous nations, and all the power, knowledge and ingenuity of your country can never *hurt* us, while you consume our luxuries, and pay for them with money, obtained by the culture and sale of the necessities of life." She signs herself Thaliska Toluda, a name that would not seem to be Chinese even to unsophisticated American readers of the time. The letter itself, however, reflects some significant sentiments. It is entirely positive in regard to the Chinese nation and specifically indicates that the laws of the kingdom are just. Also it expresses an attitude toward the China trade completely opposite to the optimistic view of Samuel Shaw, one more in line with the cautious approach of Jefferson and Freneau.

A similar display of invented Chinese names and titles designed to satirize local idiosyncracies appeared in an essay series "The Itinerant" in the *Boston Magazine*, 10 Sept. 1803 (1: 185–86). Designed to ridicule hypochondria and medical nostrums, the essay purports to be the advertisement of a Chinese physician setting up practice in Boston: "Dr. Ching-Ching-Ti-Ching, from *Pekin*, Fellow of the Imperial Medical Academy of China, Second Grand Physician to the Imperial Seraglio, Chief Counsellor of the Emperor's Chief Physician, &c.&c." The advertisement offers Dr. Chang's MAGNUM IMPERIANDUM BRANIORUM RESTORANDUM, or GRAND IMPERIAL BRAIN RESTORATIVE" as "a sure and infallible remedy for all diseases of the mind." As testimonials, Dr. Ching cites the cures worked upon Miss Fanny Flutter from overeating and overspending, upon Master William Muslin from excessive dandyism, and upon Mr. Walkbackwards from political raving. This attention to Chinese medicine is quite unusual in the American climate of opinion, although a hotly disputed debate on Chinese remedies and practices had taken place in Spain during the middle years of the eighteenth century.

Other pseudo-documents or pseudo-translations were presented in American periodicals as completely genuine. Franklin published in his *Pennsylvania Gazette*, an extract from the London *Gentleman's Magazine*, headed an "*Address of a late* Chinese *Nobleman to the Emperor*" on "*the* Pride, Luxury, *and* Corruption *of the* Chinese" (1 February 1739). In the address, the nobleman in great distress laments the corruption and lawlessness of the nation as luxury, folly, and sensual pleasures flourish all over the kingdom. Pointing out that a sincere love of virtue is no longer being inculcated as in the past, he charges that wrong measures are responsible for the spread of vice. Finally he exhorts the emperor to examine history and think of virtue and the welfare of the poor. The English essayist was no doubt using an oriental background to urge domestic reform, and his Chinese names and trappings may have deceived readers on both sides of the Atlantic.

A similar piece appeared in the *Royal American Magazine* (1 [August 1774], 310–12), a narrative titled "Princes ruined by their Ministers," designed to illustrate the principle that "those who trust all to servants are in a fair way to be undone." According to this essay, some men become bankrupt even though their business is profitable because they commit management to subordinates. In higher circles, a man of fortune runs into debt every year, but knows none of the details of his income since he has left them in the hands of his steward, who in the meantime purchases a large estate for himself. Leaders in the affairs of the nation, moreover, who do not trouble themselves about details are leaving the door open for cheating. Parliaments are checks upon ministers, but if the two arms of government engage in collusion, the nation is bought and sold. If the prince makes a bad choice, as often happens, nothing but ruin is in store for the nation. He is like a man with a bad wife who is the last to hear of her infamy. The essayist then cites an affecting example of this situation from Chinese history. Zunchin—the last emperor—had a good disposition to govern mildly, but unfortunately chose ministers who used his authority to gratify their personal ambitions and who kept people they had wronged from bringing their grievances to his attention. A rebellion against his authority was carried out by Ly and Chum, former generals, who had been abused by the ministers. When the capital city was surrendered into their hands, the emperor put his daughter to death by his own hand, and he and the empress hanged themselves. Before dispatching himself he wrote the following in his own blood.

> The Mandarins are traitors, they have perfidiously betrayed their prince, and all of them deserve to be hanged. . . . As for the people, they are not criminal, and deserve not to be punished: and therefore to use them ill will be injustice. I have lost that great empire, which descended to me by inheritance from my ancestors by the treachery of the Mandarins. In me is finished the royal line, which so many kings, my progenitors, continued down to me with all the grandeur and fame suitable to their dignity: I will therefore for ever close my eyes, that I may not see the empire . . . ruined and ruled by a tyrant. . . . It is fit the prince should die, since his whole state is now expiring: and how can I endure to live, having seen the loss and destruction of that which was dearer to me than life?

The essayist concludes with the warning that the monarch of a kingdom as large as all Europe with a population of a hundred million subjects was forced to destroy himself and his family at the age of thirty-two because of the villainy of his ministers. This essay has some basis in historical fact for Zunchin was the title given to the reign of the last Ming emperor of China, and Chum was another historical figure Wu San-kuei. I have not been able to ascertain whether this essay originated in America or whether it was taken from an English periodical, and the same uncertainty exists about other essays treated in this chapter for which I do not provide a particular provenance.

It is not clear whether the author of the narrative of Zunchin intended it to be taken as historical fact or allegory. The same is true of a rather insipid essay in the *Massachusetts Magazine* (5 [June, 1793], 337–39) titled "Oriental History / Specimen of Chinese Luxury." It concerns the reign of Kia, a person of wit, imagination, bodily graces, and great strength, born to be a hero. Unfortunately the spirit of irreligion and an excessive love of luxury made him corrupt and inhuman. After alienating all his subjects, he put to death three bonzes who remained loyal to him. He fell desperately enamoured of an ambitious woman, who persuaded him to build a palace impervious to the seasons and filled with light day and night. After he lavished the wealth and resources of the empire to build it, a neighboring enemy attacked and destroyed the palace and seized the throne. Kia fled to save his life, wandered about in misery, and at length died, "the victim of mad luxury, the scandal of his throne, and the contempt of his people."

An unmistakable allegory in the satirical vein of Swift or Voltaire appeared in the *New Haven Magazine* (1 [August 1786], 214) under the title "An Account of a controversial dispute that happened in China." The dispute concerns religion, and it portrays the Chinese as not only champions of tolerance but superior to the clergy of the West. Early in the reign of Emperor Kambi (an imaginary figure), a mandarin of Canton overheard a violent altercation in an adjoining house. He learned that it was a religious controversy between a Danish almoner, a chaplain from Batavia, and a Jesuit, the three disputants representing the Lutheran, Calvinist, and Roman Catholic faiths respectively. After the mandarin invited the adversaries to his house to settle their differences, the Jesuit declared "that it was very unhappy for him, who was always in the right, to have to do with people who were always in the wrong; that he had, at first, reasoned with great composure, but that at length his patience was quite exhausted." The mandarin, intimating that "politeness was very necessary in every dispute," asked to be told the subject of debate. The Jesuit replied simply that his two opponents both refused to "submit to the decisions of the council of Trent." The mandarin turned to the others and remarked that since a large group of people must necessarily know more than an individual, they should accept the decisions of the council. The Lutheran answered that the principle is a wise one, but that he respected the opinion of a large number of assemblies held prior to the one at Trent. The mandarin then inquired whether the Lutheran and the Calvinist held the same opinion against the Jesuit, but was told that they differed from each other as much as from the Jesuit. The Jesuit thereupon maintained that since the other two were mortal enemies and had disputed with him, it was evident that they were both wrong and only he in the right. Denying that this is self-evident, the mandarin affirmed that probably all three were wrong and suggested that each state his case. The Jesuit then began a long harangue of which the mandarin understood nothing; nor could he understand the arguments of the Jesuit's antagonists. At length all three talked at once, abusing each other in the process. Silencing them, the mandarin warned that if they were to be heard in China, "they must begin by being neither intolerant nor intolerable." The Jesuit then met a Jacobin missionary on the street to whom he confided the whole affair. The Jacobin declared that had he been present he would have convicted all three of them of falsehood and idolatry. The mandarin thereupon committed both priests to prison. When his deputy asked how long they must stay there, the mandarin replied "Till they agree." The deputy replied that they would then remain for life. The sentence was then modified to "till they forgive each other." When the deputy answered that this would amount to the same thing, the mandarin agreed that they could be released when they were "content to seem to agree."

Voltaire treats the same subject in one of his dialogues with almost the same cast of characters, a Jesuit, a Jansenist, a Quaker, an Anglican, a Lutheran, a Puritan, a Muslim, and a Jew, attempting to to confound each other and to convert a group of Chinese (1837: 6: 640–42). With appropriate deference to the renowned French satirist, I find more bite and amusement in the American tale.

A less satirical piece inculcating a more general morality appeared in the *Massachusetts Magazine* for August 1789 (1, 496–99). Titled "Tsouy, or the Philosopher: A Chinese History," this tale concerns the relationships between God, human behavior, and philosophic belief. The Emperor Tsching-Ouhan, entertaining the strange project of discovering the meaning of the word *philosopher*, issues a proclamation that all who belong to this category appear at court. The first candidate, Cham Sou, who had composed one hundred volumes on Confucius, boasted of his talents, humanity, and exemplary piety, but the emperor found on inquiry that he was vindictive and ambitious of being talked of. Next was a rhapsodic author who in his books obscured truth instead of clarifying it. His conduct was motivated by pride and singularity; he did everything to obtain notoriety; and in all his conversations he indicated how much he hated mankind. The emperor found him a "diverting animal," but dismissed him. Kiong, the most humble of the bonzes, next appeared. He depreciated himself in every way, but in doing so registered pride in his humility and debasement. The emperor gave this "religious mountebank" into the charge of his physician. He was succeeded by a mandarin with a huge triple chin who represented hedonism. His method of studying pleasure as a science the emperor rejected as disgusting egoism. Determined not to give up, however, the emperor left Pekin in disguise with his minister Tcheou Kong. Near the Great Wall they entered the hut of a hermit, who outdid the preceding mandarin in hatred of mankind. He expressed a wish to see the destruction of the entire human race and threatened to kill his visitors if they would not leave immediately. The emperor felt pity, but departed. In another city, he encountered Ouci Fong, who had written an entire treatise on the five duties and whose sentiments breathed truth, beauty, and virtue. The emperor thought he had found his man, but on inquiry discovered that Ouci Fong did not put his precepts into practice; he was rich, but did good to no one.

About to abandon his search and conclude that a philosopher is merely an imaginary being, the emperor approached a neat house in a small village. A peasant informed him that it belonged to a very even-tempered man—known for revenging himself on the villagers who play mischievous tricks on him by doing good to them in return. Entering the house, the emperor discovered a good old man, Tsouy, praying to Tien and thanking him for a morsel of bread that he is able to divide among the needy. Tsouy asked what he could do to serve his visitors and told them his story. He had been a minister during a former reign, but had been calumniated by his enemies and disgraced. He bore them no ill will, however, but was a loyal and adoring subject of his emperor. The latter exhorted him to return to the court, but Tsouy said he preferred to remain in retirement. On returning to Pekin, the emperor issued an order for Tsouy to appear. Although assuming that new charges had been leveled against him, Tsouy out of a principle of submission obeyed the summons. At the palace, Tsouy recognized the emperor and was proclaimed a philosopher. His virtuous and beneficent actions had earned him the title. After he and the emperor died, two statues were erected: that of the emperor bearing the simple inscription *The Benefactor*, that of Tsouy, *The Philosopher*.

A similar narrative in the *New York Magazine* for November 1793 (4, 682–86) describes the loyalty of two friends, thereby attributing to the Chinese people traits of honor and steadfastness; completely opposite to those in the tale of the Chinese matron. The events in "The Friend—A Chinese History" take place in the reign of the legendary Emperor Yao. Two bosom companions, Fong and Kiang, are models of perfect friendship. One night Kiang enters Fong's house and confesses he has murdered a virtuous man Outing over an imagined insult that Outing in his last breath declared he had never uttered. Fong insists on hiding Kiang and looking after him. Kiang asserts that he is willing to die, but agrees to remain alive for the sake of his family. Fong then learns that another virtuous person, Ming, has been unjustly accused of the murder. He is then in a quandary whether to allow the virtuous and innocent Ming to die or to betray his closest friend. He tells his wife the situation and leaves Kiang in her care, and, going to the place of execution, declares that he is the guilty one. He is about to be killed when Kiang arrives, having been informed of Fong's intention by the latter's wife. When Kiang declares his own guilt, the judges are not able to decide which had committed the deed. They are both taken to the emperor, Yao, who at length discovers the truth. He frees Fong, but, although pitying and admiring Kiang, says he must be condemned, for he "who sheds blood, must have his blood also shed." Kiang accepts the decision, saying that Tien himself has spoken through the mouth of the emperor and asking only permission to embrace his friend for the last time. During the embrace, Fong faints away and on recovering finds himself and Kiang seated side by side. Yao explains that he has satisfied justice by subjecting Kiang to all the terrors of death, who has thereby expiated his crime. The emperor is, therefore, able to exercise his clemency and benevolence by pardoning him.

Another account of judicious discrimination appeared in the *Universal Magazine* for June 1797 (2, 376–77), under the title "Remarkable Instance of Penetration and Advice, A Chinese Story." The intendant of a certain city appointed his close friend chief justice. After a certain time the latter noticed that the intendant had suddenly become very melancholy and seldom appeared in public. The justice insisted on being admitted to his presence and persisted in inquiries about the reasons for his friend's melancholy. The latter confessed that the imperial seal in his custody was missing from its cabinet and that without it he was unable to conduct his official duties. Yet the cabinet in which it was kept remained locked and showed no signs of having been broken into. The justice then asked whether he had any enemies, and the intendant replied that the governor of the city bore him great antipathy because he had been passed over for the intendant's position. Realizing that the governor had stolen the seal, the justice advised his friend to move his valuables to a safe place, set fire to the room containing the cabinet, and call the governor, whose duty it was to protect property from fire. He did so and turned over the cabinet as in a fright to the governor. The next day the governor returned it to him with the seal inside, for had he not done so he would have borne responsibility for its loss. "And thus the calmness of the chief justice proved a remedy, where a man of superior parts, but without constancy of mind, threw up all hopes, and abandoned himself to a wild dispair [*sic*]."

It is possible that the two previous narratives are based upon actual events and that they were extracted from European historical sources. Other stories appeared in American periodicals with appropriate indication of the works from which they had been taken. The *Massachusetts Magazine* for April 1790 (2, 236–37), for example, carried "Historical Anecdotes of an Illustrious Chinese Patriot, Statesman and Historian," taken from the *Histoire générale de la Chine* of Moyriac de Mailla. The anecdote concerns See-Ma-Koang of the eleventh century B.C., who restored Chinese history after the great fire designed to destroy all learning. A man of recognized virtue, candor, and learning, he was declared by a pupil ten years after his death to be the enemy of his country and guilty of high treason. As a result, his titles were erased, his writings denounced and burned, and his monuments torn down. "This outrage against a character so illustrious and unsullied, was the contrivance of a wicked cabal," but was condemned and its interdictions cancelled under the next emperor.

Further authentic history appeared in a "Chinese Anecdote/The Female Warrior," extracted from the abbé Grosier's *General Description of China* in the *Massachusetts Magazine* for December 1793 (5, 727). The anecdote concerns a woman warrior belonging to a group called the Maio-tse. Soldiers who had been conducting the siege of a small fort under the impression that it was being held by a detachment of men discovered that a single woman had been defending it by hurling down stones and occasionally firing her musket.

Robert Waln, Jr., whose essays on China I have considered in chapter 13, also used the genre of a dream vision of feminine beauty in order to impart some of his historical and sociological information. Early in 1824, he submitted to the first volume of the *American Magazine* in Philadelphia a manuscript titled "Voyager on Wings" that the editor described as well-written, but too long for publication. Waln presumably resubmitted a shorter version, for it appeared in two parts in the June and July numbers of the same year (1:434–446;2:8–17). In the first part, the narrator and a companion named Femino embark on an aerial tour of the world to view the various appearances of the female sex and the customs associated with them. Although professing to investigate beauties rather than deformities, the narrative dwells upon the latter. Some societies, he states, trace all evil to women, and others call them the best works of God's creation. If every man followed reason exclusively, all males would be in love with the same woman, but fancy and taste have made variety acceptable. The two voyagers visit a number of exotic sites, including Ceylon, Malabar, India, Burma, Pekin, Persia, Tripoli, and Italy. In connection with China, Waln gives a lengthy description of bound feet, and in an unusual comparison affirms that the same custom existed in Spain during the seventeenth century. He also observes physical likenesses between Spanish and Chinese women. He concludes by remarking that "female associations are the strongest links in the chain of human happiness;—sever them, and you destroy not only morals, but religion—*he who abandons female society, is an enemy to himself.*"

Dropping entirely the winged voyage motif in the second part, Waln concentrates on China under the sub-title "Chinese Feet and Long Nails." Accepting the notion of the eternal stability of Chinese culture, he affirms that the manners and customs of this ancient people have no resemblance to those of the rest of the world. Indicating that Marco Polo has no reference to the practice of footbinding, he quotes the conflicting explanations for the custom offered by a series of later authorities and concludes with his personal observations in Canton.

Much authentic Chinese fiction contains considerable magic and supernatural intervention in human affairs. In many oriental tales of the West these elements are united with descriptions of romantic scenery and plots inculcating conventional morality. At the turn of the century, a publisher in Hartford, Connecticut, brought out an illustrated pamphlet *The Trifle-Hunter: or, the Adventures of Prince Bonbennin. A Chinese Tale*, 1798, that was followed by separate editions in Newport, Rhode Island, 1799, and in Windsor, Vermont, in 1810. A moral lesson in the guise of an oriental tale, the narrative has no connection with the China of actuality, but is an allegory against being obsessed with trifling matters.

A much longer work similarly based entirely on imagination with no link to the real China issued from the pen of Henry Sherburne, a native of New Hampshire, in 1800. With the anomalous title *The Oriental Philanthropist: or True Republican*, the work has no didactic purpose, but exploits to the highest degree the conventional devices of magic and the supernatural in a vein of purified theatricalism. Like Fowler's protagonist ten years later, Sherburne's romantic hero, the son of the Chinese emperor, is described as a philanthropist, a sign perhaps that Americans in general regarded upper class Chinese as benevolent sages in the mold of Confucius. Sherburne's novel opens with a descriptive setting resembling that of *The Tale of Genji*, although Sherburne had certainly never heard of the Japanese classic, which was not introduced into the Western world until late in the nineteenth century. The rest of the novel has more in common with *The Arabian Nights* than with any work in Chinese, Japanese, or European letters. It is filled with magnificent palaces, genies, fairies, flying chambers, and instantaneous voyages from one continent to another. In addition to this constant magic, the novel is permeated with abstract sentiments of benevolence and rectitude. All of the men are virtuous and handsome; the women, pure and beautiful. Evil does not exist. Occasionally an uprising occurs or a selfish minister plots against the state, but the uprisings are put down without bloodshed, and the selfish individuals repent of their misdeeds. Supernatural monsters every now and then threaten one of the virtuous characters, but they are always saved in the nick of time by a genie, and the monster usually turns out to be under a spell which is lifted through the efforts of one of the virtuous characters.

A philosophic and contemplative prince Nytan, son of the emperor,

Rexien, is surrounded in a castle by a coterie of select friends, including his two amiable sisters, Ereng and Yerrie, and two worthy mandarins who had gained the hearts of these sisters. The names of these characters, formed by the arbitrary combination of random syllables, resemble those in the twentieth-century scientific utopias of Ursula K. Le Guin. In the propitious reign of Rexien, the miseries of poverty and oppression were scarcely known. One of the court ministers, Sanden, in an effort to blacken the character of Prince Nytan in order to ascend to the throne on the death of the emperor, makes it seem that Nytan had intrigued at court against his father. On the way to refute these charges in Pekin, Nytan is seized by Sanden's troops and taken to a gloomy castle in a deserted countryside.

At this point Sherburne combines an attempt at verisimilitude with utopian fantasy. He indicates that "the historians of *Xientien*, who wrote Memoirs of *Ravenzer*, (the nation celebrated in the following books,) do indeed give a different account of the Prince's misfortune," and refers to a purported historian Zerinn, who locates the events farther back than the period in which they are placed by "the Historian of China *Reshang*" (15). Sherburne asserts that his version rests primarily on Reshang although he occasionally consults other writers, especially Lengshan. His design in narrating the fortunes of Nytan, he affirms, is to present morality "in the most engaging view" and to "guard the mind of the reader, while he is travelling through the regions of fancy, into the world of reality" (1800: 17).

One of the obvious purposes of Sherburne's narrative is to oppose religious sectarianism. Nytan during his captivity dabbles in the occult sciences and prays to the God of nature. Approving the latter and condemning the former, Sherburne indicates that "Rexien, the Emperor, who was very learned and a great writer, had, in some of his published works, (which were of great reputation throughout all China, and other countries,) exposed the absurdities of those religious sects. . . . The sects of enthusiasts, and the promoters of fanaticism, were . . . inimical to the reigning power of China" (23). But the element of fantasy in the book far outweighs that of social criticism. Nytan possesses a magic picture that operates like a genie, carrying out the prince's commands. After he sends it to spy on an invading party of soldiers, it is brought back by a beautiful maiden, who transforms herself into a yellow bird in order to gain entrance to Nytan's cell. She is the Fairy Leingreing, who lives in a castle at the bottom of the sea. She renders Nytan's chamber invisible, sends it through the air to the summit of Mount Caucasus, and installs it in the palace of libraries, the storehouse of all the wisdom of the world.

The chamber next flies to the island of Ravenzar, where Nytan encounters thirty beautiful maidens. He orders thirty dwellings and a palace to be erected in a model city and provides handsome squires for the maidens. Then he sends a winged chariot to Pekin in order to recruit among the poorest families a population for his ideal community. He orders 100 more dwellings and a few pages later increases this number to 600. He invites the thirty couples and the other settlers to engage in a mass marriage and to choose legislators and a president. Some critics have called the land of Ravenzar a utopia, but it has nothing in common with imaginary communities which spell out their laws, customs, and principles of government. In Ravenzar everything is general, nothing specific. The reader must accept that the inhabitants are wise, beautiful, and virtuous and that the state abounds with riches without asking the source and nature of the wisdom, virtue, and wealth. The metropolis on the island is called Xientien after Pekin in China. In a footnote Sherburne informs his readers with his customary disregard for reality that "a modern name for China, is said to be Tamin, i.e. the Kingdom of Brightness" (84). In the space of two pages Xientien acquires twenty thousand buildings and Ravenzar becomes a nation protected by divine providence and dedicated to virtue.

Nytan next goes to Persia, where he guards the queen against the invasion of a disappointed suitor. A blue bird tells him to marry this queen, and in a remarkable foreshadowing of the device of the doppleganger in later Romanticism, it eventually turns out that the bird and the queen are the same person. He marries Selina, the queen, and installs her in a garden and palace exactly the same as those in Ravenzar. They rule Persia jointly with virtue and benevolence, and their subjects, like the inhabitants of Ravenzar, are uniformly happy and good. In Sherburne's words, "The ladies of highest rank, and the nobility were virtuous, generous, and exemplary" (100). In the meantime, Nytan's sisters in China marry worthy mandarins. In China also "virtue and industry generally prevailed," even though the land was peopled by "no less than three hundred millions under the government of one man (103)," an authentic touch, as we have seen in chapter 9. Embassies were not allowed from any nation except Ravenzar. A superman as well as a saint, Nytar next becomes a soldier in a European army and leads his troops to victory.

After appointing rulers to take their place in Persia, Nytan and Selina return to Ravenzar and build more roads, houses and cities with the help of fairies and genies. Everything is "magnificent, delicious and enchanting" (131). Sherburne speaks out against "the luxury, the profuse magnificence of the rich" in the ordinary world, while at the same time glorifying wealth and splendor in the happy land of Ravenzar (133). He also condemns institutional religion as an "engine of cruelty and oppression" while filling entire pages with rhapsodies over the beauties of the creation and the benevolence of the creator. Amid all the moralizing throughout the book, the only practical virtue he specifies is that of temperance, devoting a dozen or so pages to sermonizing against the abuse of alcohol. He includes very brief remarks against slavery and suddenly turns the inhabitants of Ravenzar into vegetarians. "None feasted on flesh; . . . no creature's blood was shed . . . to gratify a vicious palate" (145). Although making no connection between diet and longevity, Sherburne has "the citizens of both sexes, increase in beauty, and vigor, and every amiable accomplishment, as they advance in life" (156). Many live to be several hundred years old and retain the bloom and energy of youth.

Despite fantasy such as this, Sherburne apparently believed that his blend of magic and romance had some relevance to the emergence of the United States as an independent nation. After the citizens of Ravenzar choose a republican form of government, Nytan proclaims virtuously, "Though I am heir to the empire of China; and though my father would place me in [*sic*] the throne, I have preferred being a citizen amongst this illustrious people" (209). Sherburne also concludes his novel with a poem in which he compares his fabled realm of Ravenzar with the "Federal City" of America, which he exhorts to "rise in glory."

In a footnote, Sherburne says he has "no other apology for his attempt to imitate the Oriental tales of fiction, than the hopes of drawing the attention to interesting realities, of those who would otherwise be hardly persuaded to peruse his pages" (212). It is difficult to believe that many in Sherburne's time or later have had the persistence to wade through his pseudo-orientalism. He apparently did not realize that one of the most important ingredients of the genuine oriental tale is brevity. Not only do the "interesting realities" that he was attempting to convey fail even to materialize, but his sentimentalizing and moralizing style is repetitive and diffuse. His book contains some genuine reflections of Chinese life and culture, but it is doubtful that many readers progressed far enough to encounter them.

The China of imagination in American writers takes a poor second place to the China of reality in such historians and chroniclers as Samuel Shaw, Amasa Delano, Robert Waln, Jr., and even the admirers of Chinese agriculture. The books of Henry Sherburne and George Fowler are substantial in size, but not in content. Sherburne's has nothing whatsoever to recommend it although Fowler's has some pertinent comments on contemporary manners and political issues. Apart from Franklin's Chinese letter, the only playful utilization of China that is clearly the product of the United States is the other epistolary work "From a Chinese Lady." This is a respectable *jeu d'esprit*, but its focus is local rather than international, satirizing, as it does, female attire, subservience to British attitudes, and native cupidity. The "Controversial Dispute" between the Western clergymen of three different faiths is an even more polished example of social satire, comparable to the tales of d'Argens and Voltaire, but its vocabulary strongly suggests a European origin. "Tsouy or the Philosopher," "The Friend," and "Instance of Penetration and Advice" are excellent moral tales, but they resemble narratives taken from actual histories such as the anecdotes attributed to Moyriac de Mailla and Grosier, and they may, therefore, be extracts from European histories rather than original compositions. But if these works of the imagination are actually from American pens, they deserve recognition as readable native examples of the oriental tale.

CHAPTER

16

Conclusions and Conjectures

merican commentaries on China during the Enlightenment years
covered a highly diverse spectrum and reflected opinions equally
varied. Some writers, as one contemporary complained, extolled
the Chinese "in the highest terms," but others ran into the contrary
extreme of bitter denigration (*Boston Magazine* 1786:3:220). Religion, agriculture, and government received considerable attention; whereas little
recognition was given to Chinese priority in the development of printing,
gunpowder, and the compass or in areas of medical practice. Individuals
like Benjamin Franklin investigated other aspects of Chinese science and
technology, however, and gave favorable reports concerning them.

It may be said with certainty that information about the Middle Kingdom was almost as widespread and as readily available in America as in
Europe, particularly toward the last years of Jefferson's lifetime. Franklin
read Du Halde's *Description* no later than three years after its publication in
Paris, and by the end of the eighteenth century every major European book
about China could be found in American libraries or bookstores. Even more
important, at least twenty-five books referring to China were brought out
by American publishers before 1826; eight of these were by American
authors (Handy, Morse, Van Braam, Gibson, Sharan, Delano, Waln, and
White), and those by Pierre Poivre and Aeneas Anderson had two separate
American editions. The great interest of American readers in the accounts
of the Macartney expedition was not stimulated entirely by the glamour and
prestige associated with the British empire, for their curiosity concerning

the Middle Kingdom had been previously aroused by Shaw and other American traders.

The Library Company of Philadelphia, the oldest library in America, possessed before 1812 at least twenty-two books on China, the titles of which can be found in its delightful publication *China on our Shelves*. The catalog printed in 1812 by the Library of Congress, one of the newest libraries of the time, however, shows only eight titles: *Asiatick Researches* of the Bengal Society (London:1801), Herbelot de Molainville's *Bibliothèque Orientale* (Maestricht:1760), Du Halde's *History* (London:1738), François Catrou's *Histoire générale de l'empire du Mogul* (La Haye:1708), Barrow's *Travels in China* (Philadelphia:1805), William Coxe's *Account . . . of commerce between Russia and China* (London:1780), John Meares's *Voyages . . . from China to the West Coast of America* (London:1791), and Staunton's *Account of Lord Macartney's Embassy* (London:1798; and Philadelphia: 1799). No Confucius, no Poivre, no Aeneas Anderson, and no Van Braam, all of whom were to be found in the Library Company before 1812.

Franklin's reprint of *The Morals of Confucius*, the earliest sign of American interest in China, initiated a current of respect for Chinese ethical standards that branched out on various levels throughout the century. Hannah Adams made clear in her encyclopedias on world religion, however, that the rationalist creed of Confucius did not extend to the majority of the Chinese population, which adhered to the mysticism of Taoism and Buddhism. Samuel Shaw not only failed to join in the adulation of Confucius, but emphasized the superstition and idolatry of the joss houses, an insistence in which he was joined by Robert Waln, Jr. Paine and one or two other deists followed Franklin and Voltaire in portraying the teachings of Confucius as parallel to the Western religion of nature, but the Chinese sage did not represent for Americans as a whole one of the saints of humanity, as he was regarded by Leibniz and other Europeans. One reason is that American Protestants remained untouched by the controversy over Chinese religion in which the Jesuits were engaged against other Catholic orders. Protestant orthodoxy, moreover, did not welcome alien strains. It is not strange, therefore, that a conformist defender of the faith like Timothy Dwight should condemn Confucius as a symbol of infidelity in contrast to the more liberal Ezra Stiles, who viewed Chinese culture as a type of benevolent humanism. In America as well as in Europe, political and religious traditionalism were likely to go hand in hand. In the aftermath of the French Revolution deism was associated with French political radicalism, and a sympathetic attitude toward Chinese culture tended to be espoused by persons of a liberal bent. The anti-Chinese strictures of Proclus were right at home, therefore, in the ultra-conservative pages of the *Port-Folio*.

Franklin's deistical treatment of Indian myths represents the same attitude of broad toleration that is revealed in his respectful attitude toward Confucius. The similarities between his Indian creation myths and those of China offer one kind of an East-West literary parallel, and the resemblances in plot structure between Petronius's tale of the Ephesian Matron and the Chinese legend of the inconstancy of Madam Choang provide another. Franklin's treatment of Indian mythology, moreover, reveals significant cultural affinities between the folklore of China and that of Native Americans.

Among the scores of European works about China that were known and read in the United States in the eighteenth century, the vast majority were French rather than English. The Jesuits achieved extensive recognition through the translation of Confucius and the compilation of Du Halde. Lafitau, however, does not seem to have made his way to English-speaking America until the present century. The gospel of the Physiocrats was widely disseminated through Poivre and miscellaneous information on Chinese agriculture through Brunel and Grosier. Prior to the Macartney mission, English works on China had practically no vogue in America. Although a version of Anson's voyage around the world was published in Boston in 1760 by Franklin's nephew Benjamin Mecom, it does not seem to have evoked much interest in American readers. Arthur Murphy's play "Orphan of China," the English equivalent of Voltaire's "The Chinese Orphan," was produced in New York as early as 1768. Goldsmith's *Citizen of the World* received more attention in American periodicals than did d'Argens *Lettres chinoises*, and Thomas Percy's translation of the novel *Hau Kiou Choaan* was mentioned by Jefferson, Waln, and Freneau. After the Macartney mission, England increased its presence in the Far East while that of France diminished, and as a result the influence of English publications concerning China began to outweigh that of French ones. Mendoza and other Spanish writers were completely unknown, and the only attention to Swedish ones was the review in Paine's *Pennsylvania Magazine* of Osbeck, Toreen, and Eckeberg.

In Europe, many of the most influential books about China came from the pens of authors like Du Halde, Grosier, Liebniz, and Wolff, who had never left European shores. In America, the eminent figures who concerned themselves with China, Franklin, Paine and Jefferson, had also not touched Asian soil, but the most substantial American literary works concerning the Middle Kingdom were written by men who had come into direct contact with Chinese culture, Samuel Shaw, Amasa Delano, Andrew Van Braam, and Robert Waln, Jr., had all been in one way or another engaged in maritime trading. The least cultivated of this group, the sea-captain Amasa Delano, wrote without prejudice and without displaying a sense of superiority. The most antagonistic, Samuel Shaw, paradoxically did more than any other America to stimulate interest in China, but he advocated close connections merely for the financial returns they would presumably bring to his nation. Van Braam was no less gifted as a writer than his European counterparts, Anderson, Staunton, and Grosier, but the circumstances under which his travel account appeared worked against its receiving adequate recognition even to this day. Had it been written in English it would merit a place on the reading list of college courses in American literature.

Robert Waln, Jr.'s *China* is also a distinguished book, but it is too diffuse in style and too exotic in content to have appealed to a broad readership in his own times, and it has consequently been out of circulation ever since. But it represents a brilliant combination of historical research and literary imagination. If, like Cotton Mather's monumental *Magnalia Christi Americana*, his *China* had embraced American culture and embodied a national theme, it would probably now be regarded as one of the classics of American letters. It gives a coherent digest of the current knowledge concerning Chinese geography, history, religion, and racial origins spiced with an intriguing sprinkling of satire and personal experience. Waln's newspaper essays reveal an even greater degree of originality in their approach to such topics as food, painting, drama, secret societies, and East-West diplomatic relations. His lack of knowledge of the Chinese language may keep him from being classed as a professional Sinologist along with such European stalwarts as de Guignes, Staunton, and Davis, but his literary talents are by no means inferior to theirs.

No evidence exists that the European fascination for Chinoiserie, or arts and decoration in the style real or imagined of the Middle Kingdom, expanded to America before 1784. After the initiation of trade relations, however, porcelain, painting, tapestry, furniture, and other objects were regularly imported and displayed, and Van Braam built his house and pagoda in the Chinese manner.

Among literary works of the imagination inspired by the Middle Kingdom, the only one that has received any scholarly attention is Franklin's Chinese letter. Sharan's spurious voyage is less distinguished artistically, but it may have been more widely read in the period. One significant feature to be noticed about its China coverage is that his travels in other parts of the world had to be buttressed by harrowing or picaresque adventures, whereas the section on the Middle Kingdom depends for the most part on putative information about the geography and customs of the country. Translations and summaries of serious European works about China served a valuable purpose at the time, but today they have merely historical interest. The reason for the paucity of belletristic writing concerning China is not that the Middle Kingdom failed to inspire it, but that gifted authors had not yet been developed. Even Samuel Miller in 1803 placed his own nation among those that had not yet become literary.

Finally, there were no American Sinophiles in the eighteenth century comparable to Voltaire in France or Leibniz in Germany. Franklin shared many of Voltaire's enthusiasms for China, but they are not expressed in any of his major works. American opinion in general was, nevertheless, favorable toward China, especially in regard to its morality, government, and agriculture. Practically no trace exists of the racism that came into being during the nineteenth century. Those who criticized China did so because of its institutions and policies, not because of any physical distinctions or characteristics of its people. Paine, Jefferson and Franklin, three deists, praised Chinese culture because they perceived in it institutions compatible with their personal Enlightenment philosophy. The only devastating attack, that of Proclus in the *Port-Folio*, consisted of considerable contrived reasoning and scant reality. Samuel Shaw was better informed, but equally prejudiced; his derogatory views were balanced, however, by the favorable ones of Amasa Delano. Van Braam, who had lived for a quarter of a century in Canton, revealed that experience gained in this enclave had little relevance to the rest of the vast empire. The more he penetrated into the heart of the nation, the more he cast off earlier preconceptions. Robert Waln, Jr., had a vaster encyclopedic knowledge of China than any one else in his milieu. He found much to condemn in Chinese culture, but had occasional words of praise in his effort to be fair.

Before the middle of the eighteenth century, Americans knew little about the Chinese except that they revered Confucius and consumed ginseng, but by the end of Jefferson's administration fact had overtaken myth in regard to the religion, literature, history, and agriculture of the Middle Kingdom. Americans shared with Europeans the notion of the great antiquity of Chinese culture and its moral excellence, and some expressed the notion of its eternal standing still. During the lives of both Franklin and Jefferson, it was the Enlightenment manner of looking at the world that characterized the perception of China. Its culture was thought to embrace natural religion, strictly observed morality, a planned economy based on agriculture, and a patriarchal government combining both high ethical standards and an orderly administration. It cannot be argued that knowledge of China in America in the hundred years before 1826 approached that in France, England, or Germany, but neither can it be denied that American interest in the Middle Kingdom during the same period was continuous and extensive and that it consequently produced a considerable body of respectable and influential writing.

APPENDIX: AMERICAN IMPRINTS
CONCERNING CHINA BEFORE 1826

This list is based primarily on the holdings of the Library Company of Philadelphia and of the American Antiquarian Society, Worcester, Massachusetts. It may, therefore, not be complete.

1760. Anson, George (Dilworth, W. H.) *Lord Anson's Voyage Round the World; Performed in the Years 1740, 41, 42, 43, and 44.* Boston: B. Mecom. (The printer, Benjamin Mecom, was Franklin's nephew. The account of the voyage was not the semi-official one published in 1748, the authorship of which was attributed to Richard Walter. The latter complains severely of the "artifices, extortions and frauds" practiced by the Chinese people, but the Dilworth version published by Mecom has nothing unfavorable to the Chinese.)

1778. Poivre, Pierre. *The Life of David Hume, Esq; the philosopher and historian, written by himself. To which are added, the Travels of a philosopher, containing observations on the manners and arts of various nations, in Africa and Asia. From the French of M. le Poivre, late envoy to the King of Cochin-China, and now intendent of the Isles of Bourbon and Mauritius.* Philadelphia: Printed and sold by Robert Bell, next door to St. Paul's Church, in Third-Street. MDCCLXXVIII.

1787. Lecompte [*sic*], Louis. *The Voyage of Peter Kolben A.M. to the Cape of Good Hope. A Voyage to China by Lewis Le Compte. Anecdotes of the Elephant, from Wolfe's Travels.* Philadelphia: William Spotswood.

1791. Handy, Hast (Hastings?). *An Inaugural Dissertation on Opium submitted . . . to the College of Philadelphia.* Philadelphia: T. Lang.

1794. Crouch, Nathaniel. *A Journey to Jerusalem. Containing, the travels of fourteen Englishmen, in 1668 to Jerusalem. . . . In a letter from T. B. To which is added, a Description of the Empire of China.* Poughkeepsie, Dutchess County (New York): Printed and sold by Nicholas Power.

1795. Anderson, Aeneas. *A Narrative of the British Embassy to China, in the years 1792, 1793, & 1794.* Philadelphia: Printed by T. Dobson.

1795–96. *The World Displayed; or, A Curious Collection of Voyages and Travels, Selected and compiled from the Writers of all Nations.* . . . First American Edition, Corrected & Enlarged, in Eight Volumes. Philadelphia: Published by Doblebower, Key, and Simpson. Vol. 6, pp. 184–247 contains "A Description of China. By Louis Le Compte [*sic*] and P. Du Halde. Containing their appointment by the French king;—their adventures till their arrival in China;—their reception at court."

1795. Anderson, Aeneas. *A Narrative of the British Embassy to China, in the years 1792, 1793, and 1794.* New York: Printed by T. and J. Swords for Rogers and Berry.

1796. Morse, Jedidiah. *The American Universal Geography, or, a View of the Present State of all the Empires, Kingdoms, States, and Republics in the Known World.* Part II. Second edition of this volume. Boston: Isaiah Thomas and Ebenezer T. Andrews. (contains 46 pages on China, including 30 of extracts from Aeneas Anderson)

1796. Winterbotham, William. *An Historical, Geographical, and Philosophical View of the Chinese Empire.* 2 vols. Philadelphia: Re-printed for Richard Lee, Dunning, Hyer and Palmer.

1797. Poivre, Pierre. *Travels of a Philosopher; or, Observations on the Manners and Arts of various Nations in Africa and Asia. By M. Le Poivré* [sic], *late Envoy to the King of Cochin-China.* Augusta (Kennebeck) Maine: Reprinted by Peter Edes.

1797–1798. Van Braam, Andreas Everard. *Voyage de l'Ambassade de la Compagnie des Indes Orientales Hollandaises, vers l'Empereur de la Chine, dans les années 1794 & 1795. Philadelphie: Et se trouve chez l'Editeur.* 2 vols. (This is the first book about China written by an American and published in America. It was translated from the Dutch by the editor and publisher Moreau de Saint-Méry. Later pirated editions of the first volume were published in London in English, 1798; in Paris in French, 1798; in Leipzig in German, 1798–99; and in Harlem in Dutch, 1804–1806.)

1798. *The Trifle-Hunter: or, The Adventures of Prince Bonbennin: A Chinese Tale.* Hartford. Printed by John Babcock.

1799. Staunton, George, bart. *An Authentic Account of an Embassy.* Philadelphia: Printed for Robert Campbell, by John Bioren.

1800. [Mathias, James Thomas] *The Imperial Epistle from Kien Long, Emperor of China, to George the Third . . . in the Year 1794.* Philadelphia: H. Maxwell.

1802. Mavor, William Fordyce. *An Historical Account of the Most Celebrated Voyages.* 13 vols. Philadelphia: M. and J. Conrad. Vol. 8, pp. 237–287 contains "Travels in China by the Jesuits Le Compte [*sic*] and Du Halde." This consists of Le Comte's narrative overlaid with extracts from Du Halde.

1802. Mavor, William Fordyce. *An Historical Account of the Most Celebrated Voyages.* 14 vols. Philadelphia: S. F. Bradford. Vol. 11, pp. 237–287 contains the same text of "Travels in China" as that in the M. and J. Conrad edition above.

1802. Mavor, William Fordyce. *An Historical Account of the Most Celebrated Voyages.* 13 vols. New Haven: W. W. Morse. Vol. 11, pp. 237–287 contains the same text of "Travels in China" as that in the M. and J. Conrad edition above.

1802. Mavor, William Fordyce. *An Historical Account of the Most Celebrated Voyages.* New York: T. & J. Swords. Vol. 11, pp. 237–287 contains the same text of "Travels in China" as that in the M. and J. Conrad edition above.

1803. Bell, John. *Journey of John Bell, Esq. from St. Petersburgh to Pekin. With an embassy from His Imperial Majesty Peter the Great, to Kamhi, Emperor of China.* Philadelphia: Printed and Sold by Joseph and James Cruikshank.

1804. Mavor, William Fordyce. *The History of Hindostan; of the Mogul Empire; parts of Tartar; and of China.* New York: Printed by Hopkins and Seymour, for Samuel Stansbury and Co. (This is volume 11 of his *Universal History* in 25 volumes [New York: 1804–1805].)

1805. Barrow, John. *Travels in China.* Philadelphia: Printed and sold by W. F. M'Laughlin.

1807. Gibson, John. *Observations on the Manner of Trading at Canton.* Philadelphia. (no printer indicated. There is a unique copy at the Cornell University Library that is not reproduced in Early American Reprints, Second Series.)

1808. Sharan, James. *The Adventures of James Sharan: compiled from the Journal, written during his Voyages and Travels in the Four Quarters of the Globe.* Baltimore: Printed by G. Dobbin & Murphy . . . for James Sharan.

1810. Phillips, Sir Richard. *A Description of the character, manners and customs of the inhabitants of China.* Philadelphia: Published by Johnson & Warner. . . . J. Bouvier printer.

1810. *The Trifle-Hunter: or, The Adventures of Prince Bonbennin.* First Windsor Edition. Windsor (Vt.) Farnsworth & Churchill. (See 1798 edition Hartford)

1817. Delano, Amasa. *Narrative of Voyages and Travels, in the Northern and Southern Hemispheres, Comprising three Voyages round the World: together with a Voyage of*

Survey and Discovery, in the Pacific Ocean and Oriental Islands. Boston: E. G. House.

1818. Ellis, Henry. *Journal of the Proceedings of the Late Embassy*. Philadelphia: Printed and published by A. Small.

1818. McCleod, John. *Narrative of a Voyage, in His Majesty's late Ship Alceste, to the Yellow Sea, along the Coast of Corea . . . to the Island of Lewchew; with an Account of the Shipwreck in the Straits of Gaspar*. Philadelphia: Published by M. Carey and son.

1818. Poivre, Pierre. *Travels of a Philosopher; or, Observations on the manners & arts of various nations in Africa and Asia. By M. Le Poivre, late envoy to the king of Cochin China, and president of the Royal Society of Agriculture at Lyons*. Baltimore: N. G. Maxwell.

1819. [anon.] *Scenes in China, exhibiting the manners, customs, diversions, and singular peculiarities of the Chinese . . . taken from the best authorities*. New York: Published by Samuel Wood & Sons . . . And Samuel S. Wood & Co., Baltimore.

1823. Waln, Robert, Jr. *China, Comprehending a view of the origin antiquity, history, religion, morals, government, laws, population, literature, drama, festivals, games, women, beggars, manners, customs, &c of that empire*. Philadelphia: Printed and published for the Author, by J. Maxwell.

1823. White, John. *History of a Voyage to the China Seas*. Boston: Wells and Lilly.

1825. Morand, J. *Memoir on Acupunturation, embracing A Series of Cases, drawn up under the inspection of M. Julius Cloquet*. Philadelphia: Published by Robert Desilver, Clark & Raser, Printers. (Extracts from this work were printed, 10 March 1825, in the *National Gazette* of Philadelphia.)

BIBLIOGRAPHY

Adams, Hannah. 1784. *An Alphabetical Compendium of the Various Sects which have appeared in the World*. Boston: B. Edes & sons.

———. 1791. *A View of Religions in two parts*. 2d. ed. Boston: Manning & Loring.

———. 1817. *A Dictionary of All Religions and Religious Denominations*. New York: James Eastburn.

Aldridge, A. Owen. 1950. "Franklin's Deistical Indians" in *Proceedings of the American Philosophical Society*. 94:398–410.

———. 1957. *Franklin and His French Contemporaries*. New York: New York University Press.

———. 1971–1972. "Voltaire and the Cult of China" in *Tamkang Review* 2–3: 25–49.

———. 1982. *Early American Literature: A Comparatist Approach*. Princeton: Princeton University Press.

———. 1986. "The Perception of China in English Literature of the Enlightenment" in *Asian Culture Quarterly*. 14: 1–26.

———. 1990. "China in the Spanish Enlightenment" in *Proceedings of the XIIth Congress of the International Comparative Literature Association* 5 vols. Munich: judicium verlag. 3: 404–409.

———. 1991. "Benjamin Franklin's Letter from China" in *Asian Culture Quarterly*. 19: 62–70.

Alexander, William. 1814. *Picturesque Representations of the Dress and Manners of the Chinese*. London: John Murray.

American Philosophical Society. 1789. *Transactions*. 2d. ed., 2 vols. Philadelphia: R. Aitken.

Anderson, Aeneas. 1795. *A Narrative of the British Embassy to China, in the years 1792, 1793, & 1794*. Philadelphia: T. Dobson.

Andrews, Norwood Jr. . 1988. *The Case against Camões*. New York: Peter Lang.

Anonymous. 1775. *The Chinese Traveler containing a Geographical, Commercial, and Political History of China . . . to which is added The Life of Confucius*. 2d. ed. London: E. & C. Dilly.

Anonymous. 1868. Review of A. W. Loomis, *Confucius and the Christian Classics*, in *Christian Examiner*. 4: 175–85.

Anson, George. 1974. *A Voyage Round the World in the Years 1740–1748, 1748.* (presumed author Walter Richard; Glyndwr Williams ed.) London: Oxford University Press.

Appleby, John H. 1982–83. "Ginseng and the Royal Society" in *Notes and Records of the Royal Society of London.* 37: 121–45.

Barlow, Joel. 1970. *Works.* 2 vols. W. K. Boffort & A. L. Ford, eds. Gainesville, Florida: Scholars Facsimiles & Reprints.

Barrow, John. 1806. *Travels in China.* London: T. Cadell & W. Davis.

Berger, Willy Richard. 1990. *China-Bild und China-Mode im Europa der Aufklarung.* Koln: Bohlau Verlag.

Boxer, C. R. 1939. "Isaac Titsingh's Embassy to the Court of Ch'ien Lung (1794–1795)" in *T'ien Hsia Monthly.* 8: 9–33.

Brune, Jean de La, trans. 1691. *The Morals of Confucius: A Chinese Philosopher, Who flourished above five Hundred Years before the coming of CHRIST.* London: Randal Taylor.

Brunel, M. 1792. See Rochin 1792.

Byrd, William. 1966. *Prose Works.* Louis B. Wright, ed. Cambridge, Mass.: Belknap Press.

Cheung, Kai Chong. 1984. *Chastity and Moral Uplift in Salient Novels of China and the West.* Unpublished University of Illinois dissertation.

Christman. Margaret C. S. 1984. *Adventurous Pursuits: Americans and the China Trade 1784–1844.* Washington, D.C.: Smithsonian Institution Press.

Clark, Thomas D. 1956. *Travels in the Old South.* Norman, Oklahoma: University of Oklahoma Press.

Confucius. See Brune, Jean de La 1691.

Conner, Patrick. 1986. *The China Trade, 1600–1860.* Brighton: Royal Pavilion Arts Gallery and Museum.

Cook, James. 1784. *A Voyage to the Pacific Ocean . . . in the Years 1776, 1777, 1778, 1779 and 1790. . . . Written by Captain James Cook, F. R. S., and Captain James King, L. L. D. and F. R. S.* London: W. & A. Strahan.

Cordier, Henri. 1897–1898. "Américains et Français à Canton au XVIIIe siècle" in *Journal de la Société des Americanistes de Paris.* 2: 1–13.

Corning, Howard. 1942. "Sullivan Dorr, an Early China Merchant," in *Essex Institute Historical Collections.* 78: 158–175.

Creel, Herrlee G. 1949. *Confucius the Man and the Myth.* New York: John Day Co.

Danton, George H. 1931. *The Culture Contacts of the United States and China. The Earliest Sino-American Culture Contacts 1784–1844.* New York: Columbia University Press.

Dawson, Raymond. 1967. *The Chinese Chameleon. An Analysis of European Conceptions of Chinese Civilization.* London: Oxford University Press.

Defoe, Daniel. 1719. *Farther Adventures of Robinson Crusoe.* London: W. Taylor.

———. 1905. *Farther Adventures of Robinson Crusoe.* New York: Macmillan.

Delano, Amasa. 1817. *Narrative of Voyages and Travels, in the Northern and Southern Hemispheres, Comprising three voyages round the World; together with a Voyage of*

Survey and Discovery, in the Pacific Ocean and Oriental Islands. Boston: E. G. House.

Dennett, Tyler. 1922 *Americans in Eastern Asia; a Critical Study of the Policy of the United States with Reference to China, Japan and Korea in the 19th Century.* New York: Macmillan.

Diderot, Denis. 1955–70. *Correspondance.* 16 vols. Georges Roth, ed. Paris: Minuit.

Dorr, Sullivan. 1942. "S. D., An Early China Merchant, Extracts from a Notebook . . . 1801" in Essex Institute *Historical Collections.* 78: 158–175.

Downs, Joseph, and Margaret R. Scherer. 1941. *The China Trade and Its Influences.* New York: Metropolitan Museum of Art.

Du Halde, Jean Baptiste. 1736. *The General History of China, containing a Geographical, Historical, Chronological, Political and Physical Description of the Empire of China.* 4 vols. London: John Watts.

Dulles, Foster Rhea. 1946. *China and America: The Story of their Relations since 1784.* Princeton: Princeton University Press.

Dunn, Nathan. 1839. *"Ten Thousand Chinese Things." A Descriptive Catalogue of the Chinese Collection in Philadelphia. With Miscellaneous Remarks upon the Manners, Customs, Trade, and Government of the Celestial Empire.* Philadelphia: Printed for the Proprietor [N. Dunn].

Duyvendak, J. J. L. 1938. "The Last Dutch Embassy to the Chinese Court (1794–1795)," in *T'oung Pao: Archives concernant l'Histoire, les Langues, la Géographie, l'Ethnographie et les Arts de l'Asie Orientale.* 34: 1–137.

Dwight, Timothy. 1969. (1) *The Major Poems of Timothy Dwight.* William J. McTaggart & William K. Bottorff, eds. Gainesville, Florida: Scholars Facsimiles & Reprints.

———. 1969. (2) *Travels in New England and New York.* B. M.Solomon and P. M. King, eds. 4 vols. Cambridge, Mass.: Belknap Press.

Edwards, Jonathan. 1809. *Works.* 7 vols. Worcester, Mass.: Isaiah Thomas.

Emerson, Ralph Waldo. 1961. *Journals and Miscellaneous Notebooks.* William Gilman, ed. Cambridge: Mass: Harvard University Press.

Erkes, Eduard. 1926. "Chinesisch-Amerikanische Mythenparallelin" in *T'Oung Pao ou Archives concernant . . . 1 "Asie orientale.* 24: 32–54.

Etiemble, René. 1988–1989. *L'Europe chinoise.* 2 vols. Paris: Gallimard.

Fairbank, John King. 1975. *Chinese-American Interactions.* New Brunswick: Rutgers University Press.

———. 1979. *The United States and China.* 4th ed. Cambridge, Mass.: Harvard University Press.

Foley, Francis. 1968. *The Great Formosan Imposter.* St. Louis: St. Louis University.

Forbes, Robert B. 1844. *Remarks on China and the China Trade.* Boston: Samuel N. Dickenson.

———. 1876. *Personal Reminiscences.* Boston: Little, Brown and Company.

Fowler, George. 1810. *The Wandering Philanthropist or Letters from a Chinese , written during his residence in the United States.* Philadelphia: Bartholomew Graves.

Franklin, Benjamin. 1836–40. *Works*. Jared Sparks, ed. 10 vols. Boston: Hilliard, Gray & Co.

———. 1861. *Memoirs*. William Duane, ed. 2 vols. New York: H. W. Derby.

———. 1905–7. *Writings*. Albert Henry Smyth, ed. 10 vols. New York: The Macmillan Co.

———. 1945. *Benjamin Franklin's Autobiographical Writings*. Carl Van Doren, ed. New York: Viking Press.

———. 1950. *Benjamin Franklin's Letters to the Press*. Verner W. Crane, ed. Williamsburg: Institute of Early American History and Culture.

———. 1959—. *Papers*, various editors. 28 vols. to 1990. New Haven: Yale University Press.

———. 1987. *Benjamin Franklin*. Library of America Edition. J. A. Leo Lemay ed. New York: Library of America.

Gibson, John. 1807. *Observations on the manner of trading at Canton*. Philadelphia. (no publisher given).

Goldstein, Jonathan. 1978. *Philadelphia and the China Trade 1682–1846*. University Park, Pa.: Pennsylvania State University Press.

Greenbie, Sydney, and Marjorie Barstow Greenbie. 1937. *Gold of Ophir: The China Trade in the Making of America*. New York: Wilson-Erickson Inc.

Hamilton, Alexander. 1948. *Gentleman's Progress. The Itinerarium of Dr. Alexander Hamilton*. Carl Bridenbaugh ed. Chapel Hill: University of North Carolina Press.

Handy, Hast. 1791. *An Inaugural Dissertation on Opium . . . submitted . . . to the College of Philadelphia*. Philadelphia: T. Lang.

Hao, Yen-p'ing. 1980. "Some Reflections on the Early American Images of China" in *Mei-kuo yen chiu. American Studies*. (Taipei) 10: 47–58.

Hastings, William S. 1952. "Robert Waln, Jr.: Quaker Satirist and Historian" in *Pennsylvania Magazine of History and Biography*. 76: 71–80.

Hertzberg, Hazel W. 1966. *The Great Tree and the Longhouse*. New York: Macmillan.

Howard, David Sanctuary. 1984. *New York and the China Trade*. With an essay by Conrad Edick Wright (17–54). New York: New York Historical Society.

Hunter, William C. 1882. *The 'Fan Kwae' at Canton Before Treaty Days 1825–1844*. London: Kegan Paul, Trench & Co.

Hymowitz, Theodore. 1987. "Introduction of the Soybean to Illinois," in *Economic Botany*. 41: 28–32.

Hymowitz, Theodore and J. R. Harlan. 1983. "Introduction of the Soybean to North America by Samuel Bowen in 1765," in *Economic Botany*. 37: 371–79.

Isaacs, Harold R. 1962. *Images of Asia: American Views of China and India*. New York: Capricorn Books.

Jefferson, Thomas. 1903. *Writings*. A. A. Lipscomb & A. E. Bergh, eds. 20 vols. Washington, D.C.: Thomas Jefferson Memorial Association.

———. 1950—. *Papers*. various editors. 22 volumes to 1986. Princeton: Princeton University Press.

———. 1967. *The Jefferson Cyclopedia*. John P. Foley, ed. 2 vols. New York: Russell & Russell.

Kent, Henry W. 1931. "Van Braam Houckgeest, An Early American Collector," in *Proceedings of the American Antiquarian Society.* 40: 159–174.

Lafitau, Joseph François. 1724. *Moeurs des sauvages amériquains* . . . 2 vols. Paris: Saugrain l'ainé.

———. 1858. *Mémoire présenté à son altesse . . . le duc d'Orléans . . . précédée d'une notice biographique par M. Hospice Verreau.* Montréal: Senecal, Daniel, & Ce.

Latourette, Kenneth Scott. 1917. *The History of Early Relations between the United States and China 1784–1844. Transactions of the Connecticut Academy of Arts and Sciences.* 22: 1–209.

———. 1957. *The Chinese, Their History and Culture.* 3d. ed., New York: Macmillan.

Lee, Jean Gordon. 1984. *Philadelphians and the China Trade. 1784–1844.* (With an essay by Phiip Chadwick Foster Smith.) Philadelphia: Philadelphia Museum of Art.

Lemay, J. A. Leo. 1986. *The Canon of Benjamin Franklin 1722–1776.* Newark: University of Delaware Press.

Levi, Jean. 1984. "Dong Yong le fils pieux et le mythe formosan de l'origine des singes," in *Journal Asiatique.* 272: 83–132.

Library Company of Philadelphia. 1984. *China on Our Shelves.* Philadelphia: The Library Company of Philadelphia.

Library of Congress. 1982. *The 1812 Catalogue of the Library of Congress.* Washington, D.C.: The Library of Congress.

Linnaeus, Carolus. 1821. *Selection of the Correspondence of Linnaeus.* John Edward Smith, ed. 2 vols. London: Longman.

Liu, Kwang-Ching. 1963. *Americans and Chinese: A Historical Essay and a Bibliography.* Cambridge, Mass.: Harvard University Press.

Loehr, George R. 1954. "A. E. van Braam Houckgeest. The First American at the Court of China," in *Princeton University Library Chronicle.* 15: 179–93.

Looby, Charles. 1984. "Phonetics and Politics: Franklin's Alphabet as a Political Design," in *Eighteenth Century Studies.* 18: 1–34.

Lovejoy, Arthur O. 1948. *Essays in the History of Ideas.* Baltimore: Johns Hopkins University Press.

Macartney, George, Earl Macartney. 1963. *An Embassy to China, Being the Journal kept by Lord Macartney during his Embassy to the Emperor Ch'ien-lung 1793–1794.* J. L. Cranmer-Byng ed. Hamden, Ct.: Archon Books.

Mao, Nathan R. and Liu Ts'un-Yan. 1977. *Li Yu.* Boston: Twayne Publishers.

Maverick, Lewis A. 1946. *China a Model for Europe.* 2 vols. bound as one. San Antonio, Texas: Paul Anderson Co. (Vol. I contains a translation of Quesnay's *Le Despotisme de la Chine.*)

Miller, Samuel. [1803] 1970. *A Brief Retrospect of the Eighteenth Century.* 2 vols. New York: Burt Franklin.

Miller, Stuart Creighton. 1969. *The Unwelcome Immigrant: The American Image of the Chinese, 1785–1882.* Berkeley: University of California Press.

Milton, John. 1954. *Poetical Works.* David Masson, ed. London: Macmillan Co.

Morse, Jedidiah. 1789. *The American Geography; or a View of the Present Situation of the United States of America.* Elizabethtown: Shepard Kollock.

————. 1796. *The American Universal Geography; or a View of the Present Situation of the United States and of all the Empires, Kingdoms, States, and Republics in the Known World.* 2 vols. Part II. Second edition of this volume. Boston: Isaiah Thomas and Ebenezer T. Andrews.

Moyriac de Mailla, Joseph Anne Marie. 1777–83. *Histoire Générale de la Chine, ou Annales de cet Empire.* Paris: Chez Ph.D. Pierres [et] Clousier.

Mudge, Jean McClure. 1981. *Chinese Export Porcelain for the American Trade 1785–1835* Second ed. revised. Newark, Delaware: University of Delaware Press.

Needham, Joseph B. and Wang Ling. 1954–85. *Science and Civilization in China.* 6 vols. Cambridge: Cambridge University Press.

Nelson, Christina H. 1984. *Directly from China. Export Goods for the American Market, 1784–1930.* Salem, Mass.: Peabody Museum of Salem.

Niemcewicz, Julian Ursyn. 1965. *Under Their Vine and Fig Tree. Travels through America in 1797–1799, 1805.* Metchie J. E. Budka, trans. & ed. (Vol 14 in Collections of the New Jersey Historical Society at Newark.) Elizabeth, N. J.: Grassman Publishing Co.

Odell, George C. D. *Annals of the New York Stage.* Reprint 1970. New York: A M S Press.

Osbeck, Peter. 1771. *A Voyage to China and the West Indies by Peter Osbeck . . . A Voyage to Suratte By Olaf Toreen . . . An Account of the Chinese Husbandry. By Captain Charles Gustavus Eckeberg. Translated from the German. By John Rheinhold Foster.* 2 vols. London: Benjamin White.

Paine, Thomas. 1945. *Complete Writings.* Philip S. Foner, ed. 2 vols. New York: Garden City Press.

Pitkin, Timothy. 1817. *A Statistical View of the Commerce of the United States.* New York: J. Eastburn.

Poivre, Pierre. 1778. *The Travels of a Philosopher.* Philadelphia: Robert Bell.

————. 1797. *Travels of a Philosopher.* Augusta, Maine: Peter Edes.

Porter, Amos. 1984. *The China Journal of Amos Porter 1802–1803.* Greensboro, Vt.: Greensboro Historical Society.

Quesnay, François. 1888. *Oeuvres économiques et philosophiques.* Auguste Oncken, ed. Paris: Francfort: s/M. Baer & Cie.

Quincy, Josiah. 1847. *The Journals of Major Samuel Shaw.* Boston: Wm. Crosby and H. P. Nichols.

Raynal, Guillaume Thomas François. 1788. *A philosophical and political history of the settlements and trade of the Europeans in the East and West Indies.* 8 vols. London: A. Strahan.

Reichwein, Adolf. 1925. *China and Europe. Intellectual and Artistic Contacts in the Eighteenth Century.* J. C. Powell, trans. London: Kegan Paul, Trench Trubner.

Rochin, Alexis M. 1792. *A Voyage to Madagascar and the East Indies . . . Trans-lated from the French . . . To which is added a Memoir on the Chinese Trade (by M. Brunel).* London: G. G. J. & J. Robinson.

Ross, Alexander. 1696. *Pansebia: or, a View of all Religions in the World.* 6th ed. London: M. Gillyflower.

Rush, Benjamin. 1905. "Excerpts from the Papers of Dr. Benjamin Rush" in *Pennsylvania Magazine of History and Biography*. 29: 23–29.

Severance, Frank H. 1911 *Studies of the Niagara Frontier*. Buffalo: Buffalo Historical Society.

Seybert, Adam. 1818. *Statistical Annals of the United States*. Philadelphia: Thomas Dobson.

Shackleton, Robert. 1988. "Asia as seen by the French Enlightenment" in *Essays on Montesquieu and on the Enlightenment*. Oxford: The Voltaire Foundation.

Sharan, James. 1808. *The Adventures of James Sharan Compiled from the Journal, written during his Voyages and Travels in the Four Quarters of the Globe*. Baltimore: Printed by G. Dobbin & Murphy for James Sharan.

Shaw, Samuel. 1790. "Remarks on the Commerce of America with China" in *American Museum*. 7: 126–28.

——. 1847. See Quincy 1847.

Shen, Fu. 1979. *Six Chapters of a Floating Life*. Lin Yutan, trans. Taipei: Kai Ming Bookstore.

Sherburne, Henry. 1800. *The Oriental Philanthropist, or True Republican*. Portsmouth, New Hampshire: Treadwell.

Simpson, Henry. 1859. *The Lives of Eminent Philadelphians Now Deceased*. Philadelphia: W. Brotherhead.

Smith, Philip Chadwick Foster. 1984. (1) See Lee, Jean Gordon above.

——. 1984. (2) *The Empress of China*. Philadelphia: Philadelphia Maritime Museum.

Sowerby, E. Millicent. 1955. *Catalogue of the Library of Thomas Jefferson*. Washington, D. C.: Library of Congress.

Staunton, George. 1799. *An Authentic Account of An Embassy from the King of Great Britain to the Emperor of China*. Philadelphia: Robert Campbell.

Stiles, Ezra. 1933. *Letters and papers of Ezra Stiles* (microform). Isabel M. Calder, ed. New Haven: Yale University Library.

Swift, Jonathan. 1958. *A Tale of A Tub*. A. C. Guthkelch & D. Nichol Smith eds. London: Oxford University Press.

Swift, John White. 1885. "Letter to His Father," in *Pennsylvania Magazine of History and Biography* 9: 485.

Todd, Gary Lee. 1987. *America's Perceptions of China, 1840–1860*. Unpublished University of Illinois dissertation.

Trubner, Henry and W. J. Rathbun. 1984. *China's Influence on American Culture in the Eighteenth and Nineteenth Centuries*. New York: China Institute in America.

Van Braam Houckgeest, André Everard. 1797–8. *Voyage de l'ambassade de la Compagnie des indes orientales hollandaises vers l'Empereur de la Chine dans les années 1794 & 1795*. 2 vols. Philadelphia: M. L. E. Moreau de Saint-Méry.

Voltaire, Francois Arouet de. 1837. *Oeuvres*. 12 vols. Paris: Furne.

——. 1953–65. *Voltaire's Correspondence*. 107 vols. Theodore Besterman ed., Geneva: Musée Voltaire. [references to letter numbers, not pages]

Waln, Jr., Robert. 1822. "Chinese Delicacies" in *National Gazette*. No. 477. 16 May.

————. 1823. *China; Comprehending a view of the origin, antiquity history, religion, morals, government, laws, population, literature, drama, festivals, games, women, beggars, manners, customs, &c of that empire.* Philadelphia: J. Maxwell.

White, John. 1972. *A Voyage to Cochin China.* London: Oxford University Press.

Winterbotham, William. 1796. *An Historical, Geographical and Philosophical View of the Chinese Empire.* 2 vols. Philadelphia: Richard Lee.

Wolf, Edwin, II. 1971. *James Logan, 1674–1751, Bookman Extraordinary.* Philadelphia: Library Company of America.

Woodhouse, Samuel W. 1939. "The Voyage of the Empress of China," in *Pennsylvania Magazine of History and Biography.* 63: 24–36.

Wright, Conrad Edick. "Merchants and Mandarins: New York and the Early China Trade." See Howard, David Sanctuary 1984.

Yang, Zhouhan. 1986. "Milton's 'Canie Waggons Light' A Note on Cross-cultural Impact" in *Cowrie: A Journal of Comparative Literature.* 3: 29–45.

INDEX